The Battle We Fight
Battling Potomac Fever
To Recapture Our Homes and Communities

(Second Edition)

By

John Longenecker, Jr.

authorHOUSE™

1663 LIBERTY DRIVE, SUITE 200
BLOOMINGTON, INDIANA 47403
(800) 839-8640
WWW.AUTHORHOUSE.COM

Second Edition

First published by AuthorHouse 03/23/05

ISBN: 1-4184-9436-4 (sc)
ISBN: 1-4184-9437-2 (dj)

Printed in the United States of America
Bloomington, Indiana

This book is printed on acid-free paper.

Dedication

I'm so very thankful to my wife, Aurea. I dedicate my life to her, and thank her for saving my life by example.

Dedication also to the Founding Fathers who pledged their lives, their fortunes and all that was theirs to begin a nation in Liberty, a pledge that is handed down today to us. To you and to our Military around the globe, including our son, Edgar, United States Army: *thank you for your service.*

To my parents, John and Lillian, for giving me a start so that the rest I could do ably.

Remembering Kenny Hahn, Los Angeles County Supervisor, for bringing Paramedics to Los Angeles, among his other thoughtful service.

To Auntie June with love.

To Winnie Hobbs with love.

To friends, colleagues, authors and others who encouraged me, too numerous to mention, but most individual and individually remembered and appreciated.

And I dedicate this book to officials who follow, with the expectation that they find the courage to carry out the wishes of the People against all adversity, because our unique Liberty is so very much worth preserving.

Table Of Contents

Preface To The Second Edition.

It's after the 2004 election.

The thesis of the first and second edition is that unhappy children of three generations of broken homes don't grow up to become good leaders, and they do make good minions. And further, that such anger, is not unchangeable. People who have such *excess baggage* do manage to triumph over their adversities – their true enemy, their Angst – and as I pointed out earlier in the first edition, some do and some don't. Those who do not *remain* angry, and most of them become liberals. Sometimes, stubborn, life-long liberals.

As of the day after the election, speaking for themselves, the Democrat expert pundits are saying with greater and greater resolve that the Democrats *will have to rethink their ideas*. This is, of course, merely another way of stating agreement with my thesis. I doubt that they're thinking in terms of tactics, but – I'd like to think – in terms of content, values and world view.

Before the first edition, violent crime in the United Kingdom soared in the wake of disarming private citizens. Though this is true for nearly all of the nations which have disallowed private ownership of guns, the U.K. appears to be seeing the light and the people there are now publicly urging a reassessment of that wisdom to favor once again private ownership of guns. I wish them the very best in that endeavour.

In *The Battle We Fight*, I describe an anger from another time to explicate the Left's world view. But there can also be a righteous anger from the present, the indignity of political defamation of opposition and of attack on personal values for the liberal-minded to attempt to change externally what can be changed only internally. What won this election was the vote for those tried and true values over the immediate self-balm I elaborate at the root of liberal anger.

This book is not written to speak to the Liberals, nor the impartial; it is written to the undecided. The undecided are those individuals who are coming to change their politics, prompted by a life change. Some will be newlyweds, some couples will be expecting a child – in many ways, a life changing event may compel individuals to appreciate more those values they never gave much thought to before. Now, these people wish to run their own lives, free from the interference of official over-reach, silly causes, unrealistic regulations, puzzling impositions, and insulting intrusion they never noticed before.

So much has changed in a single night following the 2004 election, but the battle is not yet really won.

Silly, wrong-headed doctrines are still in place. Some unconstitutional laws are still in place. Rulings hostile to the home are still in place, and activist judges are still on the bench. More willing, motivated attitudes will take time to change those ideas the pundits mention.

The battle has only begun, not because any shot was fired, but because we've decided first not to become a victim. Not here, not to the United Nations, I wish, and not anywhere in the world.

JL

November, 2004

"Mr. Gorbachev, let me tell you why it is we distrust you."

— President Ronald Reagan

to Mikhail Gorbachev at the Geneva Summit.

I. The Fundamental Issues and Precisely Where We Are Under Attack.

AMERICA will always be under attack. It is not because of anything she has done, nor of where she is, except for being Liberty of the world. America is and always will be in one form or another under attack, because America is not a place, it is an idea, an idea around the world.

Your author is an average guy. Father of three, married, Catholic, average credit rating with average bills, and an average of cars in an average family home. I've had a wonderful life, with my share of stresses, heartbreaks, joys and rewards. It is because of these that I am for Liberty. Liberty means little if it's not for all. And Liberty simply doesn't register as an ideal for those without gratitude for those who made it for us.

Liberty is something you can share without losing any yourself. It's protected by alertness, and it can be passed down to heirs everywhere. It survives by handing down its history and by cultivating gratitude to the necessary sacrifices of ancestors.

How *gratitude* sprouts from Liberty is important to understand. For, Liberty as we know it today would not be possible but for the

1

unselfishness of our predecessors. Of all the praise a citizen can bestow upon teachers, policemen, mentors, and other powerful influences in our modern lives, not to mention the endeavors of strangers uncountable who take an interest in us, protect us and help us, thankfulness should be chief among them, for they gave not to themselves, but to us. We must do the same if *these* are in fact some of the things of wealth and not so much mere money as the coin of the realm. Being grateful to those who gave to us is to join a worthwhile and vital tradition.

One of the distinguishing features of modern society in comparison to the past is that of sacrifice versus self-indulgence. Self-love is a wonderful thing when we understand what love really is – not an emotion, but an action – and not self-indulgence, but self-interest, a vital distinction – and when this becomes distorted, we are fed misinformation that filters and distorts how we understand our history and values that make the United States unique in all the world. This is not an exaggeration, because only America is a Judeo-Christian society. Other societies are free, yes, but we are the only Judeo-Christian foundation. This distinction is a lamp to our path forward of us, behind us, and all around us – for us to see and be seen – and it is utterly necessary in order to complement other historical facts as to how we understand or misunderstand the sacrifices made for us, the generation to follow. Erasing our history, as is being done today, is to suggest that we are grateful to no one who went before us. This, of course, is to say to us that what we have has little value. When sacrifices are appreciated, one can then learn them, and when they are concealed, forgotten or erased, we learn them not. To snuff this light is to wish us in darkness and to lead us to a place we don't want to go.

The science, anthropology and sociology experts mention that if all knowledge were lost, we would return to the Stone Age in a single generation. We have such an important dependence on proper reporting of history – all history, including the technical, the social and the national – that a virtually instantaneous ruination would actually loom. Think of it.

This is also pretty much true of our societal values, only these are not failing in a single generation, they are consistently dropping out over a slightly lengthier span, say three or four or five generations, slowly, incrementally. And we're almost at the point where a dumber, more impartial America than several generations ago is upon us. For some, this is desirable. For those who do not see this, it is only because the damage is made over time so as to go largely unnoticed. This is what is happening today, snuffing out that lamp to the past and around us.

Good records-keeping helps, if you preserve them, interpret them correctly, and hand them down ardently. That is to say, *if you teach our History.* That is to say *if we learn from our own history.*

But with less gratitude, appreciation of the origins of what we have, these hold less and less importance in the minds of some charged with that duty. History makes the connection between what was spent, lost and sacrificed for this nation, and gratitude is the *glue* that preserves it deeply in perspective and value to hand down to others. Those who have no appreciation at all can spitefully hide the truths past generations had learned, and can refuse to furnish them. These unhappy persons have their own axe to grind. More on this later, as it is essential to understanding just how America is denigrated from within.

Imagine that: someone who hates his or her own birthplace.

Meanwhile, the appreciation and vision the Founding Fathers had for this nation – and that *thankfulness* they felt just for the very opportunity to begin it all – is embodied in a document that makes up the foundational laws and philosophy of an escape from oppression.

Inherent in the gratitude that belongs in this country is a respect and adherence to the Constitution of The United States. You can't adhere to it without an understanding respect for it, and thus, the affront is on to divide it. Many have written about the Document, but let me make this early observation: what makes the Constitution so unique and precious is that it is a document formed by a people escaping tyranny. It is appreciated modernly by other peoples who come here to escape modern tyranny. Constitutions have a way of sprouting in fights for independence. As this place is the destination for so many hopeful, themselves, to become sovereigns, and as America is so very unique in a world of misery, oppression, lies, and trading in humanity, we are the last hope on the face of the earth.

In colonizing North America, and every nation colonizes, the tyranny followed the first émigrés here, and the reach and imposition of the Crown of King George of England increased. Many nations have escaped tyranny, but few have put their loves, ambitions, their fortunes at stake for this recipe of this Judeo-Christian nation. The American Revolution broke this hold, and the Colonists created a new nation that people come to, not run from. In this revolution, as it lived on past signing of the Document, the Founders died broke, having spent their fortunes they'd pledged, as only one small evidence of their utter dedication to this movement. This survives, this pledge, in the vigilance Liberty requires, not only hourly, but from one generation to the next.

There are many facets to the Constitution which one could imagine obligate citizens to work to protect the unique liberties we enjoy, and two of them are the First and Second Amendment, respectively, the freedom of speech and the right to keep and bear arms. [The Bill of Rights is the first ten amendments to the Constitution ratified on December 15th, 1791.]

As you may know, the First Amendment permits not only free speech, but has as its purpose, in part, to be watchdog of government. The Second Amendment does not grant a right to bear arms, as if it is something to be given by officials, but recognizes it officially as a *pre-existing, creator-granted given* at the time of signing, and instead of merely delineating the right to keep and bear arms, it more importantly denies government's movement to infringe upon it; in fact, very much like the First Amendment's language that *Congress shall make no law..*, the Second Amendment simply states that this enumerated right *shall not be infringed*, period.

Putting Things Into Perspective.

I had attended college with a psychology/sociology major, and later graduated what is now known as the UCLA/Walter S. Graf Paramedic School at Daniel Freeman Memorial Hospital, Inglewood, California, and interned at Inglewood Fire Department. I worked at the Los Angeles-based Schaefer's Ambulance Service as Chief Paramedic / Paramedic Coordinator in 1977.

At that post, I sat on two Los Angeles EMS Policy Committees in the middle 1970's, *The Pre-Hospital Operations Review Committee* at Cedars-Sinai Medical Center in the West Hollywood side of Los Angeles, and the *Paramedic Continuing Education Committee*, Harbor-UCLA Medical Center.

Today, we have one son in the U.S. Army and my younger children are looking at the idea of serving in the Military, too.

What's it all for? Why mention this? Why put myself at risk and then why permit my loved ones to enter the Armed Forces?

In fact, why is it that a father of three with such blessed happiness – who is trained to come to the aid of others and who has compassion and caring for others – would be for guns among the many liberties enumerated by the Bill Of Rights? After seeing years of trauma, including gunshot wounds, why be for guns?

It is because it's not about guns – it's about *governance*.

There is a direct connection between violent crime in America and the general deterioration of our national spirit, including a refusal to impart our history correctly and to cultivate deep appreciation for what we have. I'm not asserting that one causes the other, only that there is a linear connection I would like to explain throughout this book.

The First and Second Amendments to our Constitution do not make merely for *a free speech issue* or *a gun issue*, but more importantly a *direction and governance* issue, *laying out what we are at liberty to do and laying out what Government may not do.* Much of the Constitution explains how-to in our government, how we run our country, formulas for elections, taxation, an origin of a country as a work in progress, but it also puts *limits* on government.

Freedom of speech was not crafted to be a luxury of loquacity as any kind of personal perk, but as a very insightful tool for the maintenance of all liberties for others in a foresight of what can happen with government over-reach and its silencing of the People as a part of that over-reach. And they ought to know. Furthermore, the tragic equivalent of silencing of the People is the silence *of* the People, or non-participation in their own governance. Some of these call themselves *impartial.* More on this throughout.

The purpose of free speech is to create an irrevocably powerful instrument not only as a watchdog of government, but as an individual right; the right to keep and bear arms, which is also recognized as Creator-given as freedom of speech is and *not* something granted by a government, is the right to defend against unlawful imposition of all the other rights, not to mention personal self-defense. I wouldn't be surprised if the Founding Fathers knew of the toll crime could take back then – even though they never had automobiles, televisions or personal property to protect as we know it today – and viewed *personal* self-defense as the necessary first choice as a societal loss-prevention mechanism against everything from burglary to war.

Life wasn't only simpler then, it was more *fragile* then as it was often hardy it seems. People could die from everything from starvation to accident, not to mention crime or infection. With such a high premium as what they placed on Life, and with a real appreciation for true wealth being a person's family, small wonder living and life were the true treasure worth protecting. When the community carried weapons, it was making the important statement that Life and Liberty were an identity of values, and, it seems to many, that, in vicious encounters, though they held that lives were precious, they also observed that others threw theirs away in crime. It was the statement that it was to be Liberty for all as there should be Life for all, that people *choose*, and that what you do with it is everything. This is our first illustration of how our peacetime armed citizenry did not decay into vigilanteism and chaos to destroy a society; instead, it built the nation.

Parenthetically, I recommend a look at Law Enforcement in both America and United Kingdom circa the 19th century to exhibit the next interesting history of the private citizen's role in connection with Law Enforcement's role in preserving the peace and in protection from harm.

Look at this excerpt:

> England's first police force, in London, was not instituted until 1827. The first such forces in America followed in New York, Boston, and Philadelphia during the period between 1835 and 1845. They were established only to augment citizen self-protection. It was never intended that they act affirmatively, prior to or during criminal activity or violence against individual citizens. Their duty was to protect society as a whole by deterrence; i.e., by systematically patrolling, detecting and apprehending criminals after the occurrence of crimes. There was no thought of police displacing the citizens' right of self-protection. Nor could they, even if it were intended.

For the rest of this piece, please visit: http://www.firearmsandliberty.com/kasler-protection.html (Used with permission.)

The third illustration is in the record of the current right to carry states of the Union.

The Founding Fathers knew that Government is necessary, and instead of doing without Government, they crafted a formula for a government representative of the People, where executives are appointed to carry out the business of the People so that individuals can be free to go about their personal business. Such executives are called public servants, generally. Constituents are regarded as sovereign.

But the Founders also knew very well about human nature and power, especially excessive power. Both amendments recognize the power of the People and the individual and both recognize that the individual is a sovereign; no conflict in these, but also by the spirit of the language, the Bill Of Rights recognizes that we're all just a bunch of average people, no one person unjustly having excessive power over another, not without the authority of the governed. These two amendments have always been about these, of course, and what is at-issue can be put into one word: *governance*; the very reason the break from the Crown was made and why the Document was certainly debated fully, then ultimately signed and ratified.

The concept of how Governance supercedes Liberty is this: Liberty is the ultimate ideal, far above Peace, for instance, and though Liberty is so very high on the list, it can be misled, corrupted, killed and otherwise thwarted by how a people are governed. People can be governed justly and responsively, or they can be governed unjustly, where the government is deaf or self-impressed. For Liberty to perish from the earth, governance would be one place to find one of the earliest clues to her demise, hence the emphasis on monitoring the relationship between the officials and the governed, which relationship is measured in terms of responsiveness, conflict of values, if any, and genuine public service versus over-reach to name just a few.

The concept of these two amendments, a watchdog of government and civilian, grassroots level insurance against oppression as a very sensible, workable first line of defense, work together to resist large and blatant movements against liberties and freedom, takeovers of our governance; in fact to any acts of hostility to the nation, wherever they may be. King George was a bastard, and the soldiers of his time were only too glad to be fellow bastards.

Bastards of power exist today, which is how this history recitation and review relate to your family, your loved ones outside your family, your freedom of movement and the future of the nation.

What the Bill of Rights does not stop well is the incremental movements against our liberties, the re-interpretations of law, that ever-so-subtle transfer of authority, seemingly with the consent of the governed. That, too, is up to us, but first requires the unmistakable cognizance of it. This cannot be done without a perspective, a knowledge of History.

Make no mistake: the general deterioration of our nation is a hostility from without and from within. Though this is not a takeover of our Government in the conventional sense, it is a takeover of our *governance – how we interact with our officials –* with the chief weapon being propaganda of discouragement, re-defining law, criminalization of reasonable response, including how parents discipline their children, a transfer of wealth in tort liability, and dissolving anchors of our society, with chief targets being our discernment, our resolve and our resistance to destructive change.

This is why Liberty enthusiasts do not disapprove of Government, but of *official conduct,* or the misfeasances of authority and the supporters of it (*officials, their minions and the impartial*). Liberty enthusiasts understand well the difference between Government and individual officials. For instance, Liberty enthusiasts don't object to police officers, we object to their special treatment and privilege, the code of silence, the siege mentality when we expect of our officers, probably as you presume, a sense of propriety and adherence to the laws *we* adhere to.

Most reasonable persons appreciate the frailties of human nature, but we also need those individual officers to live within the law as we must.

This reasonable objection to official misconduct is often intentionally mischaracterized as loathing of Government, for, if the reportage were to mention accurately the objection to misfeasance and governance, an extremely reasonable indignation to nearly everyone, the issue would be a non-issue. So, the media of mostly all corners fails in its being watchdog of government and simply lies or omits. What media seem to do best is intentionally re-frame the issue to one of inflammatory provocation in headlines and tone. When one turns to media for information, this values-driven reportage has an adverse affect on justice and governance, does it not? Most media do have their own values system, yes, but some will acknowledge it and some will not. Yes, this has an affect on justice and governance.

Liberty Enthusiasts of all people know that they're just average folks. I'm just average folks. But the misperceptions typical of official service and the authority and power that come with it changes *some* people to convince them that they're far above the rest of us. That, somehow, their job permits them *carte blanche* or privilege to break the law en route to their overall, continuing mission. Willing media, abdicating their responsibility to be watchdog of government (because they are values-based on a system other than that of viewers, largely), become very selective in what truths they under-report and which lies they publish or broadcast. On the one hand, media harass our police officers for over-reacting (clearly when it serves to beleaguer law enforcement), and on the other hand they investigate and announce individual acts of elitism for code of silence, which can just as easily erode public confidence in Law Enforcement.

Though this doesn't apply to everyone, it applies to *enough* to become a real problem.

This is how the conditions are changed so that our minds are changed. This is how officials can effect a transfer of wealth and authority seemingly with the consent of the governed.

The result is, among other issues, a net confusion about the very nature of the issues, among which is who should resist aggression, in what measure they should resist, how to resist, and an overall misunderstanding of values such as these. This confusion about resistance is directly related to present personal self-defense and the tools of it, and this is related directly to our governance, as I demonstrate.

Some states of the Union recognize the right to keep and bear arms on the person nearly anywhere in the jurisdiction. This recognition is generally referred to as right to carry. Moreover, such states reflect a deeper, more traditional understanding of what right to carry is all about, namely respect for the electorate and a greater harmony between constituent and law enforcement. This, too, has an impact on justice, does it not?

Put simply, Liberty is ours by law, by philosophy and by purchase of the American Revolution, and the right to carry is a barometer of government's proper governance or an indicator of its over-reach.

Where the right to carry is incrementally infringed without the promised benefits ever materializing as claimed (such as reduced crime and violence), one can surmise only that there is some incremental endeavor afoot, perhaps not a coherent conspiracy in the conventional sense, and perhaps not in itself conclusive proof of some end game, but certainly a clue or a lead as to what is likely to happen irrespective of motives.

For instance, when the outcome of increased crime and violence is so very predictable and reasonably certain, as it is in Australia, England, South Africa and the Philippines and other so-called *gun-free* countries, who cares what the motivation to disarm them was when the named benefits never come? Right to carry is the measurement of whether our Liberties and safety are safely intact or threatened, and in those countries, *gun-free* – banning guns – has spelled personal disaster.

My conclusion is that our liberties are *not* safely intact, evidenced not only by infringement of our right to carry, but also by the pre-emptive mis-characterization and the after-the-fact punishment we endure at the hands of others, namely the police who are *divided* on personal carry (many officers support right to carry in even the refuse to carry states, such as California), the courts and the editorial boards who intentionally attack right to carry as if they, as elitists, are somehow immune to the forces that threaten us all. Their immunity, it is well known, is personal protection of their own concealed carry which too many of their constituents are denied; delightful courtesies to officials when the law is broken; personal bodyguards and other measures not easily available to the public they work for. That's how they can so very easily *afford* to see things so very differently. This affects your family.

Let's take one example of how our thinking has been eroded for the purpose of reshaping our governance, say, the undermining of our values by dilution or redefinition of a common concept. Let's look at the concept of *compassion* as that example. It might be worth mentioning early on and from someone who ought to know – and we might as well clear this up now – that genuine, cultivated compassion – true compassion – isn't always the heart-melting, warm clemency that it's typified to be. Too often, what has passed for compassion is so very broadly defined as mercy and forgiveness, and then wrongly applied, overdone and misplaced, and, also too often, that it can easily be oversold and reprocessed.

What passes for compassion is actually misplaced empathy and plain good will, a desire to belong, and a combination of other psychological perceptions which have now come to favor the criminal over the victim as if somehow society is to blame for his misfeasances. As if anyone but him is to blame. Much of today's left-leaning *"compassion"* is actually a misguided substitution of great hostility to America and less concern for the victim. There is a simple explanation for this kind of thinking.

Compassion has been re-framed as part of an effort, that hostility I spoke of, which has a vested interest in altering our values and perceptions of them, perceptions of situations – one tactic for erasing history is to erase our values and erase our convention on how we assess things – and which should become most welcome once again in some not too distance future when we reflect on how we came to be here (history and gratitude for the sacrifices of ancestors), how it once *was* as evidence of what it *can be* (again, history that we were less coerced than we are today), and where the *real* power is in keeping America the happy, safe and welcoming environment for all (*more* embrace of history to know the origin and to keep the authority and wisdom of the People).

But is this excursion into Hell really necessary? Do we have to suffer the same fate as England and other gun-free societies, only to turn around and try to find our way back to personal safety? It's so very much harder, because once Liberty is lost, some – most – never get it back. What price do we have to pay to understand this inescapable truth?

Some may be understanding this for the first time: misguided compassion is to erase what compassion *really* is, and to erase what real compassion is would work to isolate us from one another, to divide. It *does* divide. If we feel inappropriately to one another, we can too easily send mixed signals to one another, which is useful in keeping people unclear on what societal rules they are observing and / or breaking. Doubt. And *doubt* can take some of the steam out of people to sense justice and injustice, and to resist.

Another example of something to erase is Marriage, another safety reinforcement or pocket of resistance. In these tactics, diversity is masquerading as something desirable, but to the excess as it is being taken, it serves to diverse too much; it divides and makes us so very easy to manipulate. Communication among diverse groups becomes harder and it often keeps us from comparing notes. Suspicion builds. Where friendship and communication would be good, how does more and more division help?

Let's get back to *compassion*. This same kind of misplaced compassion, artfully re-framed to serve the purposes of the hostility, as if society cannot tell the difference between a mistake and an intentional malfeasance, has been brought to bear on good associations, clubs and institutions where the bench or legislature or regulator somehow feels that one agency must be blatantly bullied and publicly upbraided in order to demonstrate love or pity for the other as some measure of justice in action (compassion).

One example would be the cruel treatment of The Boy Scouts Of America. The Boy Scouts Of America has explained its position, and it has the right to be a club with its own rules. To the haters who must intervene, this cannot be proportional, but absolute. This is, of course, a warped understanding of what compassion is, and it is no accident of good intentions.

Not only is it a warped perception, but it is over-used. It becomes a tool, a subtle weapon. It is part of the landscape, the lay of the land today, that darkens the horizon for the nation. Not compassion, but the mis-use of it, that false compassion, is hostile to our way of life, and this slowly makes it hostile to each of us where someone disagrees.

As Americans, as consumers, parents, employees, whatever we do, we vote a thousand times a day on as many different subjects. We choose one automobile over another, we buy one laundry detergent over another, and so on. We make choices all the time. Someone has to lose in this process, and that is the person or product or concept that wasn't chosen. The key to being chosen isn't more advertising, or to get a message out, but to build a better product or concept. On one product, improvement is impossible.

In our life together, we'll continue making choices based on what we believe is right for us and the nation, and in this process, we're being fed a great deal of misinformation to swing our choices more toward things we ordinarily wouldn't choose, that product that can never be improved. This is because one of the products or services vying for our vote isn't good enough, and has to lie to get our nod, politically speaking, of course, as opposed to, say, just plain dropping out. Key to re-taking control of our homes, our streets and our lives is to develop the ability to see through the straw arguments and bogus issues – the wrong concept of compassion is one of them – to be able to relate the facts to our core values and our enlightened self-interest. To be discerning. To have a sense of curiosity about our history to put things in perspective. Let's call it critical thinking.

This is important, because we all resonate on what constitutes our enlightened self-interest, which is to say, what's really important in life, and we all have a duty to protect what we have, not only for ourselves, but for others. We may believe that we're all pretty comfortable and that we don't see what's wrong; yet, when we think about it, we do see what we want and need in our country. We all want safe neighborhoods, we all want honest banks and honest credit reporting agencies, dependable services, good mail-order fulfillment, less infighting, more courtesy and respect in the workplace, more good faith in dealings everywhere, and so on. I doubt if there is little disagreement on this. These can erode slowly, such as safe neighborhoods becoming increasingly unsafe, and, of course, there are those which are entirely unsafe. There is also the slow but certain disrespect some Americans have for our icons and way of life. The important ingredient to agreement is having a working knowledge of what has happened historically since the formation of the country for perspective.

And part of this national loathing and blatant disrespect is the idea that we're collectively a pushover who won't fight back.

We are not merely living in the present – we're living in a time that is the work-product of intentional sacrifice and hopes; sacrifices of people who wanted the best for us, and who said it with their actions of selflessness or we wouldn't be here. They never paid lip service to it; they lived it. And they died for it. We are the direct beneficiary of their selflessness.

Many nations are built without such sacrifices; many nations fight for and win independence; but where so many have given so much with a much larger goal in mind, i.e. a Judeo-Christian haven, for instance, perhaps only that nation can become light to the world as we are. In such a country, the individual is a sovereign. In a beginning stage, it was given to us by people who knew it well, who appreciated it, and who wanted us to have it next, it was preserved for generations more, a few short centuries, and we work to maintain it so that every generation can say that they paid for the next generation's liberties. Hence the *gratitude*. I note that other nations have their history, too, and their gratitude to their ancestors. In that way, America is not exempt, but in the one way we are exempt – this Judeo-Christian haven, this tremendous advancement within only a few centuries – this is what makes the United States the destination for many is her Liberty; seeing the individual as a sovereign.

It's also worth mentioning *why* some people have little or no gratitude. Gratitude is related to self image in various ways, which is to say that you perceive yourself worthy of accepting kindness when it falls to you. Some people cannot accept gifts or kindness, because they feel themselves somehow *unworthy;* or perhaps that the donor is overly generous, mistaken, another way of saying the same thing. Some experts point out that this is rude, because it presumes that the donor doesn't know what they're doing. Other experts believe it is a psychologic expression of inner affect. With all courtesy and humility acknowledged, most do know what they're doing when saying thank you with a gift or even of gifting a nation to the next generation. The *"who ast ya?"* school of thought is to say that they're not worth it.

Well, the Founding Fathers did it anyway on the presumption that we of the future generations would share their love of Liberty. We do. Irrespective of whether some few are ungrateful, patriotism in the inception of a new nation was an expression of love, not only of Liberty of the times, but a love of their children and of their children's children. And of others' children. As the Document says, *for ourselves and our posterity.* Posterity means *descendants.* And the reason for the break from the Crown still exists today in timeless human nature of the present.

We will work to preserve it for the next generation. We do this a thousand different ways guided by our values system while others work to prevent it for the next generation, in part, by dissolving the measurement tools we use to evaluate things. Compassion is only one of them.

The New Inappropriateness.

Though some examples may seem petty at first, they are actually important, like leverage is small but important, like *clues* are important, for those examples interfere with our raising the next generation and imparting to them our sense of fairness, personal conduct and gratitude for the work of previous generations, that glue I mentioned.

The example is the enduring idea to get us to adjust to the conventions we all have to live by for a proper read of each other. It's necessary we have this reasonable expectation of each other's conduct and reactions as consistent in our society. It's wrong when we begin to undo these enduring practices which have served us for so well for so long, and its very, very wrong when the special interest group is made up of people who, themselves, can't fit into society, and it is most important to observe this motive of theirs; for, it locates imperfections in our way of life (and we have our imperfections) and tries to make a living restructuring them.

The political Left's assertions, of course, fail to recognize that this or that established practice, let's say, classroom ostracism for a child, has served us so well for generations. Changing it without a better replacement in hand is merely to undo it – undoing is something anxious people do, as we will see later – and just simply to come up with a reason to undo it at first.

Without an *announced* replacement, one that is revealed at the time of objection to convention, without an improvement in hand you might say, undoing the convention is the only objective, and it is only destruction; there is nothing societally constructive at all about this kind of interference. Delaying this adjustment, refusing to close that gap between undoing a convention and putting something better in its place, fails society and it cheats the child out of what he or she is there to learn, for instance discipline or self control. This would be one example of a seemingly small but important issue.

As this protest begins to take, and as parents are left with this discipline-gap of having removed convention and having replaced it with nothing for a while, the condition deteriorates for lack of support until parents expect some action from administrators. Left-leaning administrators, petitioned and requested enough by then, then play *another* card, and *agree* then that a child *should* be ostracized – sit in the corner for consequences, for instance – but, then substitute an undesirable value in place of the proper one, substituting something such as politically correct thinking about diversity or some other concept to erode the unity we had before. They couldn't reveal this earlier, because we'd protest too much, so they have to resort to subterfuge in concealing the ultimate objective.

The pattern is this: first, they object to the long-standing convention as cruel or exclusionary, allegedly affecting one's self-esteem, then they quench it. Cooperative parents agree or don't even know about the policy change. A period of time passes while the practice begins to fail for lack of policy (support) since the first policy was deleted without replacement. The result (troublesome children go unpunished) is the gap that must be filled in.

Next, they argue that there must be consequences for *inappropriate* conduct, but *they've* defined by then what is inappropriate. At this time, parents who wish to cooperate are only too glad, again, to accept the concept of consequences for undesirable behavior, but have not yet noticed *what* behavior is being discouraged. All they know, if even informed at all, is that a problem is being addressed. (Again, if we knew what we were in for, we'd object!) The result is that the long-standing, useful convention has been attacked and parents have cooperated in a willingness to be open-minded and *progressive to improve it,* thinking that to be *progressive* is to advance and improve things; it just sounds so good.

Of course, what has really happened is that the useful convention has been totally excised and a societally self-destructive one substituted, *and they have gotten parents to agree to it!* Furthermore, you forget about it; what has worked to children's best interests for so very long has been erased!

Without these discipline conventions in place, a child can become confused and unruly, and can grow up to be more of the same as an adult. Naturally, the confusion grows, too, and we say these individuals are maladjusted. Some become very angry and situations baffle them, and why not? Who told them right from wrong in the school? Who reinforced the teachings of the parents?

[Author's note: Some parents notice this pattern, and in objecting to officials, they are met with baffling nonsense from Administrators. Many school administrations today, in fact, live by their interpretations of some so-called studies and express blame *to the parent* for unruly children in class. I'm inclined to go along with this, believe it or not! However, while parents put the blame on recalcitrant and deaf administrations who will not reinforce their existing family values, it *seems as if* one side blaming the other; but it mustn't end there, for the parent, a sovereign, must prevail as the ultimate authority. Anything else is defiance of parental authority. Administrators utilize this when they change an entire village for the sake of a single child's allergy to peanuts, but they won't adhere to parental authority when it comes to much larger numbers of parents' objections! In selectively defying or blaming parental authority, administrators who cite those studies slowly bend the universe a little bit and incrementally get the majority of parents used to a brick wall of bureaucratic futility and custom. Children will be out of school soon, and the fight doesn't seem worth it. Thus, over time, few parents notice the value system of yesteryear being replaced by the new inappropriateness. This is a kind of erasure of history of not only American History, but of the genesis of the bureaucratic nonsense, too (values).]

Why does this work? Are parents stupid? No, parents are not stupid, but bureaucrats are tactical and they are wrong-headed, and they simply freeze parents out (while asking them to join the PTA). The bureaucrats are fully aware that parents have only their short-term involvement experience for the duration of their children's time in school and that they will see, therefore, only a snapshot of time. Knowing how good schools were at one time would certainly give a much clearer picture of what parents can expect from administrators.

࿇

Today, instead of saying it was wrong to bite or strike another child, the focus is on skin color and tolerance for the biting of other children. This is by far not in my surmise the *chief* cause of anger and confusion over how people behave, which chief cause I will delineate soon, but is certainly a venue where anger-fomented official nonsense can be found, and probably still fresh in your memory.

And this is only one venue where it can be found, this pattern of objection without replacement, a gap between removal and better replacement, then substitution of a worse policy than before.

For these young adult professionals who *grew up* under *the new inappropriateness* of political correct nonsense, their everyday adult encounters are read as exclusionary, as hateful, something overblown because it has a *mnemonic* for them much more than the meaningless everyday happenstances or innocuous boring customs they actually are. These maladjusted persons – indoctrinated is more like it – do not respond to things anymore, they simply react. This is one bone of contention for persons who believe they're cheated, slighted and hated by the unintended bump on the street, the delayed appointment, the innocent mistake, not to mention political environment.

These individuals from all professions, all walks of life, are profoundly offended by their misperception of social injustice in convention. In truth, this anger has nothing to do with anyone they're angry at, and in adult life where some can act on their anger, they chose the political party that promises to give them the most clout just *for* that purpose. To muster and to pander to this kind of unrighteous anger and to give it power for political gain (and for personal gain in glee on the sidelines) is to hurt the country. In this movement, some believe that this country is some sort of open natural resource to be mined for personal gain. It looks like a sort of claimjumping. Lawyers call it conversion. I call it political looting.

And this is only one venue. The same thing is going on in business, the arts, this idea that they listen to the experts or themselves far more than they listen to their rightful directors, their constituents. Actually, they hide behind the so-called experts as an excuse to impose their will. (I like experts, but I value constituents more.) This looting, this over-initiative, this bitter, forceful attitude is what damages the country.

Where Does This Bitterness Come From?

Why are some people so contended and others so polarizingly bitter? Why do the discontented fight so hard to change things that seemingly don't affect them? Why do they accuse any disagreeing position of being uncaring? Why are they so angry?

I've always been a people watcher. I've been very interested in how people do what they do, from historical figures to individuals at the Mall, how they go about their business and how they write their own family history book for other generations to follow, you might say. I love the case-study method and life is full of such examples to observe. I also studied sociology and psychology in college and, of course as a Paramedic, I have the experience of dealing with more than tens of thousands of individuals from minor scrapes to their darkest hour, injury, death and dying.

Some of my people watching is to see how people solve their problems. How they return merchandise, or how they praise the counterperson to their manager, how they handle fear. Some behaviors can be predictable by the way the person walks, talks, smiles or cannot smile, even the way they were born. Judgmental? No, it's science. Behavior, as a science, has always intrigued me. When it comes to political affiliation, I'm reading on my Radar specific differences between the contented and the malcontented.

When it comes to politics, individuals choose party as an expression of their world view, and some express a much deeper *anger* and *others* have non-anger interested issues to their politics. Well, who can't see that?

But I'm speaking about deep anger. I'm not speaking about liberal frustration with the way things are going for them, but of their prime motivation, something they bring to politics, not something originating in politics.

Misdirected anger. Anxiety-avoidance. It's conspicuous. A great deal of this anger was puzzling only at first, for it didn't seem to be connected with much of anything immediate. Barring the occasional misstep I, myself, took, it occurred to me long ago that, since the anger was not directed at me, it was directed at something I represented. Or maybe something entirely different, it often seemed, *as if from another time.*

My earliest clues came to me throughout life, and I really began to make a connection in my first experiences of most Paramedics: being screamed at by a drunk. This is so simple, so fundamental to EMS training, that it's almost hardly worth mentioning, except for the fact there it's an illustration that reminds us that the drunk probably isn't really angry at the Paramedics.

Let's look at a simple example. In an emergency situation, say handling a drunk who's injured himself, a rescuer can easily encounter a hostile, combative patient. Not uncommon. But, of course, many patients are angry at uniforms, authority, even helpful authorities, and the solution for the rescuers is to understand that it's nothing personal, *it's the alcohol talking*. Or it's the *fear* talking. Even in a sobering heart attack emergency, it's the sense of doom talking. Or it's the whatever talking. It's nothing personal.

There are similarities in this scenario that this same explanation is true in politics: that it may just not be anything the nation has done; it's probably some inner experience talking, anger that stood before, something from another time. Many professionals are comfortable knowing that their client's anger in session isn't really directed personally at them. They're cool with that. So am I. For the professional of any experience, we know the person is reacting to something else.

But against what? I always knew that occasionally we looked threatening in uniform, combined with the altered mentation of the patient and the patient's stress of the circumstances. Being mindful of the combination of fear, alcohol or unseen factors, it's easy to understand you're not attacked personally and therefore you're able to function optimally. (We're attacked physically, sometimes, but that's different.) Not only is this important to understand in order to get through the call, but also to integrate as part of ongoing stress management. Throughout your career, to *know* that the anger is not directed at you is useful in crossing one more stressor off your list.

In politics, there are similar perceptions and dynamics at work. In politics, it may seem that some are angry at the Right, but there are clues that this is not exactly true. Many have written on what is inside the head of a Leftist and a liberal, and more books on that subject are coming out all the time, but they have missed the mark; professionally accurate, they are, but they are also very politely understated. Dozens of books and hundreds of articles are out there on what's inside the head of a Leftist, but they have only brushed the surface, perhaps because it's hot stuff. It's painful. It can alienate the public from the professional; they're onto something, but it hasn't gone deep enough. Until now.

Personal anger rooted in *childhood disaffection – poor attachment, inner experience* – pre-empts a great deal of incidental situational anger or good faith political situational disagreement, and is at the root of a much more general anger acted out in interpersonal relationships throughout a person's lifestyle as destructive to others as much as it is self-destructive.

Of course, *political* acting out is certainly not immune to this immersion in anger; unbridled anger acting out *politically* in teen or adult life is destructive to the nation. This older anger from elsewhere (earlier inner experience) impels people to project or substitute, sublimate or deny or employ another reality distortion device for not allowing oneself to see concepts too painful to remember, and it prevents them from seeking out remedies. (These are called defense mechanisms by professionals.)

Anna Freud, daughter of Sigmund Freud and a Psychoanalyst in her own right, detailed defense mechanisms as the antecedent work for theory to follow. In her book, *The Ego And The Mechanisms Of Defense*, Dr. Anna Freud speaks of the analytic technique as a way of observing defense mechanisms as opposition while in therapy. Many laymen are already aware of this kind of stubbornness as *resistance.*

But this kind of mechanism exists also in the private life, in interpersonal relationships, *and in politics.* It exists wherever and whenever there is a conflict between the self and an encounter with something painful or threatening to the self. This, of course, can be real or imagined; all that is required is that it be perceived as a threat (anxiety-imminent).

What qualifies for such mobilization of psychic energy can be many things, but one that certainly qualifies is childhood's poor attachment, that inner experience; painful experiences that really hurt once or continuously, painful experiences real or imagined, experiences just too painful to think of any further, and where many individuals have unhappy childhoods, many elect to understand them better to overcome them while others do not. Some persons may comfortably verbalize their unhappiness, others cannot recall it from a sea of forgetfulness. Dr. Freud and others certainly agree that this is a struggle for the person, to say the least. For many, it is a constant struggle, while for some, it is a skirmish only once in a while. In either case, though, the struggle is against "...painful or unendurable ideas or affects." Dr. Freud's entire book describes the analytic process, but doesn't hesitate to mention how this enters the private life.

A large portion of her important book describes examples of "*The avoidance of objective 'pain' and objective danger.*" These unendurable ideas (danger of anxiety) must not be relived, if only in the imagination, and defense mechanisms are summoned to do their job silently and invisibly.

Page 36 makes a vital note:

"We know that there is a regular connection between particular neuroses and special modes of defence (sic) as, for instance, between hysteria and repression or between obsessional neuroses and the processes of isolation and undoing. We find the same constant connection between neurosis and defence-mechanism (sic) when we study the modes of defence (sic) which a patient employs against his affects and the form of resistance adopted by his ego. The attitude of particular individual towards (sic) his free associations in analysis and the manner in which, when left to himself, he masters the demands of his instincts and wards off unwelcome affects enable us to deduce *a priori* the nature of his symptom formation. On the other hand, the study of the latter enables us to infer *a posteriori* what is the structure of his resistance and of his defence (sic) against his affects and instincts. [*The Ego And the Mechanisms Of Defence*, International Universities Press, 1946, reprinted with permission.]

Dr. Freud speaks of the consistency of a cause and effect relationship between a trauma and how the individual selects his or her symptom formation. That is to say, what the person will become angry *about in selecting not only a defense mechanism, but in selecting the symbol objects of anxiety.* Also, note that the person does not consciously select anything, but may employ any or many defense mechanisms singly or simultaneously to avoid otherwise anxious reactions to symbols.

A priori as used there means that it can be deduced from present behavior what must have caused it (which trauma or likely which trauma before), by dint of how other similar case individuals behave afterward (*a posteriori*) when such very similar case traumas are well known. This is generally accepted not only as a conclusion, but also as a method.

The reason I go into this in such depth in such proportion in this book is because more and more Americans are beginning to remark that they're seeing something intriguing: *that, for years now, liberalism is being increasingly perceived as a mental illness.* This is not very new, it's not new at all, but they are *almost right,* as it is beginning to coalesce from the observations of decades in seeing liberal insistence, in witnessing decades of our allowance of some working room for them and funding for them, only to see failure after failure, while our tolerance and cooperation are mocked. I explain in this complaint and analysis.

In ascribing such moods to the Left and to liberals, can I read minds?

Well, yes and no. Yes, you can read minds when you listen to words and observe actions; anyone can then know what the person's intentions are; anyone can do it. No, I cannot read minds and know what people are thinking, but then how do the doctors do it?

They don't. But they do understand behaviors and motivations and make the connection between cause and effect in what Anna Freud described early as a parallelism between a cause or trauma and just how the person selects their particular symptom formation. Simply put, over time, in observational time or empirical time, a consistency emerges such that people will react a certain way the very same way others of the same given trauma will react, the basis of the excerpt in the above text. This is how, scientifically, we believe that someone with a known cause and specific behavior reaction can be a reliable indicator in persons with the same reaction and an *unknown or unproven* cause.

It's like noticing a stable patient who is stable as long as they take their medicine on time, but if they become unstable and have a sudden intensification of symptoms, it's a good bet they missed their medicine that morning. A clinician can easily suspect what happened *a priori* based on knowledge of patient behavior and science of suddenly stopping a medication in seeing results in known cases, *a posteriori*.

This behavior/cause connection is not something as a matter of conscious choice nor is it random; it follows certain psychological laws. Laymen intuitively know this kind of consistency when they comment on observable events and say things such as, *"I hate to think how those kids will turn out with that person for a parent."* They could be wrong about that individual parent, but they're in touch with something meaningful in making a subtle connection. On the subject of attachment's vital role, they don't know the half of it.

Though I don't agree with the idea that liberals are *mentally ill,* I, along with tens of millions of others, notice that they are more unruly, more willing to break the rules for the occasions, more cruel and vicious, more deceitful, uncivil and unethical than non-liberals. They are more *aggressive.* I do not mean to imply that conservatives are not these, I do mean to say that individuals who may be in the conservative camps can also be afflicted with this; it is not a matter of party, it is a matter of world view, and it is a matter of *degree,* which explains why so many religious and seemingly conservative are just as inconsistent and sound so very much like liberals.

Now, before you ask me for my Ph.D., understand that defense mechanisms are not pathologic; the behaviors mentioned here are not pathologic. And to make observations as I have made is not to diagnose. It's easy to understand and anyone can do it. Those affects exist in normal people, and to comment on them requires no diploma any more than a shrewd businessman needs a law degree to understand his own everyday contracts.

Furthermore, there is the written body of experience of recovering Leftists, such as author and publisher David Horowitz, who, like many individuals of the sixties, was very much involved in Leftist movement and who possesses great insight to the mind of the Left. As more of these individuals emerge to speak on the record, joining the cadre of experts who've been trying to tell us for years, the average constituent can finally get a clear picture of the motivation, energy, environs and origins of the Left in America.

And, as for myself, though this book may make it seem that I'm going way beyond my qualifications, I hasten to point out that anyone can certainly be a keen observer, one can follow-up and inquire more – one can investigate. There is always the qualification of insight, work experience and research. This is my report.

Unhappy Children From Three Generations Of Broken Homes Don't Grow Up To Become The Best Leaders. They Don't Make Good Leaders At All.

Potomac Fever, a specific attitude I mention often, has been mentioned by presidents, taken up as a half-serious joke, and generally recognized by insiders as a cost of doing business long before I ever heard of the term. In a perfect world, it wouldn't exist, but it can be treated to make for a *better* world by correcting or dealing with anti-social behavior, and make no mistake, excessive distortions of reality acted out politically are anti-social. I go into this in greater detail later.

As I discuss the attitude of Potomac Fever here, for recapturing our homes and communities, it is only part of the problem we constituents have with governance, the other portion of the problem being in the misperceptions of those not in office who share those same traumas, those same reactions and original anger and unstoppable energy thereafter.

Remember that the experts have been trying to tell us this all along, only they've been kindly ladies and gentlemen. They have tried to be gentle. And the *real* experts – the David Horowitzes and other recovering Leftists – have been pointing to defense mechanisms and liberal anger with authority.

My observations are an elaboration of what more and more Americans are beginning to notice as inconsistent behavior of poor ethic, rage and seemingly limitless energy; more are making the connection between that and the political choices of expression of angry people – *an anger from another time.*

In one sentence, it is the concept of original trauma, summoning defense mechanisms to stop the anxiety-imminent moments against ever-hounding symbols, and the stagnation (fixation) of being so very pre-occupied with that anxiety in every choice that most parsimoniously explicates the puzzling American Leftist behavior and left-leaning choices.

This distortion is personal most of the time, but when it enters the realm of politics, it becomes an *impairment*. Like drinking on your own time, who cares? But get behind the wheel, and it becomes my business.

This impairment is a compensatory purpose wherein people function without a *complete* separation from reality (*although it seems that way at times, does it not?*); theirs is a partial distortion of reality for self-protection. As I said, Americans observing liberal behavior and reactions – such as paying lip service to values, but exempting themselves from them and the by now familiar tactics of double-standard and ad hominem attacks – sense this inconsistency over time, though they may not be able to put their finger on it and relate it to anything clinical. Let's look at this even more closely.

Liberal behavior, liberal constructs and liberal anger – and conservatives who seem to act like liberals – are best put into perspective against a backdrop of a core moral values system. Psychology means little without a moral values system. This is because psychology means little without deference to sociology.

Put simply, some individuals have traumatic experiences in youth and handle them poorly; others handle them better; still others handle them poorly and triumph over them in adult life. During the period of handling them at all, how anxiety is *managed* comes from within from either good values system (in terms of self-restraint) or a weak one (which surrenders to it), to say the least, preferring oneself over all others in the process of every choice. Understand that this idea of self-control versus surrender to anxiety is present in most of us, and as a moral value, is a matter of degree. We all hurt from something – few of us can escape childhood inequities, some of us somehow do – and some of us work them through or triumph over them while others do not.

Most defense mechanisms are aimed at restraining anxiety from that source, among others, and this is not pathologic necessarily, but when it gets political, it spills over into our values system and begins to affect our governance. *It is the equivalent of one entire political party in America being impaired.* When anxiety-avoidance is the chief motive in every decision, as it is with the activist more than simply an issue of national interest, we have not only a clash of values, but a clash of *objectives.*

Because the opposite of love is not hate, but *selfishness or indifference,* and to become activist at anxiety-producing symbols is to be selfish beyond what most people can even comprehend. The unselfish motive, as with any act one can think of, takes the person out of the equation for the sake, or the love, of another. In terms of national politics, may people sacrifice for the sake of others. This is important to understand when we view national issues.

Because, where the person will not take himself or herself out of the equation and makes his own ego safety part of every decision, evaluation and choice, we have that clash not of values, but of objectives. Something is hidden in this selfish arrival at choices that some people find hard to comprehend. Why? Because most people are kindly, and don't imagine such things in others. For them, the thinking of the good of the nation often requires sacrifice, and these people who are willing to sacrifice have the reasonable expectation that others would be willing to sacrifice, too. Make sense? What they find hard to comprehend is how anyone would insist on keeping their own ego-safety in the decision on national issues. Well, when your ego feels that endangered or anxiety-imminent on such a wide range of issues, it's easy to understand how national safety would be among them. Ego-safety figures in every choice they make, more than the safety of the nation.

But those childhood injustices, which we know cause anxiety reactions, aren't always visible to the person. Those defense mechanisms, if they're working properly, conceal the painful truth to avoid anxiety. Like the common angry drunk mission EMS personnel frequently encounter, emergency personnel are not the object of the drunk's anger, but we are a symbol of some previous experience, probably a very unhappy one, hence the anxiety encountered upon the very next crew's arrival on scene. This is no slam against the EMS professional, but it is common that some individual patients can believe they had an earlier bad experience from their misread (or correct read) of the situation, and that's not the fault of the professionals arriving on scene now. They are only *mnemonics* of that patient's past experience.

In the liberal mind, their misread is functioning well. Projection is one of the many defense mechanisms, and it often means that the person is blind to the origins of the anger or anxiety they harbor. It's been written about a hundred times; let's look at where it comes from.

Anxiety-avoiding persons perceive threats to the person or reminders of the original pain – any anxiety-producing symbol or imminent event – as a variety of things, *including* but not limited to social injustices of others, and sometimes themselves as champions on their behalf. Truthfully, their intervention, their social or political activism, is a *balm* for their own pain much more than really solving an injustice ever can be.

As you might expect, the interpretation or the read of a given political situation is incorrect due to the distorted (projected/substituted) perception, and the product (policy) of a distorted view never works.

How *could* such policies work when they are based on self-deception of the reality of the situation and of our society? Poor values of self-soothing, anxiety-avoiding motivation figures in every decision, which clouds thinking. Naturally, this affects the values system in identifying priorities. Such a person would *of course* be impaired. When oneself is the top priority, there can never be unselfishness (national interest *first,* say) as long as anxiety figures first and which must be defeated, even if only momentarily.

Projection, in the political setting of values and perceptions of things, is a defense mechanism that distorts the perception such that the individual doesn't seem to own the action or the anxiety about to come, and cannot see who properly does own it. The values system is supplanted by what's more important to the person, namely anxiety-avoidance; it puts it on the back of someone else; projection sees qualities, actions, purposes, faults, and other characteristics as belonging to others, anyone but himself (and, in speaking about crime, anyone but the offender, with whom the person identifies for the moment as part of the protection device).

Some anxiety-producing memory or real experience is too painful to recall within, and projection redirects it outside of oneself effectively enough to defeat it for a while. Psychologically, it never sticks, though, and leaves the problem unfixed because it is never seen truthfully and is of course never resolved. As long as the defense mechanism works, whichever mechanism it is by the choice of the person – projection, substitution, denial, blocking out, rationalization, isolation, sublimation, and one of the most common, *intellectualization* – the individual is operating on misinformation filtered though his own system of hiding the truth. Some of these defense mechanisms are re-categorized over time and have been merged, but behaviorally, they are pretty much the same.

We're all imperfect. We all have our faults and we all make mistakes. But there is also such a redeeming thing as making an effort in changing personal unhappiness, stress and anxiety to an ability to cope better. That is to say, *change.*

Many defense mechanisms are at work at any time in any individual, irrespective of their political affiliation, but it's especially true in Leftists and followers who feel angry for unresolved so-called crimes against them, *some inner experience*, because old hurts lead these angry people to the party of so-called conscience of the people as a balm for that anxiety.

In trying to soothe their own pain, they seek justice through coercion instead of reconciling these misperceptions internally. Because, you can't change others, only yourself. This eludes them. And when the person refuses to see this truth of truths, there is no hope of change. No relief of the anxiety. It lives on, and is acted out politically as much as anyplace else in their lives. This is also why the anxiety-plagued oppose self-reliance.

Do Liberals Want To Destroy Society?

In a word, no. I doubt if the Left really wants to destroy society, but they do wish to interfere with the stability of society for a variety of reasons. As I've said, they have their excess baggage which they bring into politics, and they express their anxiety-avoidance motive in every choice they make, in fact in every fight they pick with society, the motivation is to eliminate anxiety-producing symbols.

People who see social injustice everywhere are anxiety-avoidance driven; they are the scavengers who hope for the hurricane so they can scour the political remains and sort the political paydirt from the political debris. When there is no hurricane, they make one, or some other crisis, as you may have noticed. Liberals thrive on crisis.

Remember that what drives Liberals insane is when they aren't needed and their connection to the soothing balm of social justice is cut off. Remember also that most of those injustices are purely in the mind of the individual (inner experience/injustice collecting), which is viewed through their slight distortion of reality. When the rest of us don't seem to notice it, we're mean-spirited, greedy or stupid.

In political dialogue amid such crises the Left like to parse; in every argument, they attempt to sound reasonable by finding an exception of some sort, and in every such parsing, the issue is slightly changed or broken down further and further so that the Leftist has yet another toss of the coin in there somewhere. Every toss of the coin gives him another chance to make his argument or to win it.

Stability, confidence, certainty, and finality on issues such as self-reliance eliminates much of the need for further discussion. The issue is closed. So the Left has to parse for another toss of the coin. One such example would be the parsing on parenting – looking for political paydirt among the crisis – a reason to interfere with parental notification. This is equivalent to tossing the coin again, making another issue, parsing, finding another way in.

Leftism and Liberalism have several motives, not the least of which is destroying icons which, for them, symbolize anxiety-imminent moments or persisting institutions. Self-reliance is one of these, because it doesn't need champions, and without the need for champions, there is no opportunity for anxiety-ridden people to fight injustice. There is, in fact, no injustice at all, at least, not in self-reliance. The *real* injustice is the manufacture of crises for the sake of personal balm – anxiety-avoidance.

Do Liberals want to destroy our society? No, they want to interfere to keep patent those pipelines to balm by attacking symbols that provoke anxiety within them, but in so doing, they are nevertheless destroying our society.

On Certainty, On Exemption From Policy, and On The Rewrite Of Personal History.

The Left dislikes the certainty the Right enjoys. More accurately, perhaps they envy us our certainty. We have our uncertainties, of course, but it seems that we're always so sure of things, so cocky about things.

Perhaps we are, but there is worth looking at why some feel so *uncertain* of things. On the issue of self reliance, there is a certainty the left cannot understand. Conservatives – most of us – have something the Left doesn't have: introspection. Sometimes expressed as doubt, the Left fully acknowledges *our* doubt or introspection because they see it as a weakness in us, they know it that well.

Meanwhile, self-reliance, certainty (or more certainty, anyway) is loathed, because it sets the can-do example in reality and suggests that such examples will inspire standards and more independence, perceived as a threat to the impaired; the threat of those standards and scrutiny enrolling more and more constituents to belong, thereby isolating the impaired more and more (more than they might want instead of adapting and joining, i.e. dropping excess baggage).

They key for them, then, is to adapt (grow) and to join society. That's what grown-ups do. We work without a net. That means dropping excess baggage.

The professionals understand that there are various periods in the life of a child which determine his mood and its source. Some authors I like to read discuss the earliest years as decisive, while they also write about later years and both intact and broken family homes. Other issues are better explained, they believe, by pointing to how the child reacts *in spite of* the best parenting as the key to understanding how a person copes or fails to cope with the environment. All of these can be true simultaneously, and for the purposes of this discussion, they are not exclusive, nor in need of real elaboration. Suffice it to say that there is a real connection between what you might want to call *excess baggage* we bring and who is able to leave it behind and who isn't, and how this surfaces politically.

You see, most people expect such excess baggage to be limited to relationships, relationships such as romance or workplace. For many of us, the idea of excess baggage never enters the political arena. But, anxiety and anxiety about social symbols, makes its way to all aspects of a person's life.

This is the key to understanding the difference between so-called conservatives and so-called liberals: the difference that some people will carry their excess baggage and others will triumph over their anxieties. (We *all* have such anxieties, but some of us grow and others won't, not by choice per se, but more of a sort of learned helplessness, another subject.)

This analysis of liberal anger and political choices explicates that we're not talking about your grandfather's excess baggage.

In these cases, the defense mechanism protects *itself* from attempts of the person to reconcile matters. It's like a science fiction super-computer that becomes self-aware and won't allow you to shut it off! This pulling the plug on that computer would be introspection and would be constructive as a goal, to reconcile things *internally*. In short, to get help.

To reconcile this pain *externally*, to act on their indignations politically, is destructive, since it is based on a distorted interpretation of reality and it unjustly subjects others to the will of the impaired. Others are made to suffer and, ultimately, they are made into the image of the sufferer as his or her only acceptable comfort and reassurance – the need for constant reassurance, a confirmation or affirmation, you might say that all is well. This blocking out, this motivated forgetting, this denial, expressed as his mental removal from the justice of his own coercive programs, laws and policies, is of course, only consistent – in that he is not accusing himself, naturally – and, deep in the mind of the person, *is an attempt to rewrite history – his own history, the part he wants to avoid most.*

One of the main reasons the Left exempts itself from policy is that they originally write these dopey rules as a remedy for a perceived social injustice – something they didn't cause – and since they do not accuse themselves of anything, they should not be subject to them. How's that?

The fact is, maybe they *didn't* cause it, but neither is it really there. More on this later.

One of the more obvious irritations of more than one political group is that they turn politically outward for self-affirmation in legislation and special interest protections. Spoken from the beginning as demanding fairness and as demanding acceptance, it is nearly absolute evidence that they do not find affirmation within themselves as sufficient, and if you can't find it there, you'll never find it in coercing others to accept you. And if you find it within, you don't *need* it from others.

Still, though, that small, vocal minority of the minority that claims to speak for the special interests as a whole is their worst enemy, undoing the social amity kind persons are most willing to give them. Others in that or *any* such social group, such as gun owners, HAM operators, long-hair music lovers or even square dancers are quite comfortable with their own affirmation and don't need approval of others. We embrace these people. Who doesn't? And you know something? Most of these individuals just want to be left alone. They're just like me: regular folks.

Of course, forcing acceptance and affirmation is not effective as a balm for these, and the more the affronted and the put-upon people object, the more affronted and affronting the Leftist becomes, simply because amity is not what he wants. Soon, we begin to realize that they will never be happy with any level of cooperation short of utter surrender, (destroying the opposition that brings about these anxieties) as some of us are contemplating today. Because changing things externally will *never* alter the traumatic inner experience that is *internal* for the anxiety-ridden person, America's cooperation means she will have surrendered all for nothing. *This is also where we are under attack.* To surrender for the sake of an ideal we do not condone and which, incidentally, will never change that *internal* anxiety, the thing that irritates the impaired the most.

Where introspection – to become cognizant of these traumas and of the person's reactions to them – is a most desirable goal solution, this is almost the *last* thing the Leftist will permit. (His computer won't let him pull the plug as it will defend itself.) The whole errand of defense mechanisms is, of course, to prevent the truth from being seen by the person. The re-write of their personal history by omission.

This Has Been Building For Generations.

I point to the immense power of childhood joys and childhood estrangements, in completeness of the household, that parental attachment, in how people become what they become. This is a major player, the Richter Scale, the Gold Standard, in how joyful people become joyful and in how angry people *become angry*, how they perceive threats to the person and which forms their entire world view. For generations, the experts have been trying to tell us just that, and they have been kindly and most patient about it, have they not? It's time to make the connection between our national governance and the insistence of the anxiety-ridden for their most selfish of motives – the protection of the self in every single choice they make.

We're *all* unwelcome somewhere, and we *all* have some sort of resentments from our earliest experiences, undoubtedly some more severe and painful than most, I know. Believing that it is personal or more than it is is a distortion. These can be perceived as crimes by them, of course, when an angry adolescent or adult person sees some action or some institution which is a mnemonic trigger or emotional reminder of past pain. Somehow, it is more painful than what others experience. Somehow, they say, this is different. This is a crime.

Anticipation of reliving that pain is anxiety. It's easy for this to slip past you and get into yer head when you're conditioned to react this way to it over time before coming of age to vote. Years of accumulated pain and sorrow. But none of us escapes sorrow. None of us escapes being unwelcome somewhere. The left-leaning seem to forget this, that sorrow is a fact of life.

The chief example of how it probably begins (in viewing consecutive generations of domestic statistics) is to grow up without a dad, or in a household where Dad was away a lot, say, on business trips. Additionally, a broken home, foster parents of incompetence, shifting around a cold system or any combination of these can be just as counterproductive and painful.

41

It's easy to see how a young child can become an angry adult, angry at parenting, angry at two parent families and angry at the idea of work and workplace. And only naturally, too! After all, it's work that takes Dad away so he's not home at nights and it's a gyp that he's not here at all. One can easily see, then, how destructive it is for a modern day single adult to *seek* single parenting as a lifestyle, and easier to understand now why the single parent *cannot* see this same cruelty. Seeking this lifestyle for the adult may seem satisfying, but what about the happiness of the child? Tuning it out, rationalizing how studies don't support the idea of trauma to a child, are all part of the selfish bent that is blinded by anxiety-avoidance. Narcissism is a proper conclusion, but what causes the Narcissism?

You see, kids don't care what the reason is for being fatherless; only selfish adults can rationalize up a reason for their ignoring the needs of their child; the child has no choice. The child – their child – is powerless, and the people who pay lip service to child rights are the same individuals who *begin* a home without two parents. All kids care about is Dad and Mom being home, and if Dad's not home every night, it hurts. The natural response to feeling unloved is anger, and you now have the main ingredient for the recipe for long term pain; pain that contributes to addictions, pain that makes for violent crime, pain that disrespects others, pain that they can't shake; Pain that can live through adolescence to adulthood and express itself in the acting out in party choice.

The statistics are simple: multiply three generations of single parents by the number of their children and you have a recipe for the next generation's increasing numbers of single parents; selfish single parents, because they don't know any better. Another thing we've been told for years, but who has made the connection between broken-hearted children and their politics of today? Who would have taught them otherwise? *Judgmental people?*

The avenues that could correct the course – the safety valves and protection devices we had in place – are being removed more and more all the time, and *politically every bit as much as personally.*

Popular choices of convenience and fad don't change human nature, and a fatherless child of three generations of fatherless children will still be very deeply angry. It hurts not to have a dad. It really does.

Against Notion And Nation.

Remember that, for decades, the liberals wished to change the household, asserting that it was more dysfunctional than not. Some households were, but not that many, for, at that time, it was *only the beginning* of newly identified, so-called dysfunctionality as liberals were articulating it. The lie was that they were interested in well-being of the children. But this was only another maneuver in taking advantage of the willing, cooperative American good nature in destroying what works and substituting something worse in its place; homes now sentenced to become more rotten than those they were denouncing.

Multiply yesteryear's broken homes times today's children and you have a recipe for tomorrow's increasing numbers of more single parents, and lonely, ignored, broken-hearted children who bring their anxiety and anger into politics. It is these who cannot see a difference between what is a solid marriage and home for a child and the highly diluted family life at best, which will give rise to yet more broken-hearted children.

But I'm not finished yet. Because we're not talking about the making of a liberal, we're talking about *anger* and the way a person contends with anxiety-producing moments arising from that sensitivity, and elects to deal with them in political terms, and as a result of this, often chooses liberalism as the most compatible expression of politics.

But, this could be *any* party. And even though I lay the blame at the door of liberals, I'm speaking about individuals, not Party.

It is that those of the bent I'm describing almost entirely choose liberalism to express their sensitivity and some even to wield their clout also as *RINOS* (*Republican In Name Only*) who go along with all of it in a confused state of cooperation and kind-heartedness, that misperception of *compassion* again.

Many, many of us want to be good to other people, but without the right values system and understanding of facts of life realities, including the reality that sorrow is a fact of life for everyone, it's easy to cooperate and be used by people who need to turn off that pain these everyday symbols bring out in them.

And where is all this anxiety-avoidance activism directed? Families and Family, parenting, employment, workplace, education, sexual conduct, bonding. Liberty. All symbols of anxiety for the impaired. Stay with me.

Not all liberals are angry, but angry people tend to become Leftists, and bitter liberals follow Leftists and their inspiring rhetoric more than anyone else on the political spectrum on the mistaken notion that the Left stands for kindness, compassion, safety, peace and equality. It does not. Frankly speaking, these values are too unwisely handed out and oftentimes outright wrong and undeserved, intentionally misused as if it were truth. This *uses* kind hearted people.

These people using people are too angry, too wrapped up in their own bitterness, too wrapped up in their own sense of seeking soothing justice and soothing reparation for themselves to be considerate of others and too far gone to see the ultimate wisdom of *withholding* such graces. This means, of course, that, because they cannot see fact-of-life truths – they dislike so much what happened to *them* – they cannot see right and wrong in moral terms. Because the balm-motivated perception figures in every choice, they cannot see right and wrong. They push it aside so they can put off the anxiety which that very convention symbolizes, no matter how well it has served us for so very long.

This is where the angry are against both notion and nation. Our values system, the things we cherish and which we see as anchors of our society, are attacked as silly notions, because, for the impaired, these are symbols of a different meaning. A hyper-sensitivity meaning. Since these emblems have an important place in our society, some of that glue I mentioned – that mutual respect combined with specific commonalities, such as family and fairness – attacking these can dissolve the nation, that is to say, the people. Country is a place of geographic borders, etc, and the nation is its people. When you dissolve the cohesion of the people – any people – you take down everything, thus the affront is on to dissolve values, or notions, and by extension, the people, the nation.

They ignore the hurting of others in the belief that they're going to do some ultimate good (sublimation/rectifying the injustice), and that this trade-off is somehow worth it; worth it as long as the constituent is picking up the check, that is; worth it as long as it compels others to live with the consequences; worth it as long as it turns off that anxiety for a while. Justifying acts painful to others is a rationalization, a cloak to make it make sense to the anxiety-ridden.

The woman who has a child intentionally without a father is one example of this kind of rationalization, asserting that there is no evidence to the contrary (denial), and certainly not willing to put plans on hold to wait for the results to come in (Narcissism) or to see the common sense cruelty of it all. To them, owning a child is the answer which will soothe their anxiety.

Necessarily, irrespective of how they claim to be the *conscience of the people*, by dint of their emotional pain and anxiety, having empathy for others (such as children first) is *not* a strength of liberals and, of late, has not been a strength of the Democrat Party. Such disrespect and a real lack of empathy betrays the true character of the troubled individual, as programs for the children, upon reflection, do not help, but in fact hurt children. Interference with parental notification is one example. Diluting family wishes and mischaracterizing junk science to make children messengers of doctrine to take home in hope that the messenger gleans the message is another example.

Over-selective, discriminating adoption is one other example. Where there are many qualified couples willing to adopt, such as white couples interested in adopting children of any race, the white couples are ignored and the child sent to uncertain homes, sometimes with disastrous outcomes. Adoption for the loving, interested couple could cure this overnight.

Of course, anger can wear others down and destroy society from within. Hippies called it a *downer, man. Don't be negative, man.* They didn't want to hear truths that could very well apply to them more than anyone else. It's a compounded problem: anger's energy can propel you to the completion of your mission, possibly, and it can also wear down the resistance of others to submit to you: and then it can wear down their energy to cooperate. Compassion fatigue sets in when we're over-lectured by people who themselves haven't even begun to contribute. People then feel fooled. And there are reasons for trying to fool us.

Of course, the person, himself or herself, must be fooled even to conceive of the proposal, that bogus compassion arising from that distorted view of reality. Make no mistake; the Leftist who conceives of such preposterous policies is the very first to be fooled, fooled by himself in a view of how, quite unconsciously, he can best avoid anxiety when encountering some anxiety-producing issue. History re-written.

The angry person who likes to compel others to contribute their fair share isn't interested in the contribution itself, but interested in the coercion; coercion is the payoff, and usually with little conscience.

Call it control if you like. This person often confuses his revenge and desire to alter the power of the symbol with so-called compassion – it was important to make that distinction up front – and fails even to comprehend that his action is to change something – to rewrite something – for the wrong reason; to defeat it *because it makes him anxious,* not because it's morally wrong, or morally right.

Although the goal seems at first noble, the method of choice is almost invariably defective from the very start because the perception of reality is impaired by the anxiety-avoidance motive. As I said, this betrays their true character and motivation: to eliminate symbols. In acting on the elimination-of-symbols motive instead of on the wishes of constituents, the officials don't really know what they're doing, do they? If they knew, and the defense mechanisms see to it that they don't, then how do they find out? Who tells them? Constituents *try* to tell them, but liberal denial and other mechanisms frustrate every attempt to get through to them; they take their cue from the path of least resistance and which best agrees with their anxiety-avoidance, destroying-of-symbols motivation, even if this clashes with a majority. What's needed is Introspection. Cognition.

If a little introspection is most helpful, even therapeutic, a little hindsight would be a good kick start. Reflection might help them to realize that their efforts at social engineering have been consistently fruitless for decades. It's important to see how this kind of inner storm can extend into adulthood where people put their anger into action. Reflection would show that, giving rise to the popular theory that liberals must be mentally ill. Let me put it another way: People who never took a day of psychology can very easily see inconsistencies in the Left. And what's more, they have had enough time to see that what liberals accuse the Right of is more true of the Left than anyone else; projection. *But you already knew that one.*

Liberal anger in politics is wrong entirely because the anger existed before the so-called injustice was even seen, such as it is. And although this isn't my chief proof of the origin of the liberal's world view, it does state that an angry person on the hunt for injustices will find them, sometimes where there are none. And a really angry person will manufacture them where there are none. The injustices that liberals really think of and try to *avoid* thinking of is so very much like what happened to them when they were little.

All of sociology and psychology operates within a framework of what we hold as social values, mores, ideals, conventions. Other cultures have their social values, and for them, specific behaviors and conduct would not be objectionable or anti-social. American values operate within the framework of what we as a society deem, and in many, many ways, the American culture is unique in all the world. Conservatives view these values as necessary for the continued, enduring integrity of our society; for the continued and improved Liberty and safety of our society; liberals view them as a vehicle meant to be manipulated for social gain in the name of justice, forgetting how justly those conventions have protected them so well for so very long, I hasten to add. This lack of gratitude is conspicuous as a real indicator of their anger. Without the sacrifice - gratitude connection of history, and without the stigma they should suffer for spitting on our history, too, Leftists open-mindedly view our values as obstacles on their path to more power (control/soothing balm), and they don't care about the future beyond anxiety-avoidance acts.

This is a rationalization that ignores what it really does to others. Politically speaking, this political rationalization is identical to that personal rationalization of interpersonal relationships where a single parent-to-be ignores the pain of the child who will live without a dad. Or where a married man seeing his mistress doesn't care if he hurts his wife and family. Simple.

Psychological defense mechanisms have the power to damage beyond repair by dint of the fact that they serve to protect the individual from anxiety when the person cannot handle routine life experiences for the symbolic power they possess, and thereby operate on reality distortion.

In that process of self-protection, they don't know when to quit, and they alter the perception of reality (though *on behalf* of the person, sure), so the person is, more or less, ill-informed you might say. This is not a good combination when such people can make law, write and enforce education policy, quarrel about elections when their candidate loses, or spit on social icons; for the duration, the person operates on misinformation input.

Like the drunk whose intoxicated perception makes it harder to discern distances and relationships, so a defense mechanism makes it hard to see reality. The job of a defense mechanism is to do just that.

How Is This Analysis Further Germane Politically?

The analysis is germane politically because emotion, clouded or clear as the case may be, plays a big part in how governance issues are perceived. It affects just how issues are sighted as friend or foe. Conventions, policies and constructs we have depended on for such a very long time have symbolic meaning for the anxiety-driven, and which seem to have a different, more pleasant or endurable meaning for others. One example of this is the anxiety over the so-called *patriarchal society*. It may be true that our society *is* largely that, but to loathe it gives away your position on what you think or feel about it, and it is a clue as to what they think about family, and Mom and Dad.

Attacking symbols, such as institutions or conventions, when they really have contributed so much to all of us for so long, is to blurt out in response to their tempting call. Others for whom the symbols are routine or beloved are not tempted or called out, it seems.

Traditions which have been anchors of our society for generations are perceived as threatening. We find our way when common sense prevails, when our core values prevail, and when the process works, and, no doubt, the Left may believe that this analysis of misperception is equally true of conservatives.

But it is not. It is, in fact, one of the differences, which the Left takes full advantage of, noting by their very indictments those differences (such as accusations they make which are more true of them than anyone else).

Yes, conservatives have their defects like most folks, but there is a marked difference *in degree* between the people who are happier and more content in life and who are more calm and conventional, and those who are ever-angry, have been for a long time, absolutely insistent on controlling others and who never rest. It is possible and likely that one majority within the total of all constituents in America irrespective of party is happy with life and others are not. It is just that most of the discontented choose the Democrat Party. Where individuals of all parties share specific traits, such as defense-mechanisms, the difference is a matter of degree.

In its indictment of the Right, the Left accuses conservatives of not caring. The Left claims it seeks social justice. The Right's reply is that it abides by facts of life and prefers the non-interference directive. What is the secret of the happy, contented people? Probably happy homes, and a brighter world view. Why is it that contentment generally spans all economic strata, from the poorest to the most wealthy? What is at the root of the angry people, which also spans all economic strata? Probably an unhappy home, and a bleaker, more cynical world view.

As I answer this, I want to point out first how liberals insert themselves unrequested, and how they get it wrong on nearly all issues, what I call political blurting out. When historians, writers and commentators reminisce on the past and how good it was, more than one famous liberal would posit, "Things were good, but *good for whom?*"

Of course, this issue-spotting forgets that things naturally weren't perfect, but that they *were* good for most everyone, including the constituents of the self-appointed, self-impressed "leaders" of the Left, and things were good for people of all social and economic strata. People were happy and on their way to being happier, and, as I mention in greater example below, liberals were, as they almost always have been, largely unneeded.

Yes, I know that some regulation had to be set in place, such as merry-go-round safety, hazardous waste, fireworks falling off of train cars, with objects set in motion to vehicles being unsafe at any speed, but when these ran out, and when the liberals were overtaken by Leftists, the Left had to look around for something new to sell.

Feeling this *'loss of inventory'* you might say, they had to insist, and spoke out on issues and conditions that may not have been unblemished, but could have worked out if left to their own devices. Oh, some needed a boost, but not entirely attributed to angry people injecting themselves uninvited. In some of the cases, Republicans made the case and the liberals just don't deserve the credit.

The "*Good for whom?*" argument is an indictment by implication, as it misrepresents historical facts in order that hungry Leftists today could obtain a meal ticket and permanent place at the table at the expense of others. This is the commerce of the Left, and if it weren't for the angry followers of the Left – if there were far fewer broken homes to create such unloved, angry children, the Left would not be as powerful here as it is today. Unhappy children of past generations of broken homes don't make good leaders. But lonely, broken-hearted children do make good minions.

These activists who blurt out to take issue were the angry in our society, taking up a notch the energy of early formation of Party now to re-writing history, raising splintering issues, heated editorial commentary, elimination of tradition in education and other underhanded tactics to alter the landscape.

One point might be claimed that if you *aren't* angry, then you don't understand the problem, but in a time when we had fewer social problems and things were looking up – the forties and fifties, then again in the seventies – who was it who insisted on upsetting the applecart, that is, when there were few problems to understand? Who had to have something to sell? Probably not for the first time, anger of people who found a home on the Left, under color of righteous outrage, laid a hand on America's conscience to lead it astray to be forever changed, and endorsing a values system that erodes family was to make for a new population of angry to follow in time.

And what is the secret of the happy people? The secret is, and I repeat this throughout, that the happy Americans understand more fully specific societal inevitabilities and accept them, specific ultimate realities, certain positive truths and some difficulties over time. ...*and who don't have such excess baggage.*

Isn't it more true that so-called injustice is more of a fact of life, or perhaps just insignificant when compared to the ultimate realities that always follow? Conservatives – individuals who have the same or lesser anxieties, but who manage them differently – see the skinned knee and losing baseball game as such realities. For them, these are not injustices to be acted upon.

Some people contentedly accept these experiences as part of life while the liberal cannot seem to stomach them long enough to appreciate that. The source of this disparity is, I believe, in how the child was attached to parents and perhaps more striking, in how the child, correctly or incorrectly, *perceives* whether he was loved or ignored – that inner experience, among others, which gives darker meaning to these symbols, which even makes them into symbols.

Divorce, cheating, cruelty, coldness all contribute to the heartbreak of a child, and where these are unknown in the life of some children, where the parents think of the child more than themselves, the child has less anxiety and more certainty in adult life. This observation negates the criticism of hypocrisy in attacks of Marriage as an institution, for, immaterial to how one lives life, honoring vows or not, putting the child first makes all the difference.

This is why true conservatives are not against Gays marrying – Gay men or Lesbians marrying opposite sex is not a threat to the institution – Gay men and women marry all the time and keep their orientation secret out of discretion for the sake of the child. Same sex marriage cannot do this, for it broadcasts the incongruence. More on this later.

Ignoring realities – distorting them to adjust them to suit the anxiety-avoidance – is consistent throughout the life of a liberal: to fail to see the greater reality and to be impelled to act on the short sighted to avoid the immediate anxiety. This includes immediate gratification, such as the me, me, me assertions of their politics. This is where they insert themselves uninvited. They blurt out how the symbol (whatever it may be) offends them while the thing is probably not, in and of itself offensive. Sort of like turning around when someone yells, "*Hey, Stupid!*" This is how they become very good at what they do. *They have a ton of experience at it.*

These symbols bait them. They call to them. They irritate and provoke them. This is where their emotional anxiety-avoiding perceptions show up a phantom bogie on their Radar; this is where their interpretations of these symbols go wrong and impel them to act to raise issues that aren't there. This is where their political actions of initiative are wrong.

These injustices, the real injustices – sometimes *life's injustices* – are seen by both sides, yes, but the world view of the Leftist is that it is an injustice to be handled and that if others are unwilling, say, because they know it is futile or ultimately wrong to interfere with a fact of life, then the Left sees only that it must be resolved by coercion (legislation, regulation, some sort of action now, etc.)

while the *contented people* understand that it will be resolved by other, more equitable forces, such as maturity, consistent enforcement of present Hornbook laws, or maybe even turning the experience into an important object lesson. Many, many conservatives believe the Lord will take care of things. All of this may sound neglectful to the angry, which is the chief insult they hurl, but it is in fact that the more contented people know things as inevitabilities or facts of life and liberals (the angry) just will not accept as performing promptly enough to suit them.

This fixation – this arrest in development circling around this or that anxiety – keeps them forever stuck in time, maturity time, that is. Totally unaware of how these can be best handled internally (a defense mechanism will defend *itself*), they elect to handle everything externally, politically, as one for instance, and this never gets it done.

Being poor and to struggle in life is not a disgrace nor is it unendurable, except in the mind of the liberal. Liberals think in economic terms because they cannot think in terms of ultimate truths, facts of life, and they cannot think in terms of ultimate truths and facts of life because they are reminded, deep inside, how much they hate prosperity, independence and maturity and things that remind them of a cold home life.

Dad and Mom mean the complete origin of those things, in most cases, anyway, and how the angry were 'raised' , as some insightful persons put it, is actually to *recognize* that the individual has anxiety about such experience, and to acknowledge that they will do almost anything to avoid a repeat of that anxiety. To admit that one was 'raised that way' is to identify the origin.

The angry understand how they, too, are subject to life's truths, but they don't like it; it confines them too much to the reminders of anxiety they'd like to do without, the cards they were dealt, so they strive to change it. Mentally. Emotionally. Externally. All simultaneously. But never internally where it really resides.

Rationalization is to make a perception conform to the needs of the person to avoid an anxiety, to give himself a reason – a better reason – to carry out something where a sense of right and wrong would otherwise prevail. This is the selfish component of the impaired. To make their own psyche safety figure prominently in every choice they make.

This would not be possible without the angry person's partial cognizance of an individual-society connection. Without values as society deems them, stigma, etc., there would be a lesser recognition of symbols and the power they have over the impaired.

Stigma is a safety valve of disapproval in our society. It has a purpose. For the sensitive angry, stigma is a criticism of the person, a painful mnemonic, hence the wish to destroy symbols like that more than anything else. People who think they're ugly won't have many mirrors in their home.

When it comes to the poor in America, what liberals fail to understand is that many poor in America are self-respecting, grown-up and contented in spite of circumstances not because of money or lack of it, but because of values. They pray to the Judge of all things for mercy, they work hard, they give thanks for what they have, they love and make love, and they contribute to their neighborhoods. *In spite* of their circumstances. Thus, to make their case, to insert itself in order to begin to re-write things, to assimilate, the Left has to continually re-define what poor *is*; neighborhoods are filled with too many good people it seems, huh, for them to be an example of liberal intervention? This is the failure of the so-called crime/

economic status thinking of the impaired. It doesn't suit them, and as an irritating source of anxiety, it must be removed.

If being poor is so bad, how is it best fixed? The defect in the logic is that poor is bad. Too many people believe that *poor* is a measure of cash. I believe that poor is a measure of emptiness. Too many people go to church, give thanks and live by a set of values they believe are being devoured more every day. They, too, feel the threat to their homes not entirely due to crime, but due to an interference and attack on what they, as parents, are trying to do. More than you know, many of these families understand that wealth is a matter of who you love and who loves you.

As another germane example, one of the greatest truths my father taught me is that *nobody cares*. In editing, I thought to delete this passage, but changed my mind. Is this a good value to hand to a kid? It is when it's another way of saying *that's life*.

As harsh as this may seem at first, it's the understanding every teen needs to comprehend when he or she contemplates getting his first job, showing up on time, saving his own money, planning his own future, and first carrying out his life plan for himself. People do care, yes, but the bottom line is that people are generally interested in *results*, and if they care more than you do about the effort and the goal (and results in how you and I interact in society), you'll never get anywhere waiting on those caring people, and whose fault is that?

Like the truth that the opposite of love is not hate, but selfishness, it is a fact of life worth teaching that it is better not to expect such personal things from strangers that you will not even grant to yourself. As you know, self-love is self-interest, such as brushing your teeth and not staying out late – self-interest. If you do not hold yourself in sufficient regard and instead look for affirmation *externally* (which is where most liberals put blame as much as credit because they externalize in their own lives), you will delay your entry into the world, and be a little more ragged when you do get in.

If you don't work hard for yourself, others will certainly work hard against you, not because they dislike you, but because they are en route to their lives and, again, people are interested in results. To believe that someone should care about you more than you do is to hand them the keys to your life (or the keys to your chains), for there will always be someone to take the lead in your life if you let them, charity notwithstanding. This is why Liberty is the ultimate respect we have for one another, and why non-interference is how we recognize it as Creator-given.

My dad cared and my mom cared. Make no mistake: I, too, have my remembered indignations, but how do you get past them?

The truth and usefulness of this concept is borne out in the reality that family is an *anchor*, a proving ground, a nest before flight, and, again, relatively speaking, there is no such anchor out there as there is in the Home. People with a good anchor in their lives tend to create their own anchors when they form their own households, to clone what they learned and how they learned it, even to improve on it, we'd like to believe, thus cementing a stronghold for the nation against adversity. Is this value not worth protecting and not dividing at nearly any cost?

America is blessed with a tremendous number of opportunities, and as such, our way of life is replete with issues or *symbols* that continually remind the angry person of earlier, painful times – anxiety-producing symbols. Those institutions will most likely be sensitive ones for them. For many, many others, life in general sees the very same concepts as non-threatening. Why?

When our way of life for someone is symbolic of happy times, these institutions can be reassuring, a source of tranquility and hope for them, and, hopefully by example, for the next generation as well. Think of it as we do: an anchor. After all, this success is what has gotten us this far, has it not? This is how it works, and it's how it works best, and it's just that simple.

The Left's drive to take initiative in things such as social justice is largely motivated by their anger and anxiety-threshold watchfulness for injustices, an anger fostered long before they ever saw a major social injustice, and followers of the Left, who believe that they are kindly, generous and tolerant. The initiative develops when enough anxiety develops to move the person to action to reduce that anxiety. Unbeknownst to the person, the sense is more that of rectifying an injustice, re-writing things, actually, within the inner experience of the person alone.

Liberal endeavors over decades don't stand up to examination: there is a specific inconsistency in such behavior that is the first clue: liberals who wish to be kindly and generous and tolerant are all too kindly with coercion of others to compel their participation, they're largely generous with other peoples' money, and tolerant enough to silence opposing views on a mission they believe cannot survive if criticized. This is becoming increasingly evident. This is not true sympathy for others, it is anxiety-avoidance behavior, and when such political issues taunt and call out the anxiety-ridden, they are summoned by the anticipated pain and they politically blurt out. The blurting out in seeing something not calling out to others, but to them.

There is a difference between a true injustice – we really know them when we see them, do we not? – and the perceived injustice which calls to someone who reacts to something only he sees, something that reminds him or her of a painful inner experience from another time. This is political blurting out.

This political blurting out brings activists to pick fights with people, the anxiety is so great. Minions who join them share their pain, the symbols speak to them, too. Others, such as those who also shared similar disaffections, but who somehow triumphed over them, see and understand, they do, but they see also a fact of life, or are otherwise not threatened by the same symbol. Thus, to reconcile that anxiety externally, activists will carp about compassion and kindness, they will coerce payments, they will carp about not being heard in the political arena, all prompted by something calling to them in a siren song no one else hears, or even better yet, the song one no longer hears.

Of course, if liberals wanted to be kindly, they would give their own money, which they do not do (except for a very, very few select billionaires who come to mind). If liberals wanted to be compassionate, they would do it themselves and not coercively put others in their stead, which they do. (No liberals come to mind in setting the example on this one.) And if they were tolerant, they would not silence opposing views for competing ideas, which they do. Instead, they go overboard, with uncouth language, poor etiquette, unbridled aggression, intensifying uncivility, loss or destruction of Archival documents, and they further silence opposition by the primitive behavior of devouring their enemies through defamation, contrivance, undermining and lying. Anxiety-avoidance against symbols is the chief motive in all choices.

Let's think about this. Why do you suppose does the allegation of the Left name their grievance as *social injustice,* or as *fraud* – and why describe a great deal of policy as *healing?*

Because in politically acting out, the person who chooses liberalism is most certainly expressing a feeling of *being wounded;* previous emotional injury, from a time long before the spotted so-called injustice. The person who sees injustice everywhere is pretty darned sensitive. And why not? They, themselves, feel cheated. They're conditioned, and in this regard, they are what Anna Freud wrote as the *injustice collectors.* It's true that nobody cares, and liberals certainly don't care about people, either, since everyone is interested in results. The angry person's objective – the results *they're* looking for – is stifling that anxiety, and if it means attacking and devouring, then attack and devour they must, any way they can. After all, every offensive act is felt more as a crime than a fact of life.

In emotional pain, removal from the painful environment is still the goal, but it cannot be done as if they can simply leave the area. They have to leave *emotionally*. Only by removal from the emotional environment, by, for instance, an untruthful perception of the situation, can emotional pain (anxiety) be reduced. In this regard, the Left is functioning like a normal human being; that is, his or her defense mechanisms are in perfect working order. (But remember: they were unattached and became angry; other Americans had a happy home or otherwise *triumphed over the same adversity and are not angry in adult life*, it's important to know.)

They may even sound intelligent and conservative by dint of eloquent lip-service to the issue, but the inconsistent actions betray it all underneath. Emotionally, they have to be a million miles away or suffer the anxiety the situation begins to bring out. There is a cure, of course, but they won't seek it; introspection. Some doctors write my local newspaper and implore liberals to get therapy. Introspection in connection with a good core values system, that is. Therapeutic. For them, life under mental health would be dull by comparison. Others would view it as more peaceful, desirable. Some would love to be pain-free, while others hang onto it.

The difference between Left and Right here are not especially clear because the Right has its share of stubborn members, too; it's not a Left/Right issue: it's an issue between right and wrong, or to put it another way, the difference between interference and perseverence on the one hand and benign neglect and a general acceptance of ultimate outcomes or reality inevitabilities on the other, facts of life.

For those Leftists not in political office, there are special interest groups, Political Action Committees, and other venues to vent their anger and devour the enemy, such as by character assassination and destruction of businesses or of land inventory, more *symbols*. For the happier, there are the same kinds of groups, but without the components of deceit, character assassination and other negative features. More of a value and emphasis on fair play.

Marriage And Home:
The Environment Of Certain Constancy
And Of Constant Certainty.

Is the original trauma – the etiology that distinguishes the angry individual from the happy individual in teen years and then into adult life – from a single source?

Edmund Bergler, M.D. wrote an interesting book called *Parents Not Guilty Of Their Children's Neuroses*. It's a very satisfying book, and Dr. Bergler points out that much of the child's etiology of neurosis is formed by his or her own interpretation of events, etc. while very young. We know that the child tends to fill in the gaps by his of her own fantasy, and often gets it wrong. Dr. Bergler adds that encouragement from parents doesn't help much to correct the perceptions. Understood.

But this is not about spotting a single etiology or cause as if it were a single event – sometimes it is – but more of an environment which can *also* contribute materially to one's view of life, and, in many cases, the person gets in wrong.

Keeping this momentum going, then, is the defense-mechanism to stave off anxiety. Some dislike it enough to get help. Others don't.

I'm not going to cite factoids and other sources overly, because this book is largely philosophical, and chiefly, because liberals would not accept the factoids anyway. *Not in their present condition.* This is why I say at the outset that I am not writing to convince the liberal, but to reach the undecided, the new adults, the newlyweds, those for whom Liberty and Freedom mean so much more to them now than ever before. For, many individuals go through a life change – reaching age of majority, perhaps a wedding, a new baby, emigration to America – all of these people are now living their lives for others like never before.

And the experts have been trying to tell us for years. Recommended reading and sources appear at the end of the book.

Psychology books are replete with illustrative quotes to give examples of familiar behaviors or lay expressions which prove that people are observing that make the point. They do this because, in being experts on behavior, those psychologist authors understand fully how laymen, too, can easily recognize behaviors and, over time, people have chronicled them in their own way so that they finally become part of the American Culture.

Generations ago, people easily recognized the juvenile delinquency-fatherless home connection. *"The boy's delinquent because he doesn't have a father,"* was so very easily understood by laymen everywhere. This could very easily be a cold, resident father as much as it is an absentee father or any mix. You can be away from home a lot, or you could be home and be a rotten dad who never expresses affection. Who on the political stage comes to mind when we talk about extreme liberalism and a fatherless home?

What movie star comes to mind, recently describing her cold, actor father as reason for her extremely liberal attitudes? She finally made the connection the best way possible: coming to her own conclusions, introspection, when it would otherwise be next to impossible to convince her. As the shrinks say, motivation; you have to be willing to change, willing to see, and perhaps Jane Fonda determined that she'd finally had enough anxiety and enough experience to see that her attitudes weren't helping it – to be *willing* to become more insightful after hurting others and covering it all up for so very long. She recently decided to make a go of it to try and triumph over her adversity and go public with it as she spoke with Oprah Winfrey and in other venues about herself and how she came to the Lord. [See Jane Fonda's interview with Oprah Winfrey available at www.jane-fonda.net and specific URL's for Part I and Part II cited at the end of this book.]

Jane Fonda's apology made the news. What really interested *me* was her conversation with Oprah on how she came to want to make it at all.

The giveaway, to revisit an earlier statement, and which distinguished the kindly liberals who shouldn't be Democrats from the angry liberals who will always be Leftist is easy: the giveaway has always been how the Left consistently characterizes traditional values as a fraud. In expressing injury, in expressing an idea of being wounded, characterizing traditional values as a fraud is certainly to express disappointment there. Disappointment for those years of childhood is critical not only as a clue to the reasons and motives of angry liberals, but it also gives emphasis to how important proper attention and love to children really is. They depend not only on adults for protection, but for the feeling or knowing of their protection, that certainty that comes from mom and dad.

I always loved taking my kids to the park where they play for a few minutes, then run back to 'check-in' with us, only to go out and play again. Children depend so very much on mom and dad not only for protection and teaching, but also for moment-to-moment certainty about their protection. That certain constancy and that constant certainty is what children need. Without it, the attachment may not be as secure.

The original juvenile delinquency - fatherless home connection was compassion properly placed. It reflected an understanding of the situation and, as such, it wasn't allowed to get out of hand back then. Different values, back then. This was one of the very reasons for the inception of places such as Boys' Town then, and the Boy and Girls' Town of today.

And there were many ways a boy might not have a father – alcoholism, excessive work, promiscuity, addictions, divorce, illness or premature death – irrespective of the cause, there was a fatherless home-delinquency connection. Without question, these juveniles, like most unloved with or without a dad, were angry.

Then came more broken homes. Then came the idea of easy divorce. Then came the idea of *saying there was a need to understand* better the problem of crime, then adult delinquency and so forth, all designed to stall penalty, a probable factor in reducing crime. All this was an interference with justice.

Then came the idea of *starting* fatherless households. Motherless homes were in the making, too. Soon, a new kind of "family' was being defined with little regard for the child who had no voice, no choice.

Naturally, this example of anger's etiology is *immense* in fatherless homes, and is common among individuals who grew up in an era of disdain for Marriage as merely *a piece of paper* – it was said a million times – and which was characterized as a fraud. No-fault divorce failed the children further and aggravated the pain of being unloved, first once, then twice, as in second-marriages/step-parents, as much as single parenting next failed the child, and then the next child, and then, of course, their children. The data is readily available for the fatherless homes - anger connection, but the data for same-sex parenting has not had time to develop.

But, without specific certainties and the recognition of the fact that certainty, consistency and grounding are some of the things essential to a child's well-being in terms of attachment, what do you believe the outcome will be? Hint: think *a priori*.

For all the lip service liberals pay to children, they have the worst record of protecting the greatest haven for children, the Home. Again, the mind-reading of clearly seeing the inconsistency of their actions and their words. The child pays the price of being ignored, being frozen out from a two-parent home. This is only too well understood by the child, and it hurts.

How can a child get both sides of examples of role models and prepare for adult life when one is absent, and how can one feel loved, even *be* loved when one of two parents won't show up to love him or her? That is to say, how can one be loved when the *action* of love is not there because of a choice on the part of the single parent to begin a home with no spouse?

Indeed, how can a child observe and learn from both examples when both present parents are same sex? *By how they act?* Gay is irrelevant; Gay is not a crime; it's *same sex* that throws the curve ball to the child as he begins his life of interacting with the rest of his community.

And here's another stick in the eye of America: when fathers are made up of men, why men as *knuckledraggers,* why attack boys, who are men in the making, and *why indict society as the patriarchal society,* as it was called? Symbols.

Why is abortion so vociferously fought for? It attacks the fruit of the man, his child, a symbol. This cuts, this gets back at men, at Dad, and they know it.

Their delusion is that a powerless child is not hurting. Their delusion is that the child, not expressing in terms the adult can perceive, is somehow alright. How ignorant. How selfish. How deliberately selfish.

Of course, I am not speaking of the tragic circumstances where a spouse - parent is lost, but of the deliberate choice of putting the child *last* in a decision to divorce-for-convenience. Or to live together for convenience. Or to begin a family of one parent for convenience.

The insistence that same-sex parenting or single parenting is the equivalent of a home that must grapple with tragedy wrongly builds on the fact that a home of then-one-parent is *truly made adequate* by brave and utterly devoted persons left behind by tragedy; but that is to do the best you can in sudden and tragic circumstances; my praise to those people for their courage in the face of such adversity. But, this is not the same as making the bed of selfishness in *beginning* a home this way; merely because some people manage to survive adverse circumstances is no imprimatur that it can be done by choice. I'm sorry, but to those, no praise. That's not courage, it's the brazenness of selfishness.

To *plan* single parenting is pure cruelty to the child. In this, you will probably instinctively recognize one of the chief defense mechanisms at work in selfish divorce and a refusal to recognize how it hurts one's own child. Divorce, day care, over-working hours, same-sex partners-parenting and an absentee pop or an absentee mom all hurt a child immensely as much as an at-home alcoholic does (absenteeism, nevertheless), yet the selfish adult refuses to see this in spite of the numbers of suffering children to become delinquent, unguided and ignored. You know this one as denial.

It's no crime to see the world through a distorted perception, but it is dangerous for such people to take power when they can so very adversely affect our nation by affecting the sense of right and wrong *to defend* their own distorted perception, their insistent choices and bogus safeties in their imposing politics, our governance. Fighting for dissolving what a home is is one of these dangers.

To elaborate on an earlier topic, the mission of psychotherapy in such cases is to give the client deeper insight, a new and permanent tool to use to cope with life's trials. *The very idea that cognitive approaches work effectively to cope with life is to recognize that facts of life are what they are; unchangeable.* One may not be able to summon the future, but summon oneself; the person cannot change others, but can change only himself, and the person cannot change without motivation to change.

Like Jane Fonda who announces a new insight. James Carville announced after the 2004 election that the Democrat Party perhaps should re-examine its ideas. This could be the beginning of something monumental. Self-examination. This kind of insight could be huge.

Until liberals elect to look within themselves, most liberals will elect to remain liberals.

We all have our problems. But, without introspection in the liberal – that kind of introspection that more normally comes with maturity – the liberal remains a liberal, and when they act out politically to coerce others to their distorted perceptions – injustice collectors – then we have a real governance problem.

Liberals who over-react to symbols do not have this insight, or there would be a lesser feeling of superiority and snobbery, that classic *intellectualization* we find so offensive and almost entirely a tool of the mean-spirited liberal. It's a pretense, or specific behavior that is almost conclusively characteristic of the affliction.

We're all just folks, and that's where most of us belong, including me. The intellectual, stuffy art snobs who disrespect others' icons are hardly superior, much less polite, much less belonging to the dignity of their craft. With introspection, you would think that artists would have respect for the emblems of others – and the work-product of others who disagree – not a challenging disrespect, unless they wish to make a statement more than adhere to a sense of professional values (which is the case).

It is because these institutions and values so attacked are irresistible *symbols, calling them out, taunting them*. To many of us, they are symbols of Liberty, freedom, home, nostalgia, and certainly respect for self and respect for others among them, communicating values we like to see alive and well, and they are symbols of a certain kind of safety (anchor) not only for the present, but of the past. To the angry Left, they are *offensive*, and that is often their term of choice.

Sometimes these symbols do great honor; sometimes they educate on something central to someone for the very first time. But they mean *also* something elemental to the angry; they enrage the angry much more than they inspire a loving bond otherwise, it seems, and thus, they become targets to devour. The Home is one of these symbols, and most enraging to some, it seems that the more beloved and cherished the Home for many, the more it becomes an object to devour.

The increasing fuming of the Left is due almost entirely to the fact that no matter what they do to reduce the inner anxiety, it doesn't work! It never will on the road they're on. Nearly everything they loathe is in one way or another an inner experience of their own perception, and which must involve a distortion of reality to keep that anxiety level down low. Thus, the primitive behavior of devouring the enemy – defamation, frustration, separation from work-product, deprivation of Liberty, etc.

The greatest mooring of the child is the Home even after the person moves into adulthood, and if the child begins unchecked to perceive his life as a fraud – who was around to say otherwise? – how are the rest of his or her relationships and encounters managed? How about their politics?

The better doctor to lead the way in introspection would be the one who helps the client to develop insight within a values system that follows a code of ethics rather than the insight that follows a code of encouraging selfishness, a stamp of approval for continuing such self-destructive conduct. In such cases where the *therapist* is selfish and without values, it is a case of the doctor gleefully doing his or her part in putting a finger in the eye of society at the expense of the patient in the process. *There are a lot of them in the popular psychology movement. And, of course, the patient wouldn't see this as predatory, or of being used for that matter.*

And when more and more of today's parents were themselves raised by selfish, self-indulgent parents to create in them their own unavoidable painful resentments instead of guidance and love, you have a real source of the problem and how the one infected transmits it by vector to others, including the professions, and that includes the Health Sciences.

Since the Left began taking hold in America around the thirties, since it first laid a hand on America, it has succeeded in changing values for Americans in business, law, education, religion, health science and family life, just to name a few. As more and more couples raised their children with these new *substituted* values – to identify and replace convention with *the new inappropriateness* – the next generation began to suffer from less and less guidance from a tried and true tradition, until the point where, today, we see more selfish couples, more selfish children, more selfish singles, as one kind of example. Folks, we wouldn't even be here alive at all if it weren't for the *unselfishness* of dozens of past generations, otherwise known as tradition. Or Love.

If I had to summarize tradition in one word, it would have to be *the passing on of unselfish values* by my reckoning. Or Love. Neglecting and even undoing all those values over time (*undoing* is also a characteristic of a defense mechanism) is purely self-indulgence in scratching an itch, and it's beginning now to have an accelerating, substantive impact.

The Left cared not for the damage it has done and continues to do for one inexorable motive: selfish power (a.k.a. soothing balm / reassurance / anxiety-avoidance). Some might simply call it *Ego* and be on the right track. Others might call it personal rights and also be on the right track, selfishness. Either way, and perhaps with even more assessments to come, it's still striving for a soothing reassurance that they are in control of things. Forget psychological control; when they are not *politically* in control, they obviously fight like they're insane, and some of them must be. When conservatives are not in control, *they* remain as ladies and gentleman. (*Thanks a lot!*)

When it comes to the subject of selfishness, most people think of greed, or something like it, but real selfishness can be so much more. Selfishness is also the simple exclusion of others from their reality, not merely taking their money in gluttony, whether the hog gets it or not. Selfishness in the political arena is not merely hogging, it is separation of people from their rights, their history, their tradition and more on an ongoing mission of a self-balming banishment of personal anxiety.

You see, the danger of the impaired is not that they attack symbols, *per se*, but that they come to realize that their attacks aren't working in soothing their anxiery, so they accelerate their attacks in the kind of slippery slope approach they are known for.

Laymen perceive this politically as the Left's insistence on more money, more effort and more sacrifice, but it is actually the perception that not enough has been done to reduce the anxiety – of course, because that won't come from changing things externally! The anxiety can be extinguished only from insightful changing of things *internally*.

No, the selfishness imposed by officials – anxiety-avoidance choices of devouring symbols – is this separation they love, separation from work-product, the fruit of a sovereign's labor; private property, another symbol of the fruit of one's labor. *And the elitism that takes them out of the authority of the very policies they impose, because in their pursuit of social justice, they do not accuse themselves in the process.* The very last thing they want is to be included in the laws they write for the rest of us, because they are the champion who remedies it all, they are not among the named accused.

This is important, because, to many of us, there was, in fact, *no crime.*

This is where so-called compassion went wrong. In encouraging the wrong to *stay* wrong (in self-destructive values and behaviors which are also deleterious to the nation), in refusing to accuse or see themselves as part of the loose morals that comprised the scene (another story in itself), the Left (including the health sciences and pop social sciences) was gutlessly passing up an opportunity to take the correct turn, painful as it might be. Sometimes facing yourself is pretty painful.

Time after time, the liberal would pass up a chance to do the right thing, in nearly every aspect of society. Multiply this times a million or so across the board, as no-fault divorce did to Marriage, and you've put upon that conduct a brand of pure selfishness. The opposite of Love.

Restoring what is good for the Nation is what we're trying to do, but it won't be done entirely on the floor of the Legislature, it will be done in people like you who realize that self-interest is different from self-indulgence, and that self-interest has a lot to do with the interests of the Nation, your home and community. Making sacrifices for the good of the nation will come from unselfish persons, and will be resisted by selfish persons who don't want you to spoil their picnic. You will know them when you see them, and it will be easier to work with them if we understand their true motivations.

It's Time To Ask: Am I Questioning People's Motives?

Ordinarily, I would say that what we are facing does not need to take into account motives, as in trying to solve nearly any criminal mystery at first; if someone grabs your child, you don't hang around trying to discover why before taking action; you may even say you already know their motives! It's not a breach of etiquette to be suspicious. And if you're too kindly, you could be wasting valuable time. Throughout this book, I say that it doesn't matter what their motives are, well intentioned or ill willed. All that matters really is that they are wrong, and it is we who have the right to say. We also need to understand solidly why.

Motives influence perception. They affect the discovery of alternatives, and this accounts for why some angry persons cannot see it the way the unimpaired see things, as it were. This is why, for the duration, they won't. They cannot. The core motive in left-leaning choices is anxiety-avoidance, and as long as they have to figure anxiety-avoidance *first* in every decision, quite unconsciously, of course, the impaired will not be unselfish, they will not be cooperative. Motives influence perception.

When we open our minds and our hearts in cooperation and express that cooperation in action and commitment, such as taxation money, in willingness to change and in tolerance, then, when we are made to regret our commitment, *we know we've been had*. Something didn't merely go wrong; we'd been had.

When retrospect shows that it was foolish to begin with, but we patiently went along with it anyway out of genuine concern and compassion, then we know we've been had.

When we are told that programs didn't work because they weren't given enough time or money or it wasn't done just right, and when we're insulted for not cooperating *enough*, we know we've been had.

And when the Left says No to a conservative project because it's not ready, and pushes their own projects *in spite* of *their* not being ready, you know we're gonna be had. It's time to question motives and professional integrity. It's time to *engage them*.

Is all this part of our national problem? Could there really be a relationship between these consistent observations of official deafness or double standard and the individual bad taste, rotten etiquette, wrong-headed rulings and doubt the country's suffering?

Could there be a real connection between the hatred of men and boys, abortion as a ruination of the fruit of the man more than an issue of so-called constitutional *privacy?* The loathing of Marriage as just a piece of paper, then, next, the puzzling insistence that it applies to everyone?

One year, Marriage is just a piece of paper in the argument that you don't have to be married to have sex and that you have the freedom to walk out; next, it's so important that everyone has to get in on the commitment wagon or we're all accused of being exclusionary. Each has the same result: to try to impeach our values and institutions, and when one didn't work, and it didn't, it is approached from a different angle, which could work. The idea is not to get in on Marriage, but to get Marriage out.

For decades, I have said that this analysis is the essence of what makes someone angry in a society which is the freest in all the world, and which *should be* the most *contented* anywhere. I believe that Leftists around the world are raised to become unhappy, not because they may or may not live in poverty, but because of similar childhood inner experiences, real or imagined, cultural humiliation within, unbridled projection and substitution cultivated by leaders, and a refusal to appreciate life in the perspective of gratitude to people who made it for them. After all, there are many poor throughout the world who do not feel as their officials do, and who are the most kindly and charitable. No, Poverty is not enough to explain *their* anger.

How Do We Deal With The Impaired?

In their present condition, you can't talk to Leftists, and in their present condition, you can't really get through to liberals, either. Their defense mechanisms are working perfectly, too perfectly, for anyone to reach them.

More of us are becoming, ourselves, angry and indignant over being kicked, tricked and a sense of being licked; we're sick of being lied to, and sick of being used for our kindness, cooperation and generosity. We feel this way largely because, though everyone experiences life's frustrations and adversities, there are those who manage to triumph over those adversities. Those who can, do, and those who do become more self-confident, more conservative. The belief is that if some can, others, can too. I've said this before.

But the impaired are filled with the urge to devour, and kidding oneself that motives are pure and idealistic is a feature of the impairment. The leftist lies to himself by his defense mechanisms which protect him from anxiety-provoking memories, say a rotten home life to name one as one probable origin. A fatherless home, or absent father at best. Uncles and other men are a poor substitute for a full-time dad. It's not entirely a question of male role model, it's more a need for ongoing presence. Think certain constancy and constant certainty.

In this, the Right's view that an intact home is vital and that it is wrong to interfere with all kinds of new definitions of Marriage, we are accused of being selfish, mean-spirited and lacking compassion.

But we counter by showing that people - everyday people - who do not adhere to liberal tenets manage to live their lives well - struggling, but well - without the interference which is the price of liberal help.

This is becoming more and more preferred by the next generation, the new hopefuls, those who can compare both Right and Left, having experienced a taste of both firsthand. This, in my opinion, is unique for a number of generations, the Left having had a monopoly on media for decades. Hopefuls see the importance of intact homes, oppostie-sex households and non-interference as the strength of the nation.

As the new hopefuls form their own households, they begin on the presumption that they had specific freedoms; they now come to appreciate that the so-called social responsibility they had been fed is actually lip-service and interference.

These households will be successful because they have the experience at the resolve, confidence and success of dealing with adversity without help. Their homes, like most, will be a proving ground, nest before flight, for dealing with adversity.

So, how do we get any political work done if we don't include the Left in the debate?

Here is the short answer.

First, we don't exclude them, we do two things; we can work around them, or we can utilize them.

In our stumping on issues, we can speak to the hopefuls and we can speak to the officials most responsive to our values. (I, for one, no longer write my Liberal representatives. Why do Republicans answer their mail, but the Dems won't?) As the new hopefuls emerge, they will be taking greater and greater interest in discovering issues that affect their homes and how they run them. They will probably find that conservatives share more of their values, or vice-versa as they come to think of their families.

How we utilize liberals is to keep doing what works, namely giving venue to the spokespeople for the Left, especially in Talkradio. In this, we wipe out their whine that they are not getting their message out, or that they are not articulating it properly. How can this be when they are being heard in their own words? The savviest Talkradio hosts do this.

And finally, we set the example. It is probably one of the toughest of all the things to do. But then, we can handle adversity better. And we want to imbue our loved ones with this ability, too.

Thus, it is not that liberals are not heard, it is simply that people do not like the message. It is now being seen for what it is, counterproductive, destructive, self-destructive.

But then, some add that the liberals have nothing to say. I am among those. Why is it that liberals really have nothing to say?

Because, as more and more households are demonstrating, a champion is not needed. Not always, anymore, anyway. We certainly don't need self-impressed, self-appointed champions.

Without injustice, real or imagined, the impaired have no sense of purpose, which purpose, incidentally, is nothing more than a search for a pipeline to balm, eliminating anxiety-provoking icons, where devouring the icon is that balm that will soothe his or her own personal anxiety. I sometimes refer to this as a search-and-destroy mission, because it seems that the Left's anxiety and injustice-collecting will smell anything in such a symbol-rich environment as Freedom. For them, so many things appear to be a legitimate military target to devour.

To be a Leftist in the freest nation in the world is to remain an impetuous youth, an angry youth, stuck in time, maturity time, the inability or unwillngness to get past traumata. To triumph over resentment is an opportunity to change that some lack the fortitude even to begin.

The new hopefuls realize that household and the values which protect it are not threats, real or imagined, but havens and strongholds of the nation.

This is the short answer on how we deal with the impaired.

Let Me Tell You Why It Is We Distrust You.

Liberals are disoriented. As if I hadn't begun this above, let me say why it is that we cannot trust liberals. Liberals, as fellow Americans, are not mistrusted because they are untrustworthy in the conventional sense, but cannot be trusted because they are *impaired*. This is not to be insulting for insult's sake, but to understand that you cannot trust *anyone* who's operating on misinformation input, or *any* impairment for that matter, which is precisely the nature of the disorientation for them.

Edmund Bergler, M.D., New York Psychoanalyst and author of *Divorce Won't Help*, among other books, points out that *neurotics can't love*. Bold statements such as these are long overdue, largely kept in the annals of psychology, or even private mutterings, until being summoned by the layman's willingness to hear. And even then...

The idea is that individuals who are so very pre-occupied with such anxiety-motivation simply have no capacity for involvement with others, for the duration. Until one can dispense with distractions such as irresistible foibles or addictions or other powerful motivations, one cannot love another person.

This is always subject to change, such as when someone makes room in one's life for another. Sometimes it takes therapy to discover the sources of those anxieties, to recognize them, to eliminate them, to work them through. Until then, and not because there is no one companion at the time, the individual remains focused on the object of his or her energy. If it's anxiety-avoiding choices, and making them a part of every move, then it's anxiety-avoiding choices. But remember: it's in a world where others see those same symbols as not anxiety-producing, a society where others are not threatened by such symbols. The impaired cannot simply look around and see those symbols as entirely harmless.

And what *is* love? Love is not an emotion, but an *action*. To be *in love* is a thing that involves thinking of the other person, a sense of anticipation, longing, devotion, you get it. And for many, this is the end of the definition. To be *in love* is to ride a high on thinking of that other person, an emotional experience. We all know that, don't we?

But to *love* another person is a much deeper concept, one of actions that help, comfort, sacrifice for the other, even a degree of vulnerability. To know them *both* is a joy. And a milestone of maturity. We already know that, too.

You see, though anxiety-avoidance is not always to the extent of being neurotic, it can be disruptive and on a national scale. And without therapy, or more precisely, without the motivation to change, little can be hoped for. Until now.

Because we *do* have motivation in many instances, such as in life-changing events. As merely one example, when one believes he's in love and finds there that motivation to change, there can be the motivation to drop that *excess baggage* I mentioned. The consistent cast to the idea of excess baggage was, of course, that it was all so very *unnecessary*. And that's what liberal anger really is. True in the sixties, probably true always. Anxiety that just isn't necessary.

But liberals go through life-changing events, too; they get married, they come of age to vote, they go through these, too.

Ah, but the difference is not in the act or the experience, but in the choice to continue carrying that excess baggage or to abandon it in favor of the beloved, or even just for other people. Liberals cannot do this in any endeavor, much less every endeavor, purely because theyhave to put themselves first in every choice, first for safety purposes. The difference between the impaired and the less impaired is the election to carry or abandon the torment and to keep this kickback/payoff in every deal. The torment of the anticipation of anxiety and therefore its reaction is not external in the real world, it is purely in the mind of the tormented, the inner experience, the injustice collecting. Until they can make choices without putting their own anxiety-avoidance first, they're going through the motions of lifestyle, a sort of acting out lip-service.

Life-changing events are largely to credit for the swing in the 2004 election. People underwent life-changing events that compelled them to begin then to live their lives more robustly for themselves, not so much in hedonism any longer, but in better self love, and perhaps more importantly, to live for others. As they began to taste this, they began to understand more deeply the meaning of reciprocity, or in many cases, just plain old unselfishness, as in the life-changing event of having a child.

In short, the demographics changed. Not only were the liberals speaking to fewer children/adults, but the constituents were only too glad to leave that childhood behind as they moved into parenthood, among other institutions, institutions they didn't appreciate being mocked now that they were becoming part of it all.

Making anxiety-avoidance part of every decision is to be, of course, necessarily selfish – self-protecting in every choice, personal and political – and selfishness is the opposite of love. If neurotics can't love, then the impaired has to come in as a close second. How can the impaired be capable of love? How can they have compassion when anxiety-avoidance must figure first in every choice as a matter of emotional survival? How can they govern?

Motivation Influences Perception.

Motivation influences perception of societal or national issues because it frames the discovery of alternatives.

When a person motivated to avoid anxiety demands that anxiety-avoidance figure first in every assessment, that person will probably see only solutions that re-assure him or her, and not solve the problem in reality.

When anxiety avoidance is the primary motivation in law, morality takes a back seat to self-reassurance or balm, and reveals to the person only a narrow field of alternatives.

When anxiety plays a much lesser role in viewing that field of solutions, the person is open to more of them, it seems. More solutions are visible.

If a person looks at a book and sees a paperweight or something to be thrown, it's possible they don't like books, and aren't likely to see books as an information or entertainment source before anything else, as one for instance.

These Impaired will be most difficult on political issues, standing firmly on only those limited possibilities they see, bolstered by their emotion to do so, and if those possibilities are limited to those which include their self-balm, one cannot expect much in the way of cooperation.

They Promise To Be Good Masters, But They Mean To Be Masters.

Before we connect all the dots, let's connect a handful to begin with. Let's talk about what we have to give our society and what we have the right to expect from others in our community and our nation, and how this, itself, is being undermined.

Another of the many features of official stubbornness, indolence and disrespect for constituents and country is a condition known in Washington as *Potomac Fever*. As I'd mentioned earlier, it has been described generations ago by presidents and authors, it is today known jokingly by official insiders and commentators. It's believed to be a very real psychological condition that overcomes individuals upon arrival in public office. It is the oftentimes defective concept of the self-impressed, making life easier, supposedly fairer and generally better for Americans, not by listening to the people, but on the legal authority initiative of *because we say so.*

Some of this is benevolent, some is malevolent. Some who aspire to such middle or high office are predisposed to this fever by dint of their earlier resentment, their world view. Some are not. And though it is often referenced jokingly from time to time, let me say that, to us constituents and other Americans who have to live with it – it's not at all funny. Potomac Fever, an urban legend of a sort, is real.

One of these misguided concepts arising from a warped view of values is to lift burdens from Americans. This idea of lifting burdens is an insidious and disgraceful tact, *irrespective of the motivation.* Our burdens are not only ours alone to carry, but they are wonderful for so many reasons. They serve a social purpose, and it would be most unwise to tamper with them. For some, this is precisely what they want. It is every bit as hurtful as the single parent who unloves the child on the premise that it will prepare him or her for life, and that it is up to him or her to later triumph over that adversity of being unloved. But we're not all living by the upbringing of *A Boy Named Sue*, are we?

In contrast, the burden of caring for a family is not only hard, but it is a privilege. It is an honor and a joy. The burden of paying bills and running a household, tough as it may be, is a degree of control we have over our lives, the freedom to choose what we choose and the freedom of movement to handle it the way we want to handle it, with all its rewards and with all its penalties.

I emphasize this, because life is life, and it has its normal, proper risks and rewards. To live life under freedom and Liberty, we really need to hear our news unfiltered and we need to live unfettered, empowered by correct information to make the choices we must make on our own, irrespective of the notions and precepts of others who cannot resist the temptation to interfere.

The desire to interfere overpowers any altruistic beliefs of beneficence. The excuse of rendering social justice is, of course, a cloak. Incrementally, or often suddenly in large chunks, these interferences attempt to lift burdens, and these lift away also our liberties with them. Take away the risk, you take away the reward.

Take away the earning, and you take away what is earned. Part of this confiscation is the separation of an individual from the fruits of their labor again, a gleeful act for the official under the delusion that lifting a burden is part of his duty. It is not.

These acts of separation and confiscation are wrong of course, because they proceed from the misperception that a burden is unwanted.

All of these responsibilities so much the subject of discourse entitle us to the liberties purchased by carrying our burdens. Yes, in addition to our liberties being God-given, and having already been purchased by the American Revolution, we *maintain* our liberties, we pay for them through eternal vigilance, as we are worthy of them daily, they are ours. And no one can take them away from us.

Or can they? The obsession of 'serving constituents' by lifting their burdens reflects a poor understanding of American values and way of life. Lifting the burden cheats us out of the Liberty of owning our actions and the rewards of good judgement, hard work, passing on our deeply felt, shared devotions and our goodness as we, the People, define it. These are *ours* to define, not for officials or their minions to *hijack and to substitute as they do against the sovereign.*

It also cheats us out of the penalties we incur when we make a mistake (and learn), and to deny our ownership of those also reflects a poor understanding when it sees only one side of the equation, namely risk, and which ignores the concept of reward; to acknowledge reward is to acknowledge that liberalism isn't really needed after all. In short, continued worthiness for such a gift is down to us to earn; by carrying our burdens and protecting our liberties, we earn the right to *keep* our liberties unquestioned.

Lifting our burdens is to make a societal statement not yet in evidence until it is molded and coerced into existence. Liberals do this a lot. Liberals make a pronouncement that cannot be proven even to exist at all, much less widely, then they mold our society so that the statement then becomes a reality; one example of this is *no-fault divorce*. The alleged burden is commitment; the pronouncement, that Marriage is just a piece of paper and is a fraud; the real truth is that (again, the impaired's re-writing of historical terms), it is an institution whose true history is erased and substituted so that it *soon becomes* what was described. Devouring and assimilation. The result is discouragement. The objective is to remove an anchor of society, a pocket of resistance to adversity. Marriage is that much of a stronghold.

Lifting our burdens also cheats us all out of the benefits of the social contract we have all formed to contribute into and from which we may expect contribution from others, that is to say, to rightfully claim and to know that this nation is all ours, not *Government's*. (individuals have rights, governments do not.) This social contract shapes our society by being another kind of *Vote* of a sort. We say what we want by building it. Insisting on lifting our burdens – interfering with how we constituents craft our society – worries me as an indirect and most subtle attack on our liberties by both the well-meaning and the ill-willed. For us, there is no difference between them. And for us, their motivation is immaterial.

For those readers who see a contradiction here, there is only elaboration; I suspect and I question motives of others, yes, and this is for understanding of the gravity of what we are up against; absolute stubbornness and why, with no hope of reconciliation and accord. It's important to acknowledge this unwillingness to cooperate and undying dedication to coercion to rub out in others the anxiety-producing symbols that should best be handled within.

Accepting first this understanding that the Left will be unmovable, there is the truth that this is all that matters, the certainty of this un-movability. From thereafter, what they believe and why they believe it is secondary or unimportant; all that matters is understanding why they won't cooperate, ever. Thus, their motivation from then on – whether well-meaning or ill-willed – is *just as incorrect* and

The Battle We Fight

damaging, because it still issues from the same etiology. With that same origin, a deluded official who ignores constituents may be well meaning and still be just as wrong and destructive as the spiteful official who also ignores constituents.

Assertion of our burdens may puzzle officials, but it's our wish to continue to carry our burdens. As I said, the need to relieve us of our liberties reflects a poor understanding of America and her values system. Of course it does, because *they arrive in office* with this reality distortion. This misplaced compassion or desire to help views our burdens as troublesome crosses to bear, and therefore is mistakenly figured to be the best route to successful public service. The defect in the logic (a defect in *their reality and therefore values*) resides in believing that our burdens purchase our liberties, and must therefore be distributed more equally, but this is incorrect; bearing our burdens may *sustain* our liberties, that ongoing worthiness and necessity to be ever-vigilant, but our liberties are God-given and we deem that to be self-evident.

Meanwhile, self-evident means what it says, except to the defective view or hostile opinion of the injustice collectors that God is nonsense. Where slavery around the globe is routine for centuries, we abolished it early after our formation. This isn't a shame in our society, it is a credit to our society. Where civil rights may have been in need of further recognition, it wasn't the Left who pushed it through. We find our way, and the Left, on reflection, has really contributed very little to America.

Their defective view, of course without a values system, sees a less-burden-purchases-Liberty relationship, which liberals believe must be encouraged for equality. But this is not the case, this is not reality, for it confuses equality of outcome with equality of opportunity. This is no accident of good intentions. One wishes the best for all, while the other is hostile to others. Again, the object is not to help, but to devour symbols of anxiety under cloak of beneficence. Modern Leftism must be seen in this perspective from now on. That its motivations are purely against anxiety-producing symbols and not for the altruistic lip-service it pronounces. Opportunity is not really in short supply for anyone for more than two generations, if you begin with 1964.

Their equality is not a function of burdens – of who has more, who has less – true equality is a function of Liberty. And, unlike opportunity, which is not really in short supply, Liberty is becoming in shorter supply.

People love a winner. People like and respect hard work and the symbols of hard work. Most people. People who loathe the successful in America have and have had and still have no less opportunity than anyone else; they simply have been talked out of it, because real opportunity is not a matter of money, it's often a matter of *choice*. The reality is that opportunity is not in short supply for anyone, so, since the Left cannot really change this to set themselves a place at the table, they have to talk people out of it to make them believe it's true. Thus, people who believe there is no opportunity for them are making a choice. People who believe otherwise have also made a choice: they don't know it can't be done.

Choice in high school effort, choice in distractions and time management, choice in listening to parents, and choice in so many things. With so many persons and organizations willing to lend a hand to help with the rest when needed, the only way to attract their attention is to prove you're a good investment. *Choice.*

It might also be worth examining one more time the idea of being unloved creating anger. If an unloved child becomes angry, is it possible that a portion of society taught that they are unloved would also feel angry and to seek *'love'* or support from other groups in society? Just asking.

The fight to *keep* our burdens, the battle to reduce what is becoming in effect *too much help*, is a conservative viewpoint. This is easily distorted by the Left to be hateful and mean-spirited, when it is actually much more respectful than liberals can even conceive and comprehend. It then becomes clear and becomes a more popular viewpoint to those who work hard, respect hard work in others as they grow older and have experience, gratitude and perspective that enables people to come together in unity. It is these who don't have to be reminded to be compassionate to others. Truly, the poor, middle class conservative traditionalists among our society are often much more charitable and understand giving to others better than some millionaire liberals understand charity. Millionaire liberals (the Limousine liberals) are the least giving of our society while making life difficult in coercing *fair share* out of others.

It's because success still breeds respect, self-respect and respect for another's hard work because you, yourself, know what hard work is, even though success on any level is disparaged and scorned by the Left as *being White – another divisive target methodology of social engineering again.* As I said; people who loathe successful persons have been *talked out of being successful.* People who are as a group angry for being unloved are told that someone owes them something and isn't giving it. Perhaps this is because they don't really know what wealth really is. Of those minorities who certainly do, they are castigated and harassed.

But there is also another truth that reaches across all racial lines: that true Liberty, like *Life,* isn't something granted by officials, including so-called leaders and their organizations. *Loss* of Liberty can be granted by officials. *Death* can be granted by officials. But Liberty, like Life, cannot be granted by officials; their job is to *protect* Liberty and Life. Official interference, then, whether desiring to help or otherwise, is destroying the nation from within. Angry people don't make good leaders.

Good intentions will always be pleaded for any assumption of power. The Constitution was made to guard the people against the dangers of good intentions. There are men in all ages who mean to govern well, but they mean to govern. They promise to be good masters, but they mean to be masters.

— DANIEL WEBSTER

The Beast.

The liberals in this country are not monolithic, and are made up of three mind-sets I can see; a) well-meaning persons (who can be most stubborn); b) wrong-headed persons (with an agenda, and who are also stubborn) who don't care about anything more than their ongoing mission, and; c) persons hostile to America and all she stands for ('nuff said here). Many of these are just angry persons. No doubt there are still other factions of liberal mind set. All are angry or misguided because of the motivation to stall anxiety. More on this below.

America didn't get this way overnight, and the recovery from the distress won't be overnight, either. But there is one corner of the problem which can be expedited back to recovery and serve as a fabulous starting point, that little bit of leverage, the problem of *violent crime.*

Violent crime is a dominant force harassing our society while it is also a pet of government officials. Unlike Welfare or taxation without representation, as far as pets go, and unlike white collar crime, this one gets out and moves through neighborhoods to ravage other homes.

Violent crime costs America billions upon billions each year and then even more in all aspects of our lives. Personal Protection is a concept which is being discouraged more and more by a combination of individuals who mean well (including the *impartial*), individuals who are completely wrong-headed, and people who are hostile to America.

But self-protection isn't only bad for the criminal, it would be bad for the Political Left, too, for it would effectively reverse the self-indulgence of officials' balm and administrative prestige and legacy. Self-protection is a necessary serious action in preserving our safety, *and* our liberties, our community costs, our community assets and indeed preserving the present and the future for our loved ones and their loved ones. The Founding Fathers and Mothers knew only too well the monstrosity of tyranny of the Crown, and the minions among them who supported it all, and they loved their children and other children enough to write law of Liberty. Today's mothers and fathers do the same in preserving it not only for themselves, but for their children and other children. Think posterity and descendants. Posterity means *descendants*. To preserve Liberty today is to preserve it for your children's society of tomorrow. To keep tradition alive is to give them the tool for them to give it to *their* children. For those of you who take steps to provide for your kids after you're gone, preserving Liberty is yet another way to say *I love you. I love you very much.*

What started as a pesky nuisance has now become a ravenous pet of someone's single-minded adoration, a pet *thing* that seeks us out and which more or less is good for its owner who is really not yet ready to put it to sleep for all its menace. The pet is not a dangerous animal, it is *we* who misunderstand, right? The thing isn't really uncontrollable, it is *we* who over-react to it, right?

Or it could be a mistress lover, visited often.

The *Beast* is not only violent crime; and The Beast is not *Satan*, and the numbers associated with him; The Beast is a shorthand name for the combination of loathing of America by fellow constituents, official deafness and defiance, violent crime and the officials who keep it all alive for personal and professional gain. It is one of the most insidious forms of looting in America.

What we're talking about here is the rightness and dignity (the personal Liberty you might say) of personal safety being in the hands of the would-be victim in a time when one must think on his or her feet, often alone without Law Enforcement, and just how this impacts the overall makeup of our nation; it also means how we survived in spite of it (thanks to previous values), how we got here over generations (keeping those same values), where we're going (the deleterious substitution of values), and what we impart to our children, indeed if we are even alive to impart anything, or worse: alive and not free.

Karl Marx pointed out the role of coercion. He described the 'dehumanizing' affect of private property. Tell that to the churchgoers who understand giving to others better than most any Limousine liberal to come to mind. Marx believed that materialism, unhappiness and other stressors could be bred out of people in a few generations through being forced, then they would come to like it as they would then ultimately be rid of economic envy, competition and disappointment. Marx's theories were built on the erroneous belief that these are undesirable burdens and that someday, we would all be equal and free from exploitation. See any parallelisms here?

Marx believed that economy was the parameter of social justice.

Marx was of the belief that his vision was good, if only he could get others to see it. He could not. He believed that if he could just get them to adopt it and experience it, they'd like it. They did not.

Karl Marx was a troubled man, angry and isolated, which gives clues to his perception of the world. Many *modern officials* believe this way, whether they even know it or not, this idea of lifting burdens whether *we like it or not!*

Modern officials may or may not be true Marxists, but let's remember the observation that people of a specific trauma (resentments they bring with them to office) can be expected to select a specific behavior to counter it (loathing of anxiety-producing symbols). *Of course* there would be an identity of reactions between Karl Marx and today's Left! And it's no surprise that, according to biographers, Karl Marx loathed his parents; small wonder he also seems to loathe symbols of his childhood. [Bio of the author in his books *Das Kapital, The Communist Manifesto* and elsewhere. Look for older editions as well as other sources.]

Truly, the concept of what is America – starting with Liberty – is being taught less and less, yes, even to the point of *disinclining self-defense.* Where the People are the Nation, changing attitudes such as the right to self-defense is an attack on America, the nation.

It is a large hostile movement, and talking down resistance to violence is only one aspect of this movement to discourage resistance. It is to remove a burden, and that is to remove another liberty. And that is to take more control and to separate people from their rights and from the fruits of their labor. And that is to devour and assimilate.

How we survived to now in spite of it was that *Justice* – real *Justice* – was done. Justice for violent crime, seemingly harsh at times, was based on a value system in opposition to what is modern liberalism. On reflection, liberalism, when it comes to social justice, has not improved things, but has undermined the concept that harsh punishment is a necessary part of justice, and refuses to acknowledge that earlier punishment worked rather well before liberal thought began to analyze it.

Well, it analyzed wrong. What we have today is a system of harassment of core values, some of which is to undermine the justice system with over-inquiry, hair-splitting and straw issues. In this, good people willing to cooperate can be duped into being more fair than fair, and this advances the Leftist agenda of getting us to try it, and we'll like it when every instinct is sending warning lights and buzzers that it is wrong.

How we survived and got here was that our ordinary system of administering a harsh justice prior to liberalism was to meet transgression with penalty, and with little regard for the watering down power of searching the how and the why as a reason to suspend penalty for the duration, liberal parsing and malignant issue-spotting.

In retrospect, say, looking back on the last fifty years or so, we can now see that the *Conscience of the People*, the Left in America, was merely lying to set itself a place at the table, rather uninvited. Running out of inventory, it had to have something new to sell. It will *always* have to find something new to sell.

The *Conscience of the People* meddled in society with abstracts such as what makes a good boy go bad (a 1960's ad campaign about car theft), and, as another wedge, the need to understand better what makes for violent crime and to study penology in connection with it. In the not letting a good boy go bad campaign, the Left would blame the motorist for leaving keys in the car, thereby tempting the boy to commit grand theft auto. It was one of the first times I saw the sway to externalize forces from the boy who would go bad, and to blame the rest on the motorist. It's the driver's fault that the boy stole the car? Is the burglary the homeowner's fault for leaving the screen door open on a warm evening?

The Left's conclusions betray their world view that there cannot be such a thing as evil (perhaps because they don't believe in deities), as they continue to play an endless hand of card after card, one such example being that poverty causes crime, and that nothing we can do short of transfer of wealth will stop it; that externalization again. That taking again. That *separation from the fruits of one's labor* again as the real goal.

Well, poverty causes crime about as much as houses cause tornadoes, or as much as pencils cause spelling errors, and officials dislike having to preside over prosperity; they aren't needed in time of prosperity, and they prefer poverty, including poverty of spirit. Where poverty of spirit is knowing the Lord but without consolation, there is this substitution of the Left as Lord now.

Crime occurs at all social strata, one of the few differences being that money permits many alternatives in choosing which crime; poverty limits or *eliminates* specific crimes, such as embezzlement, stock fraud and so forth to commit only crimes of violence and opportunity. Putting more officers on the street is a step in the right direction, but it doesn't even come close to recognizing the first line of defense, the *individual*. It's like treating heart attacks and trauma by putting more Paramedics on the street. It's a step in the right direction, but you can see where it falls far short at the moment of emergency, medical *or* criminal.

Crime is not a product of poverty, it is a product of anger, stupidity or illness. It is a product of poor values, the inability to see the hurt one does, or the willingness to accept it. The desire to take does not arise from need or hunger as much as it arises from an anger provoked by lies and intentional injustice from so-called leaders. To claim that poverty causes crime is not only to ignore the crimes of the rich, but to say that entire poor neighborhoods are criminal. Of course, this is not the case.

Meanwhile, making a perfectly sensible and coherent issue such as self-defense *even disputable* is only one example of interference and bad faith, this time with straw objections emanating from the Left and the go-limp, passive-aggressive act of the self-identified *impartial*.

Programs headed in the right direction, such as putting more officers on the street which I agree with, but not as the first line of defense, are divided to pieces by mischaracterizing them erroneously as *imperfect or incomplete*. Needs more study, right?

Objections, objections. This is not contribution, it's interference and delay. In the end, unending objections and study are nothing more than a wedge – labeling positive logical steps as divisive or any other word you might hear – which controversy is crafted not for social justice in America, but to cultivate self-doubt in people who genuinely look for safety and Justice. *No Justice long enough equals no faith in the system soon enough.*

This is to devour.

But, we are undaunted. All of this reforming and delaying is done at the expense of society and of individuals, but looting what belongs to the People has never stopped liberals before, and they always manage to derive some sort of capital out of every inch they gain. We The People are going to have to put a stop to this looting. The spirit and thesis of this book is that we recognize that no one is going to do it *for* us. In self-defense, in speaking out against bad taste and poor etiquette, the dumbing down of our kids and absolutely stupid school administrations – no one is going to do it *for* us. Officials do not care nearly as much as we do.

Conspiracy? I doubt it. Latching on to a good thing? Probably. A psychological process that they won't surrender, but would rather surrender *to*? Almost certainly. Hatred of America and contempt for those symbols of painful memories as part of how they arrive at policy and more? Absolutely.

Again, there is a direct connection *not between poverty and crime* but between violent crime in America and what is taught (or selectively ignored) in our schools, in our media and our court rulings, and in the examples of a two parent home that puts the child first in every choice.

Some people just don't want America – some people really don't want choice, or justice, not real justice, anyway, and some people make a living on her troubles – and one way to destroy this nation would be to disincline people to resist in time of torment, violent crime; to devour, to reach back in time to get back at mom and dad who ignored them. Symbols. In fact, one way to destroy a nation would be to *disincline resistance and protest everywhere.*

Because Liberty, functionality and ability, independence, and even the carrying of personal burdens and prosperity and happiness are all symbolic of something someone felt cheated out of earlier in life. The *unendurable affects (Otherwise known as feelings.).*

Naturally, in the anxiety-avoidance syndrome, these symbols have to be destroyed – devoured – but they can't be that obvious, either to others or to themselves, for there would be an irreconcilable conflict. This dissonance never occurs, because the actions appear to correspond with the lip service, but in fact have a built-in sabotage to keeping opportunity-independence and lip-service from ever meeting. It's never perfect, it's never ready to enact. *"We agree on things, but not on the method,"* is the common refrain. It is a parsing lie, of course.

Resistance to objectionable speech, resistance to re-defining our institutions, resistance to tasteless or obscene art – art that is frankly honest, but frankly unnecessary – resistance to subtle messages in media, resistance to everything objectionable, is silenced. Object to something of bad taste or political correctness and you're not met with merely an opposing view, you're kicked to the curb with the complete and total absence of another value, civility.

Restriction on free thought and free speech is the most dangerous of all subversions. It is the one un-American act that could most easily defeat us.

– Justice William O. Douglas

And discouraging resistance puts us one step away from that.

From Without And From Within.

One of the very essential issues that make up the character of the nation the world looks up to – personal Liberty and the idea of *personal worth and value* – must be taught correctly and kept alive and well if it is to be handed down from generation to generation as it has been. Even the hateful impaired have been served well by tradition; *this is where liberals are ingrates! They can't make the connection between the time line of history's events of the nation's origins and their very liberty to talk dirty about it.* Liberals would not be alive today but for the traditions which permit legally and socially their point of view, not to mention the *tolerance* for it which serves us so well today. As one famous lecturer professor announced one day, *"We will destroy you by your own Constitution!"*

Brother, it's working.

We are under attack, friends, by individuals who are of a culture that teaches that they have *more* personal worth and value (*some people are more equal than others)* and by those who have joined them, seemingly paradoxically, to scream *no* personal worth and value, that they are expendable and, by extension, you and I have no worth and value, and that *we* are expendable. Beginning to see a connection here between your personal safety and what is being endorsed in society, taught in schools, and reported or non-reported in most broadcast news? Both of these philosophies have joined to a common purpose and have, for the duration, suspended their differences.

Continuing on the idea of personal worth, it's important for every voter to know one thing and to never forget it, and I speak to liberals here: Policies that are overly harsh and over-reaching affect us all, for when an American Taxpayer – any American – falls victim to such an over-reach, the Government doesn't care how you voted. You are no friend of such policies and such administration just because you voted for them. If they're over-reaching, they'll reach you someday and they won't be thankful to you for empowering them. Just as a rising tide lifts all boats, it's obvious to me that *an ever-increasing, eventually global hatred means no safe harbor.*

You can vote for Standards which include everyone, or you can vote for a Double Standard, which puts the elite on the inside and you on the outside, too with the rest of us. When they come for you, and they will, because you impartially empowered them with powers we tried to tell you were over-reaching and wrong-headed and you told us we were hating you, they won't be looking your name up in some great book to see if you were once their supporter. It's not a matter of Party. It's a matter of personal anger, and you can be *used* for your anger.

One of the best examples of the worst conduct in recent memory is the aggressive income tax collection efforts of the early nineties. Then, tax collection was urged by Democrats, and Treasury was pretty obnoxious. SWAT teams of the IRS took real property, personal property and rights from people by force and with little notice or latitude to the taxpayer, Republican or Democrat, with the burden of proof on the back of the taxpayer and not the master prosecuting body. You may be too young to remember or you may have been a target of outrageous penalties and tax liens. Only a taxpayer revolt and inundation of testimony to Congress turned the IRS into a more empathetic, less heavy-handed wing of the Government. Can it happen here? For a time, it did.

Let me speak more to worth. Today, to the Left, something new has been added. A new principal has joined the Leftist movement of the other three principals, namely the well-meaning, the wrong-headed and the hostile; the new principal is the foreign interest now turned violent. Foreign interests have all pretty much been involved in sabotaging America and putting a thumb in her eye one way or another. Other countries, too, would like to loot our assets and make our nation an asset of the globe.

To this end, they erode our sovereignty (discouraging resistance on a global scale) in subtle ways, try to get us to share everything, but for the most part, they had pretty much been non-violent. Today, they root in the cheering section for the violent demise of the United States.

As President Bush has stated: *Liberty is not a gift of America to the world; Liberty is God's gift to all of mankind.* I believe The President said it more than once. I support President Bush. Instead of making assets of the United States a single sweet plum to be picked, why not bring Liberty to their nation and eradicate the desire to loot by bringing them a brand new fruit tree? With their own prosperity, their hatred and looting could disappear.

That is, *if* their poverty and their forcing us to share what we have was their desire. It is not. Too many Americans – and too many in other countries – believe that if we resolve poverty, we'll resolve hostility. To presume that their friendship or hostility is a function of economy is another misread. For those who are hostile to America, eradication of the United States is their true desire, you see, not the desire to steal and own what we have in terms of resources (not entirely, anyway), but to destroy us as a magnet for their people. To those leaders, this is humiliating. To bullies, it *would* be humiliating, of course.

The refusal to acknowledge Liberty for all and the interference with those who do is a clue to the deeper thinking and *Weltanschauung* of what we call the Left in America and the miserable forces of nihilism and rage around the globe which align with the American Left now. This includes the outside tradesmen of hate against America who collaborate with the American Left in common purpose; the shared idea that Liberty as America practices it in the 21st century is not something necessarily inherently contemptible to them, but merely an obstacle to their purpose, something to be destroyed as a living force that is anti-death. America is a *rival* for the devotion of many peoples, including theirs. These anti-life Monarchs are simply in distress, and they are clawing to maintain their power in light of a great egress. We are in their way; we are a magnet for Peoples, either as an ultimate destination or as *an example*. America chooses Life and Liberty, and we are ready to die for it. The anti-life forces choose Death and are ready to kill and die for it.

It's important to understand that Americans are willing to fight for *Liberty*. Peace is not the highest objective, *Liberty* is the goal. Peace, a won peace or almost any other peace, is not. One can have peace and be restrained, and without Liberty, life under constant harassment is not worth living. Eternal vigilance, non-peace at times, is one price for Liberty, the higher goal.

Ask the people who emigrate to America, for unlike the children of much of America today, horror of totalitarian states is well known and is even still fresh in the memories. The Socialist Parties, according to the 1960's editions of *Encyclopedia Britannica* and elsewhere, would use goals of Peace and Equality as a carrot to social change, but would ultimately control the populace through increasing legislation and punitive action under color of progress. Incrementalism. The Progressive Party. Whether the Communist Party felt itself wise and altruistic or knew itself only too well as just plain cruel and powerful is immaterial. Concentration of power would reside more and more with those officials and, by incremental legislative action, less and less with the People. Some speculate that tragedy, in America on American soil and abroad, is a tool as an excuse to legislate further and further as part of such incrementalism. Some speculate further that *contrived* tragedy is carried out just for that same purpose. With the cooperation of the sheep, any lamb can be led to the slaughter. This *Britannica* text is no longer published, but may be found if you can locate a middle sixties edition in older private libraries.

Has Socialism changed and somehow become less malevolent? No, it hasn't, but editors and publishers feel its description, its bloody history and recognizable tactics are not to be published in the same detail any longer. Why?

Truth is what liberals dread – truth and history's perspective – because the idea that no one needs them is what they dislike *most* – the reality that their route to soothing balm is over – that it is only one step away and which could be easily made self-evident by the combination of hearing both sides and within a framework of good core values. Remember that they do not simply desire to be leaders, it is that they must avoid anxiety, and part of that anxiety is letting others run things. This they cannot tolerate. Whether they can fly or not, they want to control the stick.

Truth will expedite their ruin, or at least retire them to some museum as historical footnotes or token Professors. It is this kind of movement that we battle; the confiscation of our rights including guns and not including guns to empower the liberal who is the very *last* person who should hold office.

Let me relate guns, Liberty and a choice of national direction, and let us distinguish criminal violence (menace) from moral force (resistance). More than 47,000 of our fellow citizens are injured or killed each year by guns. [FBI Uniform Crime Report or visit *http://*

www.fbi.gov/ucr/ucr.htm for further information. See also *More Guns, Less Crime* by John Lott, Jr.] This is a fact. But also a fact is that more than two million crimes each year are foiled by the use of a gun, and predominantly by private citizens, and often without firing a shot. [Ibid.] That's an impressive comparison, in that it is largely unchanging from year to year and presents an interesting observation: that some people in the menace category used a gun and accidentally or necessarily discharged it, while the preponderance of the *defense* category found a way to use the weapon *properly, yet without* discharging it.

Incidentally, if you'd like to look over more digestible reports more easily relatable to real-life, visit *http://www.keepandbeararms. com/OpSD/* on the web. Gun owners, Liberty Enthusiasts and others knew early that such stories were certain to be under-reported. You can always find the average story of the criminal use of a gun, but if it's true that more than two million use a gun in self-defense each year, then *where are the stories?*

This referenced website doesn't exhibit *the two million* stories, of course, but if you're wondering where the stories are that don't seem to make it to mainstream media, just visit that address.

It's worth noting that gun owners aren't interested in shooting people, as you will no doubt be told by the Left, but owners *are* interested in Liberty, you know, that freedom of movement you enjoy and the right to do and think what you like, really. You know, that barometer that indicates the level of health of all those other liberties. We're interested in protecting it, and personal self-defense is an integral part of it.

As in the cases of unreported rape – where experts believe that for every report of rape, there are somewhere ten instances which are not reported [Rape Treatment Center, Santa Monica Hospital, California and elsewhere] – there is every reason to believe that there are similarly further figures of unreported thwartings of crime to add to the total, where, in contrast, it would be nearly impossible to under report *injuries* by guns; specifically, because gunshot wounds are usually treated in some facility and then by law must be reported; discouraging or foiling a crime is many times just simply handled by the homeowner or motorist and sometimes *not* reported. Thus, there may be an undisputed 47,000 individuals killed or injured each year, but there may be *much, much more than two million thwartings of crime each year.*

Furthermore, the breakdown of shootings falls into categories of police shootings of suspects in commission of crime, crime-on-crime homicides among denizens of crime, and a high percentage of suicides using guns, all of which substantially clarify the *character* of shootings to one other than immense gun tragedy.

Put another way, we know of almost all if not all shootings and we know how they break down statistically, but we have *thwartings* of crime, *two million of which we know about and much of which didn't fire a shot.* It could be much more, where it is very doubtful that there are more shootings to be uncovered, and of those shootings known, it is also know precisely how the shooting went down, actually.

There are probably thousands of individuals who simply stop a crime that would-have-been by the action of drawing down on their aggressor. Aggressor flees: end of problem. What's to report, right? Not only is self-defense our right, but it is also most practically the only sensible thing to do under the circumstances when the alternative is certainly an injury and personal loss to the victim and thereby the community.

Crime To Others Affects You.

Crime affects your taxes, it affects the appropriation and the missions of local assets, and it affects how government officials view their constituents. That has a lot to do with whether they even listen to you. After all, if you do nothing in the way of notifying officials, how are they to know what you'll tolerate and won't tolerate? How are they to know what the community needs beyond painting fire hydrants and fixing potholes? How do they know what kind of initiative to take? Instead, they take their own initiative.

It is important for the average Joe and Josephine Taxpayer to understand one important thing: much of the information which may interest you on this subject (the other side of the story) is either actively kept from people until now (such as under-reporting self-defense stories of record) or in some way distorted from a truth to a half-truth or an intentional mischaracterization (i.e. reporting a self-defense against an armed robber as a *shoot-out, or even when two sides using the very same kind of gun, where the assailant is said to be using an assault weapon while the officer is using a high-powered rifle*) that serves better the opposition than the truth ever could.

Another example of media irresponsibility is to describe *compliance* with the law as using *loopholes*. It's a slander. Propaganda. In short, the opposition cheats.

The media hides or distorts facts out of contempt or, more likely, *incompetence. They can't seem to report accurately and with consistency.* They have to fudge and distort, because most sensible people agree on self-defense, and that means disagreeing with liberals (and their failure to report facts), and most people don't know where to look to find the other side of the story. Many people are just now becoming interested in this for the first time. This means the new adults, the newlyweds, new businesspeople, and more who now come to place greater and greater emphasis and understanding on their freedoms. Their true freedoms.

The non-release of news and information – a sort of lying by omission in news reporting – can be negated by visiting websites which do release news of how individuals are using weapons properly, for their intended purpose.

Not for hunting, but for self-defense. Not for collecting, but for practical self-defense. All you need do is look for it. These are not Hate Sites, but information sites serving different purposes. Some of these sites are purely factual repositories where you can discover details such as statistics. Others are banks of news items where you can view reports, others are very, very commentary and raise important questions, and still others are any combination of these. But *Hate*, they are not. They have one common principle: Liberty for all, and that's not hate. Take the time to visit a few just to check references if nothing else.

You won't find very many true stories of local self-defense from Rather, Brokaw or Jennings, and you won't hear of them in their true numbers.

Author's note: *Rather, Jennings, and Brokaw* is merely an expression now, and probably not especially long-lived, denoting the anchors of the alphabet news networks, especially the kind which seems to present more Politically Correct stories and slant to the content than the kind of stories of substance Americans need to hear to be informed in making their political decisions. Since the first edition of this book, Rather has announced retirement slated for March, 2005 following a scandal that, for some, would seem to betray a blatant political agenda, the humiliation being that the anchor was the last to know; (Both his agenda and the truth of that story he was the last to know.) Brokaw has retired on December 1st, 2004, and Jennings remains. Each of these men has occupied the seat of Anchorman for decades, and though, from time to time, they do their own research and reporting, their individual and otherwise handed-them reportage is still the same, PC. How this breakup will alter the PC content and slant of future network news remains to be seen, as some mention that these retirements won't change a thing.

The sheer number of successful, lawful and justified self-defense stories may surprise you. Where crime to others affects you, so does improper reporting. This participation in omitting such fair-sided news is to befriend the Beast. Media are part of the problem.

Acts Of Interference.

Let's make an historical observation of one of the most objectionable changes in our society as it relates to the downward trend of core values, and how this is related to other unwanted afflictions such as crime and other loathing of the country. Let's look at another aspect of the Beast, the cooperation between misguided officials and destructive special interest groups.

As one domestic example, one of the most insidious movements was the introduction of no-fault divorce. The argument was that one should not be forced to remain in a relationship against his or her will, and it was part of the Feminist Movement at the time, among other special interest movements. Making it easier to divorce was foreseeably going to undermine Marriage as *a commitment,* which is the heart of the institution, whether you're making the friendly religious argument or the friendly civil argument for Marriage. Staying against your will weakens a person a little at one time or another, and is part of commitment's trials, and if you allow the dissolution more easily, then you dissolve the concept of commitment, too. This is compassion? This is good for kids?

Hardly, since some of us expect commitment in return when we give it. When your commitment is unappreciated and unsupported by the legal system without regard for the ripple effect on society – by hurting children, discouraging faith in the institution, and failing to realize the true scope of the institution, etc. – it's easy to become weak. It's easier to get that stamp of approval for a choice you, yourself, probably wouldn't have the guts to make alone.

As I point out that today's kids have only a snapshot for perspective, they may be entirely used to the concept of no-fault divorce. Perhaps today's newlyweds and others don't know that no-fault divorce is a relatively new concept, and that generations ago, no-fault didn't exist. Earlier, one of the two principals of a marriage had to prove something substantial in order to receive a divorce. Back then, divorce and divorce attorneys were expensive. Back then, you really had to have a good reason to dissolve the marriage. Sometimes, those reasons were valid. Today, when it's so very easy, no-fault threatens the institution by dissolving the very binding of that agreement.

The problem is not only in staying in a marriage, but in the quality of principals *entering* a marriage. And this applies to *all people*, people who are too young to comprehend the idea of life-long commitment, people who are addicted, people who are too unwell, and this does not apply to persons who will die married, but who are simply unable to keep a life-long promise. It is these who cannot live for others. The impaired having children of impairment makes for new generations of impaired, and so it goes.

These are the people who weasel out of their word by ideas such as *"Well, I didn't know it was going to be like this,"* and other such seemingly acceptable excuses to permit them to beg off and leave. But such feeble excuses (betraying character traits and more) are easily torn apart and exposed by the critical thinking examination of questioning why someone *didn't* know and what they *did* expect to aspire to. Just what did they really expect out of their marriage? Did they fully understand what it means to them and to the nation? Or was it a lark, which could easily be dissolved by a simple court filing?

Making it easier to weasel out of Marriage also puts the stamp of approval on weaseling out of less important conventions. Surprised? Instead of testing their mettle in staying with an institution that is a stronghold of society, they quit and never have to face the difficult, and Marriage is a place where you can certainly find some difficulties. Marriage is also a place where you can defeat difficulties as a stronghold of the nation.

Small wonder such learned helplessness prevails and guts seems to skip a generation. Or two. Small wonder others put such a high value on Marriage.

In connection with easy divorce, I have my objection to rotten sitcom television morals and editorials masquerading as News: that peers and others *approve* or seem to, and this makes it easier to advance a desire – any desire – you wouldn't ordinarily follow through with. It works the other way, too: if you see stronger, heartier values, you're more inclined to keep a commitment than abandon it if you wouldn't have been led astray without a shove, or on the other side, if you wouldn't stay but for your promise and a little encouraging support. Marriage has its trials, of course, and knowing this, individuals solemnizing the wedding routinely summon added commitment from the witnesses and guests to support the marriage in time of trials.

Today, about half of marriages end in divorce, probably made easier by no-fault divorce. I still believe that the one out of two statistic is reserved for couples *in their first two years only,* but figures from various modern sources in my most recent research don't answer this entirely for me. I wish they did. I believe that, at one time, one out of two applied only to the first twenty-four months: namely, that one out of two marriages will end in the first two years, and that if you could make it to five years, you had a better overall chance for surviving together even longer, and so forth. The statistics improved with every passing year as I recall, but it seems to have changed now that one out of two will divorce period, no matter what reference I read. Still, no matter which inference you draw, the odds are in your favor, and at 50% at worst, the odds are never against you.

Now, if I wanted to attack a nation over time, any nation, I would discredit its institutions, its *anchors*, for they are pockets of resistance to adversity, *including my adversity, my unpopular ideas (Leftism, let's say)*, and make no mistake, attack of Marriage would be to loosen an anchor, and where it's appreciated for what it really is, it would be unpopular, too.

The cohesion of couples, the resources and values held by a marriage, make them able to survive nearly anything, including my temptations to get them to stray, unless I can dishearten them at the outset, and make them doubt and ridicule their faithful institutions as old-fashioned and passé. Again: at the outset. A pre-emptive strike you might say.

Picture me for a moment to be a devil who lurks around homes and seeks ways to undermine family. Just for a minute. It can come from many directions, including school curriculum you disapprove, endorsement of children suing parents, extolling child defiance of parents and interference with in-home discipline . . . well, I could go on. Meanwhile, if the couple expects less from Marriage, perhaps I can get them to put *in* less. With less optimism to begin with, I have an edge on destroying Marriage. Their marriage. That's why, if I were a hater of America, I would make fun of Marriage (among other institutions), lie about it and try and redefine it down more every day with half-truths.

The thing about half-truths is that to the speaker, he or she or they feel they are speaking truth, and will not own the lie they utter as a half-lie; also, it's partly the fault of the listener who will not investigate. Eventually, people lose interest and accept the statements as fact. This is where tradition comes in. Hiding or erasing history – traditional values – is truly an attack on an institution that could be the redeeming stronghold of a society. This is what Marriage is: a stronghold, a pocket of resistance, to adversity. A haven. An anchor.

If the institutions and their viability become less and less distinct and less and less respected with lesser and lesser expectations for others who vow to support the young couple at the moment of their wedding, maybe there won't be *any* believers soon, and without believers in this beautiful pocket of resistance to adversity, this anchor of the nation, I can set the nation adrift. Lies don't cost much to manufacture. I can be patient.   . . *If I hated America.*

Conservatives who believe in traditional values and useful pillars of society, institutions such as Marriage, are not opposed to change as conservatives are often mischaracterized: they know – we know – these institutions as safe havens that have guided us all for so long, all of us, these pockets of strength to adversity, nearly any adversity. Marriage, as an institution, is a survival tool, recognized as such by both sides, by those who retreat to it for comfort and by those who target it to dissolve resistance to their agenda. It's not as valuable as a religious institution as it is a life-saving anchor of society. And the Left knows this. Marriage, in itself, is good for the Nation.

Thus, conservatives are opposed not to *change* per se, but to destruction; destruction of their homes, their place of safety, and, like most of us, they can sense danger when it comes masquerading as open-mindedness and change, progressive or otherwise. You've heard the expression that it's alright to be open-minded as long as you don't let your brains fall out: kindly, willing, cooperative nit-wits would like to help, but in the process can't see through the straw arguments; they let their brains fall out. Some of today's educators have done this, as I will illustrate later.

Many corners of our society are simultaneously under attack in the form of improving America – asking for tolerance and open-mindedness – and retrospect has proven them wrong. The history of Leftist failures, too, is being erased over time, it's worth noting.

The attack on Marriage comes in the form of redefining it to make it more and more *'inclusive'* and thereby more and more vague, to permit new quasi-legal doctrines, such as the understanding of the *compassion* of no-fault divorce, and to discredit it and discourage people from believing in it by cowardly lying about its character and about its place in goodness for society. Again, the concept of seeing Marriage as a *fraud. Again, the concept of making the institution to suit the misperception.* Leftism is exquisite anger, powerful, mistaken anger that devours everything that makes it anxious.

Of course, that Marriage is a fraud is a lie. Making perception to conform to some sort of statistical truth is an attack, not a public service, because the nation has a vested interest in Marriage. Knowing that America will have its adversity, the nation has an interest in preserving and protecting pockets of resistance. To target Marriage is to recognize that it is a vital area of strength against adversity.

People are raised better in Marriage, taught kindness, patience, faithfulness, strength and courage, hard work, resource, commitment, and, yes, Justice. To say that this can be done better outside this institution is to lie, because the one basket of things that cannot be taught outside of Marriage is parental love, expressed as closeness, the parent-child Bond, the skinetics, the sacrifice and consistency, the protection and warmth of home, and almost supremely important, *setting the example – the how-to of it all for them when the child someday becomes an adult and perhaps a parent.*

On the matter of certain constancy and constant certainty in the home, there is so much more a set of together parents give to children than can ever be even closely matched by anything outside family, that the proposal of any alternative is not well-meaning, but is knowingly and purely hostile. The hostility – the absence of any well-meaning – lies in the fact that the selfish refuse to understand the importance of supporting an institution they cannot be a part of.

I'll say this again; I concede that for the liberal, perhaps Marriage and family were a fraud, only insofar as this was the origin of their anger. I emphasize again that this was perhaps true for them, and certainly not true for the majority of Americans. This anger doesn't end at the water's edge of the liberal's household even today, but extends out into society as a search and destroy mission for families that are the life of the nation.

This smoldering is never satisfied merely with the truth that perhaps one's life maybe wasn't so great, but neither will it ever be satisfied with the destruction of others'. This is another giveaway that this quest for so-called progressive change is nothing more than retaliation against symbols: it attacks symbols – all symbols – of the pain that was at home, but which can never change their history and will never cure the pain. They just can't let go. Amid the affliction, it's too satisfying to have something to fight about, this itch to scratch – even to keep it alive just to have something to scratch – because that payoff is more satisfying than helping build and improve, more satisfying than healing. This is a feature of the impairment.

Meanwhile, under color of inclusion, fairness and, (*I'm nauseated to think of it) compassion*, the destructive alternatives are not only allowed, they are encouraged. More and more alternatives are found. They dissolve the institution from a distance, as the Left, the party of inclusion, can carve it up into pieces, wash their hands of it, have some sort of that Washingtonian *plausible deniability* for instigating it, and permit it to continue to erode the concept on autopilot.

Think Like A Parent.

If you believed that half of all marriages end in divorce, and forgot that divorce itself was made easier to contribute to this figure along the way with a little shove from the Left's no-fault, you, as a parent, may not be so very delighted to learn of your daughter's engagement, necessarily. But if you knew that half will end in the first two years *anyway* and rather *understandably* and *not* due to some cynic's view of just plain rottenness of Marriage, (it's quite an adjustment) would you have a new optimism when you know more about the odds? It's no longer some foreordained force, but more of something a couple can actually grapple with (*and thereby gain experience at dealing with adversity to begin a life that gives even more holy meaning to the institution; a hard contribution to societal survival*). The very idea that the first two years are the hardest is one ordeal that adds to the strength of the institution as a pocket of resistance to adversity; *experience.* Making this vulnerable period – or any vulnerable period – easier to walk out on is not compassion for the imprisoned, it is an attack on the nation, for it nips in the bud the thing that makes Marriage so strong: *gaining experience at handling adversity.*

Where the individual household must fight adversity from time to time and thereby gain experience to hand down to the next generation in wisdom, each household is a pocket of resistance to adversity, a small place where it occurs. Multiplying this by the number of households is to know Marriage as an institution of resistance to adversity. It can be both. If they can get past the most difficult time – the first two years – they're on their way to playing an important role in protecting the Nation.

Learning this, do you believe that, if your child and your new in-law marry and work hard as newlyweds, their marriage will have better and better chances for survival now? Understanding that, at worst, the odds are never against them, does it now change how you feel about their future? Now, with this new clarity about the idea, do you feel much more hopeful for your children who contemplate Marriage? Can you now stand up at their wedding with greater optimism now and take an oath as a witness that you will support their marriage?

This is just one example of how forces are eroding our sense of optimism and underpinnings of personal worth, commitment and sacrifice now by targeting the associations we someday aspire to and contribute our own help to maintain. It's so important that we even have pre-marital counseling for principals to truly contemplate what they are doing and what is expected of them for the sake of others. It is vital to comprehend this as an attack and it is vital to understand that only a posture of self-defense will prevail. Discouraging resistance everywhere, including resistance to destructive change, is directly related to attacks on Marriage. And is a feature of the Beast.

The Kitchen Countermeasure.

Other aspects of our society are under equal attack from the same recognizable weapon, *discouragement.* With crime on the increase or at least remaining the same while encroaching on every neighborhood now, *the theme is to discourage resistance.* We're told that resistance is futile; worse, that it contributes to the ire of the predator and improves your chances of injury.

Well, the concept of non-resistance (like the concept that no-fault divorce is more compassionate because it releases people from 'inappropriate' obligation) *isn't true.* Crime stats emphasize that resistance *improves* your chances of lesser injury, in fact of even not losing your pocketbook! Or your life! [FBI Uniform Crime Report, and *More Guns, Less Crime* by John Lott, Jr., not to mention those hundreds of training facilities that emphasize not becoming a victim.] In fact, if you don't look like an easy target, you may not even be approached at all! Why would anybody want to furnish you any disinformation that works against you? *Opinion?*

No, it's not their opinion; those same people who furnish misinformation also want to tie the hands of persons who choose to resist violent crime. And to hear the Left speak, you'd think they're only trying to help. But trying to help or not, they're working against us and, trying to help or not, the People have the right to choose how they want to handle the problem.

But disinformation can attack you only if you believe it (or if enough people believe it); and you can easily fall for it when it's not countered, when you don't get the other side, or when you don't seek it out. You psyche yourself out absorbing the atomic stink bomb of their pre-emptive lies, *discouragement at the outset,* with all its fallout instead of hearing information with an educated degree of skepticism, *critical thinking — and deciding more for yourself.*

Let's think about this countermeasure for a sec. Critical thinking isn't what it's touted to be lately by Leftists. Self-proclaimed experts on the subject, some professors, describe it as a useful skill, but in substance, they depart from the proper definition thereafter to endorse criticism and carping in order to embarrass opposing views and erode credibility of opponents as the primary objective. Like many tools, it can be abused.

Critical thinking is not a weapon to direct at opponents who are targeted for elimination, critical thinking is a tool for your own edification, which may result in your siding with your subject, instead of disproving their statements. Insulting, haranguing and interrupting is only Carping. Carping is a weapon where one has already made up his mind and has nothing to ask, really; the former is a tool for the individual who has not yet made up his mind and wishes to evaluate through a process of further discovery by follow-up and taking little at face value (unless you already know the fact or non-fact).

Critical thinking is not spotting the most *embarrassing* questions, it's raising germane issues that are possibly hidden or suppressed and unexplored, unresolved. It's follow-up. In fact, critical thinking is not aggressive against the speaker or writer of any given issue *ad hominem,* but investigating the *substance of the information with increasing sophistication.* The more you learn, the closer you get to the truth, and that truth has meaning for you dependent upon your values system. Hitting the *messenger* ad hominem is the giveaway of carping and is not critical thinking.

Critical thinking does not cross-examine the person to death, playing an endless hand of cards of literary or verbal harassment, but confirms or denies the truth and relevance of statements by way of follow-up. It verifies, investigates and challenges with follow-through, emphasis on follow-up, and then emphasis on follow-through. *(Follow-through is completion of something, follow-up is persistence in getting there.)* It may discover lies or it may verify truths, all of which are researched against the value system of you, the investigator. As for myself, I live by the maxim of *fiat justicia, ruat coelum – let justice be done, though the heavens fall.*

I don't mind losing from time to time. I only wish opposing views wouldn't mind either when they have to lose. This is what makes Leftism wrong: it is self-serving instead of securing a present and future of Liberty by working for Liberty for all. Leftism masquerades as thinking of others, but insinuates itself to think *for* others. This is interference to devour anxiety-producing symbols, namely, your Liberty – freedom of thought.

Critical thinking is a fabulous kitchen countermeasure to the political correctness and propaganda at work to erode our resolve in America. Critical thinking for the new-to-politics parent or constituent is, itself, most encouraging, it's really such an easy and fun tool to use. One of the greatest objections to Talkradio, for instance, is that it has become a forum of critical thinking where Leftist ideas are out there naked for all to see and to appraise where they are met by conservative ideas. Unable to really defend themselves, Leftists groan and make ad hominem attacks on hosts and callers. The most successful hosts who endure despite this are fabulous critical thinkers who exhibit true analysis, manners, tolerance and veracity instead of carping and chopfighting, as some would like to factor into the dialogue to water it down. And the loudest objections are from the Left who somehow believe that its message is not being heard, or, get this, that they're not articulating it clearly. Your critical thinking spotted *that* lie right off, didn't it?

It's also a great *parenting tool* to counter bureaucratic schools who dispense half-witted pronouncements, incorrect or edited historical facts and gutless policies which deeply indoctrinate your children their way, offsetting your wishes. So much for the doctrine of *in loco parentis (in the place of the parent,* the doctrine that presumes that officials will take as good a care of pupils as the parents would*).* Liberalism cannot stand up to critical thinking, and when it tries, it's actually conservative-sounding *lip-service.* This is where most people arguing with liberals become intimidated. But, where eternal vigilance is the price of Liberty and your way of child raising, and where suspicions are warranted, *good critical thinking skills are indispensable.*

Where information, interpretation and good habits are vital to your child's education, so resistance is vital in time of violent crime and its tolerance by society.

Resistance is proven worthwhile by the under-reported two million persons who defend themselves against the over-emphasized 47,000 accidents, crimes of violence and, yes, necessarily *undefended* injuries each year. What happens when people choose to defend themselves? The lawful use of a weapon patently outnumbers the criminal uses of a weapon against the undefended victims more than forty to one. *Q.E.D.*

Are We Worth It?

Let's look now at the supreme fundamental issue in relation to The Beast, subtle loathing attacks on our nation, personal worth in relation to violent crime, and the official misfeasance of allowing crime. Americans differ from some cultures in the world and resonate with others on the subject of *personal worth.* In some parts of the world, life is cheap. The belligerent cultures around the world hold out on their citizens, then train them to accept this as a value.

America's humanitarian efforts around the world are delivered, but often intercepted by cruel officials upon arrival. Yes, many nations, free and otherwise, emphasize personal worth, people do mourn the loss of loved ones, they do, but many of them want to flee to America, to find a better quality of life, perhaps even a better quality of science and medical care, and, yes, Justice; a higher level of what is done, and most importantly, *a higher level of what an individual can do.*

This is not western arrogance, nor is it the silly notion of self-esteem as it's touted by facile nit-wits. It's respect for others and having the moral right to expect it in return as a component of happiness. It's self-respect. It's to be cultivated in the child by teaching and by example, then the teen and then the adult. Call it courtesy. Call it true equality if you like. Call it respecting another person's hard work, because you yourself know what hard work is. *You get out what you put in,* and that kindness to others, generosity, tolerance and fairness works itself out well without the need for overseers coercing it from you to their perspective and doing it for a living, and part of that living is to get you to surrender on certain issues.

We are under attack not only by belligerents around the globe who hate us and operate on a culture of death and a discouraging of personal worth, but we are also under attack from within by fellow Americans who hate America and all of the values that have served us all, even them, for so very long. We could hear from authorities comment on the question, but it matters not, because, for the present, such analysis will never change the minds and hearts of the hostile in time; we're going to have to summon the People.

Understanding the criminal with a view toward some sort of exoneration in the name of compassion was never high on my list. All we need do is battle them and survive, hopefully to turn back the later minions who have misguided empathy for them and pass along our values to resist the recidivist and outside forces aiding them wherever and whenever they are, in this century or the next. Because, as I mention often, America will always be under attack, if not from this clique, another clique in the future. *Always.* Because America isn't a place, it is an idea.

Our supreme fundamental issue is that every individual American has personal worth, that an individual citizen here is a sovereign, that people come to America because they know that they have personal worth and they want to live in an environment that fosters that value, and that each person here sharing that value has a sense of safety in their worth and freedom of movement unlike any other country in the world. Ours is a culture of Life, and of hope and unselfishness expressed to each other a hundred different ways. We welcome others of like mind.

Ours is a culture of true prosperity, where wealth isn't measured in the coin of the realm, but of joy, peace of mind, friendship and love, trust of others, contact, health, good faith and the respect and courtesy we give one another. *This* is wealth.

Almost everything we know and love is built around the value that we, as individuals, touch the lives of each other and that we contribute a great deal more to those lives of others than we can immediately remember. And they touch us. They think of us when we are sick, and they stop for us when we cross the street. They hand us the mail that went to the wrong address, they make sure we get the right change, and they carry a package to the car for us. They wave to firefighters. They give us what they would like us to give in return. They listen when we cry and they cry for us when they can't help it. This genuine joy of life threatens some unfriendly states by our very existence, sometimes individual citizen nationals, sometimes whole governments. To these small minds, our existence is an unavoidable superior comparison leading to their indisputable humiliation on a global stage.

Some people may believe that we are magnetizing the world by our electronics, our movies, our monetary and commercial prowess among our world peers, our decadent culture, but my impression is that we are magnetizing other people to emigrate here because here a person can be a sovereign.

Until today, we have been a pest and perhaps legend, hated for our handouts and perhaps even our intrusions. But today, we are the destination of egress, and to the way of thinking of those heads of state where humanity is the coin of the realm, they should be embarrassed before their monarch peers. They are, and it drives them insane. Most importantly, it moves them to action.

It is also worth mentioning that poverty has been the way of the world since the beginning of time, and that prosperity for many, many persons, in the monetary sense, anyway, is relatively new to societies. As long as there has been family, true wealth has been with us all along. As the world begins to know having money, it grapples with a relatively new concept, and some peoples defy it as if it were a sin. Some nations envy us and hate us, but they forget that the world has always been poor.

But remember, friends, we are not under attack for our prosperity in monetary terms, but for our prosperity in terms of our *Liberty – as a destination, in fact a magnet and model to the world* — and their claim of our economic superiority is only a cloak to hide their true rage, to lie to minions, though we may be attacked on all fronts, including through our economy. Today, there are reports of economic attack, such as Internet foul-ups, oil disruptions and taking of key employees as hostages.

Our existence is an intolerable temptation to emigrate here, to resist, to egress their homeland, and where minions – people in slavery and poverty – are regarded as assets of a different sort of coin of the realm, an Exodus such as is feared by Monarch and Dictator is to fear the political equivalent of financial bankruptcy and utter abandonment. Like the American Impaired, the dread is that of ultimately being unneeded (balm connection severed), and worse, rejected and abandoned, even when one defies a regime under threat of death. Those who love to remain and thrive under those conditions hate Life itself, enchanted by something to make them surrender up all manner of humanity, their hate is so very deep. So they join with American haters and control freaks, whose hate is also so very deep.

We are under attack because we are free and because we are a light to the world which humiliates Monarchs who breed minions otherwise. People are not leaving America, they are coming to America, not because America is a place, but, again, because America is an idea. Understand that it is not something we have done wrong among our endeavors, but that *we and any* nation whoever happens to be the example to the world would be the object of hatred and attack. As a magnet to the peoples of the world, America is a place of personal worth, not of money, but of what someone can become, and for family, it is true wealth; America's Liberty permits people this, and to become anything they can be. Now, the enemies of this kind of wealth have come to our shores to join the American Left.

II. National Direction,
Our Governance.

The Perniciousness Of Potomac Fever And Of The Impaired

True Second Amendment enthusiasts aren't wild about guns, we are wild about *Liberty*. Right to carry is the barometer of all Liberty in America. It is not we who are wild about guns, it is the Left who is wild about guns. Also, the objections to its implementation are most similar to those raised by the gun nuts.

(Author's Note: Remember that we've always had guns since before the country's birth. Any mania to take them away is an attack on the norm, so gun owners are not the gun nuts, the liberals are the ones who are nuts about guns. They're outright *hysterical!* We're *Liberty* Nuts, the *supposed* original mission of liberals, remember?)

The Left resents guns as the symbols of independence, greater independence than they would like to see. Liberty for ourselves and Liberty for others is the value, and the more, the better. The

Left objects to Liberty, because it states by its very existence that a Left as it is today is not needed because of broad self-reliance and, more, that when people are free, something is out of control of the impaired.

Where people are free, they have little need for champions. Constituents are their own champions. Fathers and Mothers are champion enough. Where a government comes in is to furnish hired executives to carry out the needs of the country under our authority. That's where their role ends.

There is so much more respect and security of everyone when respect for others is generated from a much deeper, more profound value of a Creator-given right than a construct to be coerced under defective theories and a warped sense of social justice arising from anger at mom and dad. For a portion of the populace who wishes to restrict actions they mistakenly believe are done in anger, they really need the introspection admitting and surrendering their motives will bring.

Personal weapons for personal protection are merely *tools,* much like your computer is a tool for writing your opinion, or bill-paying, or for publishing your newsletter. I doubt that anyone who knows the Bill of Rights would ever believe that they should have to show cause for the free exercise of any of their rights.

Where you may have at one time objected to personal ownership of firearms and never seen the connection between the First and Second Amendments, you may now be noticing an encroachment on your right to free speech because of an encroachment *tested* on the right to keep and bear arms in the proving ground of endless debate and endless interference, generally focusing on violence and the intentional mischaracterization of violence. When the Left isn't talking us out of our second amendment rights, they're talking *minions* into eliminating them to become a formidable force. *Would this have an affect on justice?*

This is harder to maintain when people become discouraged by being talked out of rights or if their history is erased.

Through this mix of Liberty and tolerance, we somehow manage to find our way and sort it out as we go and settle in. In the vast majority of cases, we don't need much in the way of interference from the Left or from anyone; there should be only proper and honest education of our history (good and bad) and of our rights. Knowing what it took to secure our liberties develops respect and appreciation for what we have. This makes for one's value system. Call it gratitude for the sacrifices others have made for us. We need rulings from time to time, yes, but not *excessive initiative* from the Left where there may be a perceived cause to be fought, but no Plaintiff except for the Left. It's only when the Left sees an opening to make a change to benefit and advance *itself* (such as eliminating the historical symbols on somebody's County seal) does it file a pleading. It even proceeds when no one supports the group. Laws to enforce criminal abuses of the First Amendment are sufficient, however the perceived need for more and more laws against free speech which, as I just mentioned, are mounting, and are beginning to rival the mounting of laws against the Second Amendment, Liberty.

Restricting the donations of private citizens in McCain-Feingold is another such example. Where you can vote only once, but yet cast another vote in fiscal support of your candidate, it's recognized as such and stubbed out by the Left in the name of, you guessed it, campaign finance reform. As if. Any critical thinking would enable one to see that it's a restraint of free speech. This is why McCain-Feingold is nick-named *The Incumbent Protection Act*.

This kind of harassment was predicted by Liberty enthusiasts for decades in articles and speeches, commentaries and elsewhere. It's also predicted by statesmen and philosophers over the centuries. It's really beginning to surface now, and people are just now taking notice for the first time. Except, of course, where its not reported to the People in mainstream. Imagine that!

This is important to understand. The Second Amendment (the statement that right to carry is a right and that the Amendment limits infringement of it by saying *shall not be infringed*) has been under incremental attack for a very long time, and right to carry advocates were able to foresee the eventual attacks on the First Amendment early on. On the issue of whether an individual is Militia, it's already *been* through the examinations of what is a Militia and all the other insulting queries. Militia refers to all men in the country capable of bearing arms. Militia, organized militia, and unorganized militia are all different things, and they are all well defined in 10 U.S.C. 311(a)-(c). For easy reference, the section is printed here:

Sec. 311. - Militia: composition and classes

(a) The militia of the United States consists of all able-bodied males at least 17 years of age and, except as provided in section 313 of title 32, under 45 years of age who are, or who have made a declaration of intention to become, citizens of the United States and of female citizens of the United States who are members of the National Guard.

(b) The classes of the militia are -

(1) the organized militia, which consists of the National Guard and the Naval Militia; and

(2) the unorganized militia, which consists of the members of the militia who are not members of the National Guard or the Naval Militia.

In short, part (2) applies to you and me. If you're an able-bodied citizen between certain ages, you're Militia.

Put another way, individuals have rights, governments do not.

And furthermore,

I ask, sir, what is the militia? It is the whole people. To disarm the people is the best and most effectual way to enslave them.
— George Mason, during
Virginia's Convention to Ratify the Constitution (1788)

He ought to know!

I would even go so far as to say that the mind of the Liberty enthusiast could rather easily foresee by his or her value system an interesting kind of Radar – that is, the *kind* of person who would notice and become a Second Amendment enthusiast or supporter would also be the kind of person who could foresee danger for all, gun enthusiasts or not – that the Second Amendment protected all the others much like the watchdog of Government amendment, and that the demise of either would herald the erosion and subsequent demise of the entire Document.

Do you believe that professional writers, broadcasters and artists can easily spot encroachments to *their* civil right, the First Amendment? You'd better believe it! This is because the individual is perceiving on their Radar threats not to guns or speech, but threats to Liberty. Everybody's Liberty. (I'd like to think)

As I mentioned, the right to carry personal weapons is a barometer of how our other liberties are respected, and it's as easy to see as a falling temperature on a cold day. Looking at the barometer or a thermometer is great, but it's just as sensible just to look around you. Without resistance, and with enough people believing that it was the Republicans shredding the Document and not the Left, it was only a matter of time, you see, that things would begin to disintegrate on an increasing scale, and many were able to make that connection as a prediction early.

Today, we are experiencing the greatest attack of free speech in the history of the nation, and it's not coming from the Right, though the Left is using fascist tactics. Just try and give a speech at college campuses and bill your talk as conservative and see how the students receive you. As I mentioned, it's not a right or left issue, but for the present and foreseeable future, it's entirely Leftist in origin.

When we hear both sides, we find our way. In the sixties, the Left was out of power, and advocated free speech so their side could be heard. They published newspapers, they took over college campuses, they bombed buildings, they kidnaped and they held people hostage and, brother, they were heard. And things went Left. Of course, needless to say, these actions, like assassination, circumvented due process. The only solution for the Left is to silence discussion. And they not only want to silence Liberty, they also try to silence Talkradio, a medium without editorial board.

But let me say now that the government indolence isn't the chief case for the Right To Carry. Right to carry is only clearing our throat, only warming up, to deliver a one-two punch to defeat the Beast wherever it exists in America, and this includes the fellow citizen disrespect for our values and way of life. I elaborate this below. Meanwhile, why interfere with someone's right to speak by enacting McCain-Feingold for donations so close to an election, and why interfere with a person's right to defend his person and home? Are these connected? Yes, they are.

Because it's not the violence they want to stop any more than it's the illegal campaign finance money they want to stop. What the Left *really* wants to stop is your ability to resist, no matter where it appears, in the *Vote* or in the *School* or in the *Home* while enjoying both their freedom of movement the language and spirit of the law permit and the never-ending benefits that crime brings to the office.

They – stubborn officials and their minions – want to stop your ability to resist violent crime, your willingness to resist PC ideas, to resist stupid and counterproductive court rulings, destruction of traditional values, rights to practice religion, oppressive rhetoric, how little or when or how at all you can donate to your political candidate, and they want to stop your interest in resisting anything they impose. They are changing the rules when they can, And when they can't talk us out of it, they are changing the conditions to compel us to beg for change. (Changing the conditions is how officials can transfer authority and wealth seemingly with the consent of the governed.)

Both are targeted to discourage resistance. It's a vote of a kind, and the Left wants to cancel your vote of campaign contribution as one avenue.

It all bubbles down to *Potomac Fever* to be tolerated by citizen indifference or to be rejected by citizen involvement, which indifference can lead to career opportunities for most overly ambitious candidates. Officials.

I emphasize Potomac Fever in this book because I view this as an extension of incorrect perceptions, *disorientation*. Impairment. It explains a lot in the ludicrous, stupid and impulsive choices our officials make, professionally and personally. *The willingness to contract Potomac Fever* as unavoidable along the way is itself one of the earliest behavioral signs of over-ambition. Or, perhaps that the likelihood of catching it once resident in Washington (or other office) is perceived as an agreeable trade-off of one's mental health and views in order to satisfy the obscene ambition and immense gratification that can be enjoyed. Sort of like selling your Soul. For them, selling their soul, as they would in a manner of speaking, is to underappreciate their own essence. A soul, if you believe in this sort of thing, is not merely something you own and something you have to trade, but a soul is something of immense value, obviously much more than they can imagine.

Thus, to trade your integrity for ambition, a sort of selling your soul, is to go to office for all the wrong reasons, and to show up on Day One without the same sense of values as constituents. How can this personality possibly understand public service? This is the lethality, the perniciousness, of the impairment of the officials, Potomac Fever.

Understand, also, that Potomac Fever applies almost entirely to officials, and not that much to media, professors or others as much, though they may have their own strain of it. Potomac Fever is a complex one develops upon arriving in Washington, elected to public office, where, of course, they had long been predisposed to it, hence the willingness to trade integrity for ambition. Authority is the catalyst. The disease that comes over media - types, professors and others is just plain old angry Leftism protected by an insulated lifestyle. Perhaps, to them, life in Hell isn't so bad if you're given your own pitchfork to rule over other souls sent there, the media being distinguished further by the reporting appearance or stand-up high adrenaline rush and the desire to be so very much a part of the story. In *making social change* by way of the printed word or the broadcast stand-up in being so kindly, so tearfully merciful and generous, which reminds me of the largess of the fifties and sixties television show, *Queen For A Day*, the soothing balm is to the reporter perhaps even more than it is to the subject matter of the story!

It's a kind of degraded personal integrity trade-off for *pulpit power* so similar to Potomac Fever, but without the authority of office.

> *Amplifying fears is our job and our pleasure. The one bias I'll concede all of us in this business fall prey to: we want there to be a story, and "no problems" is not much of a story.*

> — RICK HOLMES, METROWEST NEWS.

A short bout of gloating Potomac Fever or spiritual confession?

In between Washington and any Broadcast Network Headquarters or Newspaper Publisher are the constituents who are interested in learning more about our national direction and governance, and are looking for a place to start. As new parents, as newlyweds, as new entrepreneurs, as taxpayers and citizens, as émigrés and as senior men and women – as constituents go through a life change – all are sensing something is wrong, that something is going too far. They sense, perhaps unable to put their finger on it, that Leftist positions aren't good for newlyweds, new businesspeople, taxpayers and parents, and it's not good for Baby. In this, there will probably be much agreement, simply because most people aren't always angry at the world, but contented – struggling, but contented – who find themselves more and more necessarily assuming a defensive posture. Who wouldn't see this after being continually attacked sooner or later as the Left eventually gets around to attacking everyone sooner or later, and being slapped in the face and defamed? In this, they come to realize that the Left in America isn't working for the Working Man, but working for *itself*.

As part of this illusion to make constituents believe that officials are their Champions, I know that the Left likes to methodically portray conservatives monolithically as the *Angry White Male*, intolerant, greedy and unsympathetic, but it is a myth, conjured up by the Left to create a common enemy any right-minded person would only naturally be against.

But when the right-minded apply critical analysis to the message of the Left, when we listen carefully, the Left can lose and lose big. Hence the endeavor to silence those opposing views. They don't want us talking and comparing notes. At least they understand that much.

This stab in the chest of labeling one targeted corner of our society as Angry White Male may just make white males angry for a time, but it may make others over an even longer time take notice and think twice about how they may be next on the list in the divisive hate of the Left. In one form or another, no one is safe from the Left. White Males may be becoming angry with all this defamation, probably, but we weren't angry to begin with. We're tolerant, kind and generous, and frankly offended at intentionally being mischaracterized for Leftist political gain. In fact, many people of all races and ethnic backgrounds are becoming angrier and offended at the same thing, the stereotypes of pity stuck to them by the divisive Left; the unfounded rage of the Left, the fraud of social injustice and intrusive penchant for taking over everything from the bedroom to the kitchen.

For generations, the special interest groups in America have made gains not entirely by the efforts of the Left, but with a great deal of cooperation from constituents of all persuasions including Republicans. This explains the subsequent resentment constituents are expressing, this sense of betrayal and of being had. It's a living. The Right seems to be suckered half the time, and weak the other half.

Yes, the taxpayer recognizes that violent crime takes an excessive toll on our nation, but has not yet made the connection to bring together taking back our homes and the retaking of direction of America on the one hand and affirming and fortifying the First and Second Liberty Amendments as the solution on the other. After all, in many, many instances, individuals have only the perspective of their own lifetimes, amounting to little more than a snapshot in present time; a peek at more history and origins of our values system – not merely the religious values systems – would greatly help to bring things into proper perspective.

Fundamentally, the solution is really simple, not simplistic. The argument style of the Left is of parsing, splitting hairs, changing the subject, in order to defeat the restoration of the Second Amendment and thereby self-protection, and by extension the defeat of violent crime, and then (stay with me), by extension, a respect by and of our fellow Americans, which, again by further extension, reduces crudeness, rotten, tasteless art, education indoctrination against parental will and hostile rhetoric to unpopular, undesirable conduct. It's all crafted to stall *understanding of what is happening to us.* In the meantime, in the debate, the anxiety-ridden individual keeps playing card after card in a parry and thrust that at first seems like an intelligent matching of wits, but which is actually mechanism after mechanism coming into play to protect him or her from the anxiety they are fighting to stall.

In this flow, I note the arguments of people who like to make the issue seem much more complicated than it is, in order just to stall that understanding. Of course, these people are lying to maintain the status quo. The solution really is uncomplicated, and will work for two reasons: first, it will work because all of these are interconnected, and it will work because it *has* in the right-to-carry states of America. It's about as complicated as a paper clip: One can argue that it has several turns to it, but it's just simple when you really look at it.

Let me be more specific. It will work because it will use due process and it will succeed because of follow-through. It will endure because of vigilance once more. By dint of this convincing success, disrespect for parents, defiance of constituents and other malfeasances and other attacks on our values which make some people anxious will diminish not out of pure respect for us so much, but from the knowledge that we are much more likely now to complete the missions we next undertake.

This is what heartens constituents most – the idea that such crap *can* be defeated. There's a reason it doesn't exist absolutely everywhere in America, and that is that the people there won't tolerate it. The reason it does exist where it does is because they know we don't fight back. *Too long have we been tolerant and permitted the Left to steal our milk money and eat our lunch.*

The Secret of previous happiness and domestic tranquility was, basically, *self-respect and respect for others*. It was confidence; confidence in self and confidence in governance. Liberty. And there was government respect for the individual.

There was a time when the government official respected the governed much more than today. It was unthinkable for most any decent person to steal a car just because the keys were there, much less break into a home and sue the owner because the intruder slips through a ceiling panel, not to mention lying under oath or looting the nation. It was unthinkable that government officials would ever perceive constituents as a threat to them. In those days, the indecent were in much fewer numbers. Today, rotten appreciation of tradition and disrespect for institutions and icons blows decency out the window with help from others who encourage them. It's almost like a mob psychology that could never exist before. Helping them, because there is a commission in it for them, is the official afflicted with Potomac Fever.

Oh, some Officials have their heads screwed on right, but too many don't. It is these bull-headed among the officials who stall, argue against common sense, and ram their views down our throats and refuse to carry out the Will of the People. Judges do this, too. It's not a conspiracy, it's just that, in their twisted values system, *not only do some believe they're doing the right thing, but also that the looting mentality believes they've got a good thing going, and they don't want to give it up.* The impaired strike their blow for the Bourgeoisie or Proletariat, perhaps both (or so they think in their endeavors). They stall, they obfuscate, they invent straw arguments, they lie to protect the perks of their career. The looters look for legal methods of transferring wealth. And this isn't even a party thing, this Potomac Fever.

Welcome To The Fight.

One way for constituents to get started early is to monitor officials in their performance past and present, that is, whether they do what they say, whether they trick you and won't do what they said, or whether they do what we need to get done. I don't care what they do in their kitchen or their bedroom – most Americans don't: I care what they do on our highways, in our schools, on the floor of the legislature. We monitor them and vote them in or out by citizen involvement in our authoritative assessment of their professional performance. We recall if necessary. Now that we have seen how Recall works as it did in California, we must never fail to utilize it when necessary.

In working other than the bureaucracy, citizens can be taking personal action such as becoming more informed, understanding the issues and *most of all, understanding what is at stake.* Welcome. What you read here may be most agreeable to you, irrespective of your world view, Gay or Straight, rich or poor, it doesn't matter. It really doesn't. Groups such as *The Pink Pistols*, a Gay Second Amendment Group, exhibit such welcome to Liberty loving of all groups. [Visit pinkpistols.org]

Conservatives don't harbor the bigoted sentiments we are portrayed to harbor as divisive of people; there are just too many Gay conservatives and too many poor conservatives, especially among émigrés, for that lie to stand, understanding, of course, how there are the embarrassing in every group of people, including ours.

In fact, perhaps this might be the very best place to say this. Gun owners may very much agree on this one thing: that gun owners are members of a group separated from the rest of society by pre-emptive legislation. It's just my little old opinion that one of the greatest indignities is to be the subject of specific crimes of pre-emption, rather than to be truly criminal.

And it's the law. Specifically, it is illegal in many places even to carry, but this is only a *malum in prohibitum* kind of thinking from the legislature. How the weapon is used – lawfully or unlawfully – is a set of circumstances or an act yet to occur, if it ever occurs at all, thus making the carrying of the gun not a real offense in itself. Why punish law abiding for the crimes of a criminal? Indeed, why criminalize otherwise legally permitted behaviors? Remember that transfer of authority in this country can be accomplished by criminalizing otherwise non-criminal conduct. That same objective can be achieved by dividing people, and convincing people that resistance is wrong heads things in that direction.

After all, more than two million times a year, guns are used lawfully to protect persons, compared to the paltry 47,000 used unlawfully.

A *malum in se* law is one that makes something a crime because it is wrong or evil in itself, a morality question; a *malum prohibitum* law is one that makes an act unlawful because they say so.

How do you want to live your life, and how would you like to be governed?

As a newlywed, a new businessman, as an émigré – do you want to be treated as a sovereign individual until such time as you come to break a law, if ever, or do you want to be prior-restrained because their distorted reality makes make them figure that you might, sooner or later? Do you want to be governed by the anxieties of officials?

This type of *because-we-say-so* governance affects all races, social strata and orientation. It covers a lot of constituents, and it covers *you*. Many constituents are discouraged from joining, not because of the subject matter, but of the hate that is directed at gun owners on disinformation and harassment such as this kind of law. Minions of their own impaired sense of realities contribute to this.

Still, though, many people buy guns for practical reasons and just keep their mouths shut. Keeping a law-abiding constituent from carrying doesn't stop the criminal from carrying, but only ties the hands of the voter. Is this why officials are pushing to restore the felons their right to vote? Is this why the Left is registering people in jail, individuals not yet convicted of a felony? Just asking.

Officials have to be told to give up their mistress – violent crime and the policies which keep her in the lifestyle to which she has become accustomed.

What matters is the understanding that this is not really a battle between liberal and conservative; it is a battle between America and its attackers who may, for the present, be hiding within the Democrat Party. And they hate *everyone*, including Gays, minorities, émigrés and so forth for their right-mindedness and emancipation from the liberal attitude. The Left can't afford to like a single person in any group, and that includes any loyalties to their bygone supporters.

What we're talking about here is the idea that your rights and liberties – our way of life – are under attack as a political party would attack them, yes, but from foreign powers now hiding within the Democrat Party and compounding its thrust. It is a worldwide movement, bent now on pre-emptive attack and guerilla attack, for our freedom is for them the last straw in a long-seething culture of mania which, actually and all along has had very little to do with anything we've done abroad, but what we do at home: Liberty. Like most rage, it is blind, seeing only anxiety-producing symbols and with vision enough to use political division as a wedge and meeting up with the experts on that. Conspiracy *now?* Possibly. And it doesn't really matter what your race, creed, color or affiliation.

Thus, it is not *diversity* which will save us, but *unity*. We have to get together on this, and knowing this, the Left tries to drive a political division and continually keep us apart. It's a generations old formula by now. The wedge would then work to destroy us, as

America becomes more splintered, then with a majority won over to turn against the remainder of the nation.

The connection between violent crime and erosion of our liberties because of it is part of the greater attack on America; the connection between defeating violent crime and restoring Liberty for all – and a better respect and cooperation from our fellow Americans – is the beginning of the solution.

Do you want to be governed by the anxieties of officials?

If you are willing to resist this as part of our nation's right to self-determination and for the sake of the next generation and for their next generation, and if you're willing to advocate the First and Second Amendments, then, *welcome to the fight.*

Violence and Force – Menace versus Resistance.

Although we are a culture of personal worth, here is a challenge: Is a violent criminal's life equal to that of yours at the moment the crime is underway? Well, what does *he* think? *What does he think his life is worth?* What is the cost of crime each year to America? What is the cost to society for every person who chooses to throw his life away by committing crime, presumably in an environment that becomes safer and safer for him with each passing day? Is it our job to protect him from himself when he enters our home at night? Why don't you commit violent crime? What stops you?

What would be the cost of a rape or mayhem to you and your family? The true costs, I mean. And why the rush to stop violence, all violence, including the violence that may necessarily arise from resistance meeting menace? What trap would you fall into if you held the criminal's life to be more valuable than he or she believes it to be? And that *would be* a trap.

Against that cost on the great balance sheet of life and on the great book of society, what is the cost – I'm sorry, I mean the *Savings* – of self-protection each year? Self-determination as a nation is good, and that self-protection is a necessary aspect of that eternal vigilance we must pay for self-determination and for Liberty. As such, it is one of those things that doesn't cost a community, but one that pays the community by its contribution to the societal equilibrium of tranquility and Justice. We'll never eliminate violent crime, but we can cut it to the quick, and quick, and that becomes greater prosperity for all.

For the predator who chooses violent crime, society must take the position that he has chosen assumption of risk. It is in this framework that I describe violence for what it is. And for what it isn't.

The children who run campuses for the people of all age groups, the people who call themselves *Educators*, collectively have the wrong concept of violence. I have not loved educators for a long time now. On this they are utterly childlike in some of their pronouncements on school violence and self-defense when they should be most adult.

Violence itself is not something to be discouraged, because in many cases resistance is vital to the preservation of individual sovereignty in time of aggression. Where aggression and resistance meet, you'll have violence, probably. At what point would you resist aggression with force? Do you believe that nothing is worth fighting for? How about your personal safety when you are alone? How about the safety of your family when you are alone?

Understand that when violence ensues because an aggressor crossed the line and put you in danger, it is not you disrespecting the authority of the law, it is the aggressor disrespecting the law. In responding with reasonable force, which you are entitled to do under the law, you are not only taking necessary action, but you are taking action that is legal, generally speaking.

But this is hard to understand when our next generation – and the adults of the current generation – are being taught that violence and conflict are wrong. That resistance is wrong. In this, there appears to be no room for distinction of aggressor and respondent.

Conflict. Resistance. Yes, the Educators have it correct on *one* aspect where many individuals think they can solve their problems with fighting, but this attitude wrongly lumps bullying and self-defense into the mix and disallows a justice that a victim is striving to preserve, not to mention his or her dignity or personal safety.

The refusal to recognize that there is fighting and then there is fighting is a simpleton's assessment of the dilemma. To think that all violence and conflict are wrong and failing to acknowledge that some violence is a product of personal resistance to menace.

Some students will agree to meet at 3 p.m. to duke it out to decide the issue, and other students will be picked on and will fight back. I dislike intensely the Educators' narrow view that kids may not defend themselves without penalty as if all fighting is under the umbrella of *violence* and that all violence is bad. This is to say that it is their official value system in the workplace and that, if they really believe this doctrine, their own homes and communities would not be defended because it could mean *violence*. I doubt, I really doubt, that they believe this in their own homes, don't you? Then why teach it to our children? Because it is their job? How do you go to work each day with one set of values and live by another set in your own bedroom and kitchen?

One example is a January 30th, 2004 letter to parents from the Bellflower [California] Unified School District. Effective February

2nd, Administrators may direct the School Community policing deputy to issue a citation to a student who fights. Furthermore, families could be fined as much as $800 or more, and that this citation would not involve investigation of who started what.

In response to a commentary of mine published in *The Long Beach Press Telegram* of Sunday, February 8th, 2004, "*A zero-tolerance policy for fighting ignores self-defense*," some parents e-mailed me that, when their children were bullied on district's campus as recently as several weeks earlier, there was no inquiry as to who started it. I've always been a proponent of self-defense and of discovering *for the record* who started it when it came not only to adults, but to kids. I knew that administrators of the Bellflower Unified School District were paying me, personally, lip-service to the subject when I had given them to chance to explain policy. The policy as they enunciated it conflicted with parents' reports of actual experience with school fighting incidents.

I discovered on direct inquiry to the District Officials that without discovering who started it, the law could easily add the citation to the child's academic record, criminal record and, as they'd mentioned in conversations, the child's later DMV record; I concluded that all of this recording could be unjust if the child was merely resisting aggression of a bully.

In my further investigation with the Los Angeles Sheriff's Office, I was informed that it was *always* illegal to fight on campus (well, guys, *I already knew that!*), as they cited Section 242 of the California Penal Code and other sections involving campus squabbles, but deputies at the desk would not comment on the newly announced policy of the school. The Sheriff's Office said that it was already illegal; the Bellflower Unified School District's announcement stated that it was new. Who's right?

Is this going on in *your* community?

This is one example of the larger movement to discourage resistance, and must be taken as such. Little by little, our kids are being told that fighting is violence, and that self-defense, because it is violence, will be punished. Three BUSD officials I have spoken with state that they investigate fights to determine who started it, but this is not supported on interviews I've held with individual parents who have had to live with real life incidents and who say that there was *no* investigation. I endorse forceful resistance to bullies young and old, foreign and domestic.

Earlier, Educators wanted to teach that *conflict* was wrong, and that it should be managed by surrendering, compromise and other forms of personal sacrifice; in this approach, there was no room for plain old Justice, and, as a policy or doctrine, it was so far out, few took it seriously. But others wanted to cooperate. They were willing to bite on the instruction to *give the perpetrator what he wants*, or *don't resist, just be a good witness.*

Abating conflict was serious as the prelude to discouraging *resistance, which prelude is now quite clear.* Accept the idea that conflict is something to be discouraged, and it's easy to sell the idea that violence is to be discouraged and punished. Now, we're being sold that *resistance* is wrong and is to be punished. This is an example of the slippery slope the Left seems to object to all the time.

The Battle We Fight.

Where personal self-defense is a right, owning and carrying a gun is a right, just like owning and using a desktop publisher is a right. (This right does not apply to felons, underage persons or non-citizens or others who are not eligible to own a gun, though some purists believe that it does and that this will societally reconcile itself.)

It's what you *do* with it that makes you responsible or irresponsible, the reality of the Right being entirely independent of individual conduct. Just because a person defames another criminally doesn't mean we further constrain the right to free speech; if someone wants to lie and ruin the reputation of another person, another law isn't going to stop him, necessarily, if he's *already* broken the law in his defamation, is it? We already have black letter law on defamation. The right to self-defense is becoming increasingly vague and punishable, and in political or demographic areas where that is not entirely possible, we are being talked out of it and talked out of all resistance in general.

Official interference through the judicial system and through general persuasion (deceiving the public by ignoring certain rulings of record and dishonestly framing the issues in specific court cases, for instance [see KeepAndBearArms.com]) has some people convinced that this right is not as straightforward as it appears to be when in fact *it always has been straightforward and unambiguous*. You just haven't been so informed. Until now. See my Epilogue at the end of the book.

One thing about gun owners I love: they have a tremendous amount of information that is documented in court cases, official position, historical record and elsewhere that the Left simply cannot match. No one individual can master it, I'm sure.

Friends, we're not talking about crackpots who interpret the law to prove they don't have to pay income taxes: we're talking about a civil right where officials have an interest in suppressing it. We're not talking about hate groups who want to overthrow the government; we're talking about our own *governance* where we already have the authority to make change, and where good people want to know, to participate and deal with the adolescents in office. But the 2004 election worked. It made the statement heard round the world. And it is only the beginning.

Visiting these sites can be most illuminating. Uncovering reports that don't seem to make it to mainstream media is a superb start. For instance, keepandbeararms.com's operation self-defense category as an excellent mother lode of resource any interested constituent can tap into. This is how I make the point that we do not insist on our right being restored at gunpoint, but at counterpoint.

In discouraging discovery of this kind of information, officials have their own prestigious interest in presiding over an unarmed, dependent public. In spite of the numbers of guns in the hands of private owners, the concept of the Right To Carry is demoralized a hundred different ways – like resistance is discouraged in your child – including under-reporting the many cases of lawful self-defense and to misinform on the subject of resistance. This is good business if you're a politician who believes in force for only one class of the nation, *officials*, but that any use of force by an individual acting in his or her own immediate interests is something to be discouraged. And why not? It demonstrates more than 40 to 1[FBI Uniform Crime Report and *More Guns, Less Crime* by John Lott, Jr.] independence in instances that the fixated official cannot tolerate.

Like the woman who handles her own case of sexual harassment, so individuals may manage their own personal defense and end of story. Some people just have self-respect in taking care of themselves before a situation escalates so that small stuff stays small stuff. It's officials who blow things out of proportion for their own interests to illustrate more of a demand for their involvement, and the feeble who cannot find their spines.

But officials *believe* in force, even though they strive to discourage not only force in constituents, but strive to discourage resistance, too.

Please note that *all laws are backed by the threat of force,* from parking tickets to child-support to income tax evasion; break nearly any one law deeply enough, and they'll come for you and your assets with force; moreover, as long as the citizenry has no force of its own, *for other matters*, a sub-set of at least two additional things can happen:

1) Government continues to justify the ongoing need for its own force to protect us more and more from anything they can name (stupid policies we agree to because too many constituents are *permissively 'impartial'*), you might even call it *Government's own form* of eternal vigilance, looking out for its own interests, and;

2)the citizenry has little force of its own to resist immediate violence emergencies such as civil disturbance, local crime, etc., thus continuing its dependence on officials.

It's all too one-sided now; the servant is running the ranch, and has gotten not only into the liquor cabinet and become intoxicated, but has raided the pantry, has control of a good portion of the available house cash and is looking for the gun cabinet.

But, again I emphasize what I said above about this not being the chief reason for right to carry; disagreements with official conduct and recalcitrance aren't imagined to develop into an endless series of shoot-outs between government troops and civilians – no matter what they predict and no matter what they're afraid of – but to disable officials' effort to continuously reassure themselves and at our expense to soothe their personal fear of an established self-sufficiency of civilians with a much lesser need for government beneficence; its feel-good, irresistible proclivity to issue imposing rules to ensure this, its so very heavy-handed use of coercion upon civic contradiction and its discouragement through the use of ever-restricting laws, and indoctrination, peer pressure and judicial fiat.

Put another way, official service has taken on a life of its own and fights to stay alive where it is largely unneeded; sound familiar? It strives to be needed, and does so by continuing rotten policies instead of permitting us to vanquish it in the most useful, legal manner.

The disagreement isn't with Government *per se*, but with the officials who have wedded themselves to public service and clout as a career perk which includes their own divine vision, and a permanent hardwired connection to power to wipe out anxiety-provoking symbols.

Of course, what would rule of law be without threat of force? How would roads be fixed, taxes collected to repair roads with fines and other penalties for negligent driving? That makes sense.

But there is such a thing as over-reach, and use of that force to snuff out our constituent grievance with officials. Part of this comes from simply being so powerful that they are out of touch with the constituent who has to live with such stupid decisions. In many ways, it's just that simple.

Some of these dopes never worked a day in their lives, but caught their law degree on Senator's Row; how could they really know what it's like to get fired or laid off, get into a fight at work and get blamed for causing trouble, live alone and deal with a home or car broken into, being robbed or mugged or even being single and being hospitalized for a time with no one to take care of your stuff?

All the fears we average Joes and Josephines have to live with, they don't, thanks to bodyguards, secured gates, perks, plenty of money, job security, and probably a job or appointment after this one, and all kinds of worry-free living. How can they *not* be wrong when they second-guess what we really need?

Movie stars and limousine liberals will *never* know what it's like to be scared in their own neighborhoods, and for what they lived through to get there, they've probably forgotten already. It is these who lecture us on how to plan our lives and deal with adversity, these who wouldn't know, because they're surrounded by those who do it *for* them, and probably spend a lot of time reassuring them and isolating them from *our realities*. To them, their read on how they serve is to do *for* us!

Why the indoctrination, peer pressure and ostracism or other punishment for mere objection or redress of grievances? Why the official refusal to do as they're instructed? Why the argument? Why does the Los Angeles County Board of Supervisors blow off the voices of the People in their urging to find their backbone and fight the ACLU? Who cares what the reason is, well intentioned or ill-willed? All we need know is that they're angry and vengeful and won't listen.

In contradiction with their stated positions at first, actions again betray the true motives; for a political persuasion that wants oversight out of the bedroom and other aspects of life, they sure do furnish a lot of engraved invitations, road maps and landing lights. Fellow electorate become emboldened over time to join a throng of contempt for tradition, in moviemaking, arts, business ethics, education and nearly anything you can think of where your voice is silenced or mischaracterized.

In this social environment of official and non-official hostility, of this misguided penchant to do everything *for* us, *your child is going to be more subject to this than you are today.* **This is the battle we fight.**

Imagine a return to a society where high officials, Senators and Representatives, local officials respect more the individual's sense of fairness – that deep sense of dignity, not even-handedness and equal outcome or fair share, *but that very deep sense of personal dignity of friendly give and take and of achievement* – understand it fully and abide by it, where the individual respects the Government more? That day could be restored.

Speaking for myself, I would love to live in a country where Government never forgets that it's a servant of the People, and the People never fail to appreciate the fairness and trustworthiness of their servants, each individual immune to *Potomac Fever*. But that country's already been formed. America. It just needs a check-up from the neck up, a little compulsory sensitivity counseling, you might say.

Potomac Fever and The Immortality of Violent Crime.

There is a friendship between the affliction of Potomac Fever and the immortality of violent crime in America. One of the most objectionable directions for many Americans, if not most Americans, is the personal losses and necessarily the overall societal losses we suffer from violent crime, the maw and claw of the Beast, that multi-faceted creature made up of loathing of America, ignorance and individual growth arrest stuck in time of childhood, the prestige of go-nowhere policies and programs and irrevocable violence.

When it comes to *allowing* the indignity of crime, the pain and suffering, the life changes, the losses of loved ones and the loss of quiet enjoyment and the outright defiance of constituents when we plead for cooperation – *how are they going to make it right?*

Violent crime takes a heavy toll on our expense accounts, broken hearts, our spirit, our creativity, our personal resolve and certainties, our overall net productivity. Having clarified response from menace, and also how media portray crime and resistance in any given report, I naturally advocate force, lethal force if necessary, to protect myself and my family, not necessarily in that order. It's hard to do this when we're all under pressure to abandon resistance, and perhaps even be punished for it. I endorse it not only for myself, but for my neighbors, too.

*N*ow think of this: when we summon the Police, are we not hoping for them to arrive with the right amount of *force and authority?* Of course. But to throw someone out of our home or to resist crime, we have all the authority we need at the moment. We don't really summon Law Enforcement because of their authority, do we? For the burglar in my home, or the mugger on the street who lays a heavy hand on me and places me in reasonable apprehension of immediate battery or worse, my authority trumps theirs (and it is this which is under attack by activist jurists and others). We do not summon officers for their authority, we summon them for their superior force on our behalf, and maybe then the authority that is necessary thereafter. You might say that they are our back-up. At the moment of the crime, I have all the authority I need.

We summon the Police for their documentation and reporting, we summon them for other things, but in an emergency, after authority, we summon them for their force, whether it's one officer or a whole squadron. At least, this is one aspect that needs to be understood: we already have the authority to evict unwanted persons from our person and our property; to enforce it, some of us may require an officer, but it's not realistic to expect this for many reasons anymore, not the least of which is that the intruder doesn't respect authority at all, not mine, not yours, not anyone's. This is the legal concept, but it is not the reality a homeowner might meet. More on force and authority later.

Meanwhile, violent crime – and even non-violent crime – in connection with Potomac Fever has eroded some of our essence as a people. Individuals mistrust Law Enforcement – and too many mistrust the Judiciary, the Executive and the whole process, for that matter – and too many professionals feed on this mistrust as a career as I've commented. This self-perpetuating penchant at the expense of the community is a real *Cash Cow*, brought to life by principals joining the cause of so-called *social justice*.

The progenitor association of experimental social engineering with the defective slide rule of their emotional guesswork, and immense, unchecked scope of granted authority changes what was once a greedy perk into the better-keep-it-in-the-cellar Beast, the association of violent crime, loathing of our country and Potomac Fever.

The association, which now has taken on a life of its own, it seems, springs from the idea that government is a butler with real clout for social justice (to the naive), only to stun constituents on the fact that, as legitimate or customary as it seems at first glance, deep down inside, government officials are actually opportunistic and are now becoming increasingly infected to help themselves to more of the pie (so, what else is new?); a mental sense of entitlement traceable to the present political environment that draws them, traceable to their childhood resentments in anger which predispose them to it all, and the self-impressed distorted thinking that convinces them they're fit for the tasks, of course. A perfect match. Or a terrible combination.

Within them is blind ambition. Irresistible, the draw poisons. Escape is, of course, impossible. The equal opportunity, scorched earth policy of non-performing anti-crime programs (such as gun-free zones) then spares no one, especially those it was allegedly crafted to protect.

Yet, we can see that violent crime discriminates, or perhaps it is *allowed* to. Surprise, surprise, it's only consistent. Black on Black crime is a distinct, known example, a well documented reality, and is disproportionate in relation to violent crime in general; this serves officials and special interest groups alike, but basically, though falling to some more than others, crime affects us all. To *permit* such – in fact to draft it as such – is to do what liberals do best, and which is an obscenity in itself – to manipulate and steal an entity or resource that does not belong to them as an individual official, but to apply their authority and nevertheless profit from it individually on some personal level, such as prestige, campaign contribution, kickback or office appointment. As long as it works, where's the incentive to put it to sleep?

The longer these programs and policies live on and fail to work, the longer the return on investment for the official. And the object isn't even theirs to trade away, it belongs to the public. Still, the practice, this cloaked, gluttonous practice of conversion of what is not theirs to convert becomes a looting of U.S. resources, namely people and their energies, their safety and dignity, quiet enjoyment and more; a cash cow of kickbacks for that narrow fraternity and sorority known as officials.

For the minions of the special interests, beyond plain old money or power, the payoff is the glee of witnessing our decline while being funded from a variety of sources who contribute further talent and materiel. You might say they're holding the coats of the officials, in addition to carrying the water for them.

Officials serve themselves and we may get only *some* minor service along the way, but they will never cure the problem, which would be to kill the cash cow, whatever the political issue may be.

In this case, it's violent crime and official deafness coupled with the refusal to put the adored pet to sleep. The prestige of public office can be most compelling, but so can milkfat and, if overdone, can be equally bad for you. For, this feel-good sensation can be taken too far – become addictive – and can be abused, where societal problems are not solved, but sought, are maintained and visited repeatedly like a well, even created (via initiative/excessive ambition) for the sake of making work for the office and department. This policy, of course, needs funding. This, largess, of course, identifies and attracts more beneficiaries – people who apply for and use the system and the department's benefits – who then must never be disappointed, because they probably mean votes. And the cycle of further justification continues. This mining of America, this stringing people along is demagoguery, a survival tactic, and it's a feature of the impairment.

Our government is not against us; it is simply stupid. It is selfish. Government – more precisely the officials who operate it – is locked in a death struggle of self-preservation now, and has been in a panic – perhaps a siege mentality — throughout the last few decades. Perhaps, in this, Government officials are against *anyone* who threatens their prestige while trying to carry out their mission of goodness, equality and vision, including, yes, lifting of burdens, one of which is our keeping vigilant for the Beast now.

The offense against society is that it wishes to carry out its vision and not that of the People and make a living of service to us, such as lifting burdens. The dangerous aspect of this is of allowing dangers to our society to fester, thereby making themselves ever-needed to resolve them, but they are never resolved. Things only get worse, remember? That bogus concept of unintended consequences, to put it charitably. Another dangerous portion of that vision is one of spotting opportunities to market U.S. assets – whatever they may be. It may be technical secrets, it may be coal, or it may be other assets. *Conversion.*

I suppose we deserve this (somewhat) for refusing to get involved over the years, perhaps even as a natural consequence of inattention and of taking things for granted (ingratitude) but for those of us who have gratitude, getting involved now means that we wish our authority and Liberty back. We reserve the right to revoke governmental authority when it is so clearly over-reach and where the better asset resides within affirming the People's right to protect themselves. It's time to take on the Beast, violent crime and its master, officials with Potomac Fever.

Taking On The Beast First.

At present, the issue at hand is that officials, in their over-reach, in their objection to personal protection, because the notion would be enormously successful, proves certain things to me so that I draw this inference and make this forecast: 1) that officials' dirty secret, or should I say, one of the best kept secrets, is that they cannot protect us (individuals, not public, per se) and that personal protection can do it much better in most individual cases, and certainly enough to reduce violent crime and its costs. [FBI Crime Statistics and the records of the right-to-carry states of the Union]. [Also, see Bowers v. DeVito, 686 F. 2nd 616, 618 (7th Cir. 1982) no federal constitutional right to police protection.] The real doublecross is that the chance to work *together* with Law Enforcement or vice-versa is denied us.

Our officials take an oath in one form or another to defend the Constitution and to protect the public, of course, but you and I are not the public. We are individuals. Police have no mandate to protect individuals. Only *the public.*

As one illustration of this distinction, we have the difference between a telephone call and a classified ad. A telephone call comes for you, while a classified ad simply goes out to all. When you are required to give what the lawyers call constructive notice, you would be complying by placing that ad or recording the document at the recorder's Office. In this, you are speaking to the public, and yet to no one in particular. If your mandate was to give constructive notice, you satisfied it by placing the ad in the town it had to be placed in or recording it with the Recorder.

Now, whether you met the idea of reaching that one person is another thought, but you were not required to do that: all that was required of you was to do something in more general terms. Done.

This is also true for Law Enforcement when it comes to actions it is mandated to take in connection with the Public, but not for individuals. We're on our own. As I mentioned, it's interesting to read the history of Law Enforcement in America and in the United Kingdom; in each country, police *never did* have a mandate to protect individuals. They still don't. This is how the so-called '*Paper Protection*' of a court ordered restraining order is next to useless. Police have a duty to detect crime, to arrest persons and to protect the public, but this is not the same as a duty to protect an individual.

The right to protect yourself is enunciated all the time, but when it comes to backing it with action, officials are too concerned that you will take reasonable action to protect yourself and prove again how little we need to depend so heavily on officials.

This, of course, would prove that people can handle the responsibility and would confirm that it is do-able as it has in the right-to-carry states for decades. I'm not speaking of feuds, and we're not talking about summary justice; I'm speaking of situations that can be kept from escalating. The danger of violent crime isn't in the resistance, *it's in the lack of it.*

This is a threat to the career survival of individuals with Potomac Fever. Government, itself, is not necessarily utterly sinister, it can become sinister if managed by the wrong talent. Remember that Government is made up of individuals; over-ambitious, unwell individuals in many instances, and that self-determination – a non-need for many, many government programs, including policies which discourage resistance to violent crime – is a threat to the prestige of office. This is why and how the violent crime is the sweet, adorable mistress of officials.

2) Officials can foresee that courts and Law Enforcement would no longer be choked by a lack of personal protection – let's say from, oh, how about. . . *crimes of violence* – and its attendant costs, but relieved of administrative logjams by dint of effective personal protection, and thereby once again automatically relieving officials of prestige (*unless it's sabotaged and undermined as some officials will*).

It is vital to fully comprehend this. With the established concept that, overwhelmingly, many a crime is discouraged and foiled by the use of a gun without even discharging it (*but with the absolute knowledge that it will be used*), there is a very poor likelihood that such actions will, themselves, escalate and ever be reported. In newsmedia, if it bleeds, it leads, which is great for the bad news, but good news and such self-defense non-events are just non-stories for many media outlets. A lot of self-defense isn't ever reported to Law Enforcement because the encounter didn't escalate; they also don't agree with the media's agenda.

Predicting – insisting – that large numbers of legal damages cases would materialize due to armed citizens taking necessary action would be to sabotage the movement to recover our homes and communities, and would go against the will of the People. Having responded with some straw arguments, officials have already spoken on the subject of personal protection developing into vigilanteism and anarchy; they have gone on record predicting jamming courts, shoot-outs, road rage and other dire predictions, but this has not been the case in those states where concealed carry or open carry are the norm. And, again, these right to carry states have had decades of experience at it.

What do they know that other states' officials don't? Indeed, what do the concealed carry state officials know that stubborn other state officials won't hear?

Part of the mistake is that officials elsewhere think they are more enlightened on the subject of gun ownership, statistics and values; they are mistaken. Those officials are behind in sophistication when it comes to right to carry as much as they are on how a gun works. Most liberals think they are behind specific issues, but the fact is that they're just *behind* in a lot of issues, period. If they really wanted to reduce crime, they could follow the right to carry model where it has been successful, irrespective of what they believe.

3) Crime's cost to society would be diminished, productivity and spirit would grow once again, and the nation would move in a new direction of propriety and prosperity for all with a new sense of clarity

and certainty, something officials are against. If President Ronald Reagan was hated because he cultivated optimism and hope for the nation, the Left will naturally oppose right to carry and concealed carry for that very same reason. As I state as a goal, this could have even further reaching effects (through due process) on what many Americans feel are contributory to the nation's exhaustion, such as offensive taste, dumbing down of students, open borders and so much more where officials simply do not listen.

4) With official cooperation, other change would follow. Those feeding on diversity would be exposed as Quacks and Charlatans, and be made obsolete and defeated by unity, unity of community, mutual respect and friendship of neighbors by the clarity of recognizing crime for what it is, a *beast*. Some might even say it's a useful golden goose, for what it does for individuals who benefit from it in so many different ways, from the laying of an endless stream of golden eggs. I wouldn't dispute that.

With the truth out there and the glad results of implementing it, the uninformed minions would follow in smaller and smaller numbers until they dropped off altogether. Decency could return almost entirely on the knowledge of our demonstrated due process and follow-through.

Dream on, John?

We unfold this at the Polls at the first opportunity. We begin to correct now by notifying officials of our wishes. We observe their responses and gauge them accordingly. California has proven that Recall isn't as hard as we thought. It wasn't that hard in Lynwood, California, in 2004, either, where the Mayor of Lynwood was recalled.

And in time of financial crises, this is an excellent solution. The cost of crime is a non-performing asset that needs to be removed from the books. It performs for *officials*, but not for constituents.

Furthermore, each state has to decriminalize the lawful self-defense without oppressive castigation and costly investigation and litigation; this is reduced by a change in the moral values system of officials to resonate more with the sense of right and wrong of constituent homeowners – and that means getting healthy people into office.

Officials can no longer impose such unfair laws and expensive consequences on constituents under initiative, but must realize the savings to be had by resonating more with homeowners rights. They must surrender personal prestige for a superior political success and public service.

We need to remember that official propensity for over-reach can be reversed on various levels and direction of governance taken back by the People by the beginning of a single objective to initiate the process. This is not an argument with government, but instruction to officials to make a relatively minor paradigm shift; there is no argument about it, we give the orders, specifically, to decriminalize not only self-defense, but also the harassing rules that seek to discourage right to carry outside the right to carry states of the Union. Stop the looting of our energy.

I am advocating the legalization of carrying concealed weapons on the person in all fifty states. I advocate the legalization of concealed carry of handguns on any property, private or public, at any time. I am advocating the decriminalization of civilian/constituent lethal force in foiling crimes of violence to them by way of the abusive, pre-emptive denial of right to carry weapons anywhere, including churches, schools, airports. Anywhere police could be summoned and needed, a citizen should be allowed to carry. Not to play police officer, but for constituents to be recognized as the true authority of the community and to put violent crime on notice that the first line of defense is present.

And I am advocating tort reform for the protection of personal assets and freedom in time of use of that lethal force or in time of non-lethality against possible liabilities as may be adjudicated from time to time in civil actions to further enrich the persons (and counsel) who sue their intended victim and who never should have menaced the constituent to begin with. That is to say, menace forfeits rights to be made whole when committing a crime so that, as a matter of public policy and interest, the would-be victim need no longer answer to defend himself in court for having injured his aggressor in his own self-defense.

The defeat, or at least the severe reduction, of violent crime through the carrying of weapons, the decriminalization of response and subduing the Potomac Fever of officials is to take on the Beast first. It is to more fully understand that a great deal of misdirection in our society is linked to a general disrespect for constituents, members, customers, parents, audiences, subscribers and the public in general by way of how long we have put up with the biggest bullies of all, violent criminals, their supportive officials and the minions who loathe us all – people who love to eat our lunch. And we let them!

We have tolerated criminals because of our kind hearts, and we have come to regret it. We've been fools.

We have tolerated stupid policies and have sent the message to others that we're a pushover for compassion, cooperation and destructive programs. We've been fools.

In our desire to be kind, we have been duped by those who first started out by telling us that we were in part responsible for the teenage car thief. Soon, we were conditioned to believe that we, and thereby society, are to blame for all the anti-social constructs I just mentioned, and make no mistake – all of the objectionable behaviors against our institutions are simply anti-social hysteria.

This is why it will work to take on the Beast first. Precisely because all these are anti-social constructs, this in-yer-face art of such bad taste, the education curricula against parental authority, and so forth are all anti-social at the core to go against what they really know are our wishes with the full knowledge that they can harangue us into not fighting back or objecting. This what're-ya-gonna-do-about-it? attitude pervades nearly everything political from the Left.

These minions are the unhappy resentful children who are now adults, incorrectly superimposing their perceptions into fears and anticipations of others, and denial in refusing to see the societal damage they do.

To take on the Beast first, and to succeed, we make an indisputable statement that commands more heed and cooperation than we have now from officials and our fellow Americans. As part of their wrong hate against institutions and symbols of their anxiety, their pain is not our problem to solve, it is theirs. The *cure* for their anxiety is not to dislocate and devour the object of anxiety, but to work it through in introspection; to themselves dissolve the cause of their anxiety so that whenever one encounters that symbol thereafter, it's harmless. Only this way can they become what they now loathe: American.

Until then, their anxiety is not our problem. *They* and the Beast are the problem. It's up to them to clean up their act, and for now it's up to us to cope with them as they presently are: disrespectful, unlawful, undermining and destructive to our nation.

How this relates to retaking our homes and communities is simple. Officials are *complicit* with the bad taste in art, the poor etiquette, uncouth rhetoric, falls in standards and the double standards of the rude here, not to mention the lack of backbone when it comes to such anti-leftist action. If officials set a better example, more constituents would feel less comfortable being the lone jerk in a crowd. Civility could return. Honor could return, and it then might someday again *be enough* to summon one's honor to keeping a promise or to go by the rules of fair play. A lot to expect? We had it once.

If the public service environment is more compatible with life, more decent people could run without fear of being incinerated by the directed energy weapon of the liberal campaign style or devouring methods of debate.

Idealistic? I don't think so. How are things in Middle America compared to Washington or California? I think my point is taken.

How is it done?

We remember our civics class and we employ due process.

We also employ follow-through.

We study. We take refresher if necessary. We learn.

If the officials are healthy, they will respond to our wishes without objection: unlike the Los Angeles County Board of Supervisors, they will serve and carry out the duties of their office. If not healthy, then officials will object to our wishes, make some sort of straw argument to protect their fiefdoms, at which time we will have to assert the right and authority to make it healthy through due process. Recall.

We're not bluffing.

Government, once perceived as a servant of the People, as *part* of the people, has chosen to separate itself from us, their decision, not ours. Ambitious individuals seek more and more benefits from public service, all too often at the expense of the very people they serve. Potomac Fever.

On the other hand, the healthier officials can be recognized by their reaction time and just how they respond to the needs of the political majority, not the political minority, and the Left, the extreme Left, happens to be that minority. Not to change the subject, but who in Hell ever came up with the idea that the political minority didn't get their say or was somehow stomped on? Who in Hell came out with the idea that the minority has to prevail? They did get their say, they are always heard, and were voted down. That's how the system works. And when one faction of constituents notifies officials and other factions are silent, the official can presume that he or she is hearing from constituents.

When the minority is loud and coercive and gets its way, and when the majority is ignored, then officials have circumvented due process *by definition*, and must be disregarded on that alone. It's time now for some critical thinking and to understand that for all its wedging of issues and parsing ideas and never-ending energy, listen long enough and it's obvious that the Left really has nothing to say.

Officials who cannot see that the public can first awaken, then change its mind and issue new directives (as a true majority, not merely loud) would naturally see us as a threat, and it is not as if we are overthrowing our very own government, but that Government is mutinying. It means that they forget that they're not private, but public servants and that they get input, cues and clues from us on what we constituents say we need as part of the day-to-day service they have sworn to do. What frightens me and which should frighten anyone is when officials see the People as a threat, which would explain why they disagree with us instead of obeying us. The moment officials forget they are servants is when we know we're in trouble. If the people speak and servants object and resist, we are in trouble. Guess what: we're in trouble.

In the initiative of individual officials and the professional conduct of what passes for public service leadership, officials do not think we are stupid; they perceive us as a threat to their prestige and power grab in that we can be more independent of them and they don't want to allow it. (They don't *really* fear materialization of their dire forecasts; all they fear is being out of a job and cut off from the ability to challenge anxiety-avoidance symbols!) The fears they enunciate, say, chaos and vigilanteism arising from more individuals carrying guns, are straw, panic-studded and disingenuous. Parsing. Straw issues. Besides, *they* work for *us*. Unless they believe otherwise. Guess what: they believe otherwise.

The Second Amendment doesn't make any mention of what might happen if everyone enjoys and exercises their right to carry. It merely states as part of the complete Document that it is Creator-given and self-evident, not Government-given, and that it shall not be infringed, period. Not by state, federal or local government, or by anyone or any entity, including courts, neighbors, schools, libraries, universities, hospitals, editorial boards, well, the list goes on, because it simply says *shall not be infringed*. Infringed by just whom, the Document is silent. It simply states that it shall not be infringed. Guess what: it's being infringed. *And it demonstrates just how the Second Amendment is an indicator of the health of all other liberties.*

There is also another maxim we live by: *let's cross that bridge when we come to it.* That is to say, if we may elect even to *consider* our opponents' dire forecasts, then let's deal with them all when and if they materialize. (This is where gun crime stories seem to outnumber gun-defense stories, but if you know where to look, you can see that it's backwards.)

And until those fears do materialize – and until they do for real and not artificially through specious rhetoric – officials should not be so anticipatory; let us re-affirm our liberties first, instruct officials to carry out our wishes in recognizing our right to carry, and then worry about problems if and when they appear. Guess what: those problems won't appear. The generations-old record of the concealed carry states speaks for itself.

But in the meantime, someone could get hurt, as we are all at risk for mugging, in-home daytime burglary or robbery, violent crimes of all sorts, perpetrated more and more in all neighborhoods if the debate continues. The inability of police to actually stop criminal activity and the interference from attorneys coming to the aid of troublemakers contributes to the situation officials first point to when demanding more guns off the streets, and other proposals. They won't stop the bad guys, so they punish the good guys who didn't do the shooting. On this, there is no debate, only obfuscation and stalling tactics by the disoriented officials looking out for themselves. As long as crime exists and as long as individuals are not permitted to respond, they have us by the throat. This is no accident.

One of the chief objections which in my mind are valid, is whether individuals can be trusted to protect themselves, be it with a bat, kitchen knife or handgun. I make the case for this below – people can be trusted – demonstrating the proud record of good people, my fellow Americans, who have proven themselves as a whole to be trustworthy and possessed of good judgement. This is, of course, quite different from what officials have gone on record as saying about you and me.

Today, it is the Left who lectures the rest of us on how we must behave, share and cooperate while they do the least of any of us. This complaint and comparison is not a matter of grudge, but a matter of pointing to *personal integrity*, because they are receiving a distorted perception of reality.

Are we to have pity on these persons for their encumbrances and for their impairment?

No, because, for all their Gestalt, they wouldn't ever appreciate it. And because as long as we pity them, we delay ending their impairment. Tolerating them any further is to become enablers. But I address this again in the last paragraphs.

Leftists, liberals and the impartial and the conservatives who join them hate America for her symbols of childhood resentment. Yes, some *conservatives* cave in to Leftist values on the mistaken notion of compassion, cooperation, and can't-we-just-all-get-along kind of weak thinking. That open-mindedness where *their* brains fall out.

I believe that the liberal sees himself in the criminal by way of identification, and that this is why the Left likes to blame society; it's still angry at Dad and Mom!

Violent crime is a harassment of America and it is also a loving mistress of officials, and it's not likely they'll see it our way cooperatively and rescind oppressive, infringing laws, rulings and regulations without some sword of Damocles hanging over their heads. Officials are to be instructed and obey, or be removed by the counterpoint of due process; election or recall.

Until that hour, call crime a magic lamp or a magic carpet for officials. The Beast is the union of violent crime, minions of the impartial and loathing in America, and Potomac Fever that nurses it. Officials *love* violent crime. Violent Crime in America serves officials in that it is a cause which, as long as it exists, keeps officials prestigious, and officials want to keep it in existence.

We will never eradicate crime altogether, but we can shrink it so that it drinks up so much less of our hard work, revenues and time. And we must. Violent crime is not a fact of life. Sex and aging are facts of life; violent crime is not. We all know the toll it takes on society, but how many of us know that we don't really have to stand for it (the object lesson of recall in California and of the 2004 presidential election) and that we have been making a horrible mistake in permitting officials complete control of all avenues of fighting crime? There is one avenue that is well charted – one of the avenues being discouraged, also – and that is in the areas of personal protection when help is not available; handling the emergency *ourselves, in propria persona.* Let's take a little time to examine other areas of frustration to our purpose.

Judicial / Bureaucratic Strain Potomac Fever

Judicial Strain or an otherwise Bureaucratic Strain of Potomac Fever is in local politics from the Bench to Board of Education to City or County Council. One of the examples that worries me is that it's getting harder and harder to protect yourself on the street, in school or even in your own home these days *as if* crime does not visit churches, schools and publicly owned places.

With officials refusing to protect the laws of right to carry states, and not permitting that lesson to take hold in places such as California, it's becoming unimportant whether you're defending your home with a gun, a baseball bat or even your fists. (*And why the big push for non-resistance anyway?*) What are you going to do when you really don't want to hurt that robber in your home, but you manage to protect yourself without taking a life and the system finds against you and it costs you the home you were defending?

The answer to these obnoxious happenings is not really in official policy, nor in the courtroom over individual cases, but in how we instruct our officials on policy we don't approve of and policy we do approve of. If we tolerate their nonsense, and stupid rulings as well, not to mention their complete unwillingness to back up our value system on issues such as bullying and self-defense, it is only because fellow citizens are already intimidated or ill-informed and puzzled on why failed policies fail.

The truth is that the policies are crafted to fail and do *nothing* about "violence", in order to extend the life of violent crime and give only the appearance of battling it.

Where the proof of the pudding is in the eating, simply look to how personal self-defense is punished and discouraged before-the-fact, such as on middle school and high school campuses, labeling – in fact, putting parents on notice – that all participation, just and unjust, is *"fighting"*. This fails to distinguish between aggressor and defender and characterizes *all* activity as simply violent (i.e. undesirable).

As part of my research for this book, and as a continuation of the earlier topic of the Bellflower Unified School District's position, I was personally informed by a highly placed local BUSD official that the administration does not want to see children settling their disputes *in anger*. This is different from the policy as announced in January of 2004, and it stands as an older position of the District, it seems.

This operates, again, on an ill-informed – I'm going to say *distorted* – perception that all fighting is anger *(very interesting)* and therefore undesirable, and demonstrates that self-defense isn't even in the thinking process of the official in appraising any given incident.

In repeated discussions with one highly placed official source on that subject, she *said to me* that she and the Board *understand* the concept of self-defense, but, as I mentioned to her, this has not been the experience of other parents and their children.

This disparity between seemingly school-friendly enunciated policy and the evidently child-hostile reality handling of schoolyard scuffles indicates how they as professionals were taught, and taught incorrectly, without parent-resonant values and without discernment.

Not only do they pay lip service to the parent and say that they investigate, then double-cross parents in an actual incident, but the concept of aggressor and response eludes them in the later, follow-up discussion, and, of course, it's missing from a report. The District can agree that self-defense is justified, but in an actual incident, as was the experience of parents who write me, the policy emphasis then changes to zero-tolerance for fighting, and for fighting *in anger*. (That assignment of *anger* again!)

Disgracefully, theirs is the mind of a child. Or worse, another angry child in office, locked up in time to simply taking the word of agenda-driven, so-called experts without any critical thinking question.

You see, where this is poor personal or professional integrity lies in the disparity between what they should know is right and wrong (distinguishing bully from victim, for example) instead and accepting a policy they *say* they understand, but which they blatantly ignore in their workplace.

Another experience I had with an educator of some decades of teaching was just as recent. An educator met my children only moments earlier, and privately she mentioned how intelligent and beautiful they are, but that she could not praise one because it would be a put-down to the other.

Naturally (and you could anticipate this) my reply was, "*I beg your pardon?*"

As she explained, it was the experts who had taught her that you can't praise a child in the presence of another without offending and excluding the one who overheard it. And, of course, they're experts.

Do you believe this?

Of course, her position was unmovable. And this experience is not at all unusual. You get the feeling that their kids have the same kind of home at night you do, for the most part, but when it comes to educating and supervising kids at school, they're living an entirely different life.

These persons are probably well-meaning, but they're very stubborn; they're very articulate and very good at defending themselves, and very stubborn on holding their position – polite, but stubborn – but they're not very good at protecting our children throughout the school day as we would.

*W*hen we defend ourselves in matters large and small, *many* are not responding in *anger*, as if there could be only that singular response, which, all too conveniently and delightfully matches perfectly — plays into the hands of – the stated mission of reducing anger in the overall resistance confusion.

It sounds great to the fellow officials and to civic groups and parents congratulating each other, this mission to fight anger, but anger is not a major emotional component in self-defense. Fear is present, reflexes, brains, indignity and other things come into play in kids, and that and more comes into play in adults, such as training, experience, authority, liability, thinking of others, etc., and then anger sets in later, oftentimes long after the situation is over. We're not talking road rage, we're talking about self-defense, an entirely different more purposeful concept when it comes to the responses of the would-be victim.

This movement to discourage *anger* and especially to discourage a *response in anger* is pointless everywhere in the process, it's premature in every incident, and it's very often just plain wrong; it profoundly reflects another poor understanding of a fact-of-life situation. Principals and Superintendents think that all fights are a product of anger on both sides, kids who solve their problems with fighting, and they fail to comprehend that many if not most schoolyard fights are bullies picking on kids in an entirely one-sided aggression. And they also think a *lot* of silly things incorrectly about our kids.

They fail to include peer pressure, personal indignity and constant haranguing, not to mention predatory kids who simply wait for the Teacher or Supervisor to look the other way, and though they may pay lip service to it all, they fail to include self-defense in the assessment of individual situations. Educators have stopped becoming adults teaching children, and have become overseers and bureaucrats, themselves children, doing what they're told without question. In fact, where their thinking is certainly that of a child, they are almost certainly promoted purely because they don't ask too many questions.

This is how not only *some parental* thinking has been redirected, but the thinking of the *educators*, too. If they really believe otherwise, such as if they hold the same values at home as the parents they are and are merely *doing their job during the day*, then we have, as I said before, a problem with their personal integrity.

You see, administrators have been taught, in a way, to think like lawyers, specifically to deny whether they can judge something as legal or moral today, on the spot, and to palm it off as something to be decided later and by another.

One of the objections people have with business is that the laws can be broken and remedies are through the system at some later days.

For professionals or businesspersons who really ought to know the law while conducting individual business, they too can violate the rules, hope that no one will notice or object, and if they do, well, then, they can just go through the process to a higher authority, which issue is to be judged *later*. In a word, "So, *sue me.* "

Like the educators, the idea of not knowing any better at the time of the incident is a problem of personal and professional integrity.

In the meantime, the individual parent is powerless to convince the administrators of just what the school's role and authority is and isn't, and of the authority of the parent. More *because-we-say-so* policy.

*N*ow the doctrine of *in loco parentis* takes on a new complexion; the doctrine presumes that the school administration will protect our kids as parents would. In fact, they have not, and the assessment is no longer opinion, but fact; too many administrations stubbornly impose their own values instead of our parental values, imposing the values which are enunciated by the Board, and which lack the common sense of the community, and which present *the new inappropriateness*. They have violated the spirit of parental wishes (and the overall spirit of the doctrine), it seems, and perhaps parents should seek legal counsel on how to enforce what can be determined to be the will of the parents. Where the entire student body and administration must yield to a single child who has an allergy to peanuts, it makes just as much sense of consistency for the school to yield to the will of the parents in individual cases, does it not?

Though Police have no mandate to protect individuals, do school administrators have a mandate to protect students from bullies, from injustice, etc. under the doctrine of *in loco parentis?* Or not? Irrespective of what is on the books, new decisions should be sought that reflect more the values of the parent than those of the bureaucracy who lives in private family at night, but ingrains public family by day.

This movement to discourage so-called anger is hand in hand with the movement to discourage resistance, and they are both terribly misguided, to put it charitably. It sets the stage to point a finger at anyone who protests the policy and to label them – *you* – as irrational and out of step with the calm of the rules, now involving the rest of your family if you ever see one of those expensive, sweeping citations.

Be alert to this lie. Just because the school administration says you're out of step doesn't make it so. Stupid judicial rulings (or deliberately hostile rulings or those hostile, passive-aggressive policies of school educators) have an interesting effect of when the average citizen cannot understand the law with any degree of predictability any longer.

This is important, friends, because if you or I cannot see any predictability in the law, how do we know we're following it? When they say so? The baffling rulings have the net effect of really keeping people off balance, don't they? A sort of interesting method of eroding your resolve to resist, isn't it?

Conferring with other parents privately to compare notes on the subject could be decisive in beginning to recapture your communities; as long as you don't compare notes, the bureaucracy is safe in overruling your values and in not protecting your child.

Where Does The Money Go?

*N*ow look at this: What would happen if the *violence* of crime dropped? What would happen if *the nature and the degree of violence* dropped*?*

By this question, friends, suppose crime went down, and the rate of decrease in violence overtook it substantially in a happy trend downward. Imagine a tremendous reduction in completed rapes, robbery or mayhem – just some of the injuries of crime – so eradicated that fewer persons were hurt by the horrors of these crimes. What if the damage of crime were frustrated and foiled by resistance of the victim? Let me answer that.

We'd all be spending a lot less tax money on this stuff. Victims would be in fewer numbers. Seriously injured victims would be in even fewer numbers. Losses to the community would be lower. Spirit of the community would be higher if fewer people were injured when the violence component of these crimes or attempted crimes were greatly reduced. And there would be fewer bureaucratic wastes in time and energy resources and in assets, too. There would be a commensurate drop in prestige of political administration as well. Oh, and we'd be a lot safer in our homes, our cars, family and property, did I fail to mention that? Turn to the records of the right to carry states of the Union. And take a long look at what crime really costs. Where would the money go if crime were reduced?

The courts might be a little less jammed, because maybe there would be a lot less squeezed onto the calendar thanks to shorter trials if the predator is stopped and caught red-handed. Shorter trials, maybe for lesser crimes, I mean. Fewer releases on technicalities, too, when laws against self-defense are repealed and the crime is prevented from escalating into a more elaborate case. Instead of charging the predator with a capital crime (namely, your murder if they're even caught!), they're apprehended in the act by the would-be victim (namely, *you!*) and charged with a lesser crime, say, attempted rape and illegal nighttime entry.

...unless catching more criminals in the act for lesser crimes would jam the courts. Ahh, we'll cross that bridge when we come to it.

Many constituents – male and female – have the guts to defend themselves. It is at this point that liberals carp, "*You don't take the law into your own hands!"* It is at this point that we answer that self-defense is *already* the law, and self-defense is not taking the law into one's own hands. Next case.

Imagine the embarrassment of the perpetrator to being held (safely) by the victim. Then, the witness testifies and puts the Defendant away for a lesser crime, perhaps, but at least you're alive. Just a thought.

It is at this point that we may hear more of those frivolous straw questions from the Left, such as: *"What are we going to do, lock up everybody?" "Are we going to return to the shoot'em up cowboy days of the old west?"*

I'll answer that question: *No*, only the *bad guys* get locked up. Even if we have to put away more criminals, so be it. And there's also the likelihood that with lesser crimes, there would be lesser sentences, improving the occupancy rate at The Graybar Hotel.

After all, what are we trying to accomplish here? We're either going to resist and be serious about it, or we're not really serious, and if we're not, they'll know it. Then *they* get to do a mind-reading act: they'll see that we're weak and unresolved. And make no mistake – the bold loathing of America, the brazen contempt America-haters show for the rest of us is almost entirely due to their perception of us as weak and unresolved. This is why we take on the Beast first.

Which do you choose? Before you answer, look at the United Kingdom, Australia and parts of South Africa and the Philippines, all so-called gun-free zones. Reports are emerging daily from those countries where gun-free policy signals the dinner bell for predators who know their victims are unarmed. Take a quick visit to www.keepandbeararms.com for Monday thru Saturday Newslinks from around the world. I visit KABA every morning for news items you won't usually find outside the locale of their covered news events, but which tell an interesting story.

When it comes to increasing numbers of lesser but certain sentences, we could have an increased criminal population. If necessary, we lock up more criminals, period.

But one of the bits of good news is that, if these crimes are thwarted in the act, there is probably a lesser charge, and lesser sentence, but same message, less cost. With so many crimes committed by individual perpetrators, and repeat perps at that, the inference to be drawn is that crime can be controlled better just by catching or stopping the crime before it escalates, lesser or smaller offense, as this is more meaningful as a workable deterrent to the perp than committing several crimes and being caught for only one of them. Maybe.

A contributory factor in the majority of those many crimes committed by one repeating individual may have been the common thread of non-resistance in the victims. And most murders aren't even solved.

Violence doesn't come entirely from resistance, but more from the combination of surprise and a lack of resistance.

Of course, I know there is the career crimal, the serial offender, the incorrigible repeat offender, but what I want to reduce is his serial victims

If a sentence is imposed to the fullest and not reduced, is recidivism less? If jail time is unpleasant, is recidivism less? This could mean shorter terms, because of lesser charges, sure, but fuller and more complete prosecutions and most certain terms. You can choose. You can resist a violent crime, suffer less injury and put the criminal away for a lesser but more certain term, or you can become a victim and maybe the criminal isn't even caught.

One of the chief benefits would be that once everyone feels safer, it will only be because more criminals are treated seriously. Translation: fewer violent criminals. But this isn't the entirety of my complaint and analysis.

My position is that, if we retake our homes and communities, if we take on the Beast first and obtain serious homogeneity due to our complete follow-through, there will probably – even likely – be fewer disoriented, impaired persons who even *become* criminals. This is why taking on the Beast first is so vital, and why the method of due process and follow-through is the best formula to make it happen for the sake of our homes and communities, and for the next generation and the next. I'm going to emphasize this a lot.

Imagine a nation where commitment was something people decided upon with fewer *exits* made easy. Imagine where good faith was the norm and people didn't enter business, university teaching or the arts to be ugly and shocking for some reason, but to express beauty in so many ways. Just imagine more intact homes because adults saw more clearly the value of it on the children, children they love. Just imagine. It's easy when you remember that it was that way once until undermined by the hateful Left. It really was. It was good.

But, *good for whom?* Good for everyone who counts on one another and who lives with others in a community, that's who.

To return to the vexing and hostile accusation of whether we will instruct our officials at gunpoint, the answer is still No, we do not instruct our officials at gunpoint; we make the *counterpoint* and we do insist on being free to *protect ourselves* at gunpoint if necessary, thank you very much. We do not speak exclusively to the officials, but to the undecided – that's you! – to rouse your involvement in all our own governance.

Right to carry alone would restore a great deal of security in the community through the reality of a legally well armed citizenry. The right to carry alone would reduce violence a great deal – excuse me, *has* kept civility a great deal – and the violence of it all by example of those states where concealed carry and open carry are popular and legal.

Note that, *nearly every case* out of *millions every year* where the lawful and appropriate use of a gun is recorded, the necessary truth is that the condition did not escalate to the detriment of the would-be victim. Where these outnumber predatory shootings more than forty to one, the only inference to be drawn is that it works. It certainly works better than those silly gun-free zones. Criminals either don't read or they ignore the rules, or didn't the policy-makers think of that? *How can officials really be in touch with our realities when they have an armed guard with them most of the time?*

The right to carry alone would save billions of dollars if affirmed permanently. This does not mean that everyone should carry a gun, but it does mean that those who wish to shall be allowed to carry without ridiculous and immaterial qualification, without registration of weapon nor ammunition, nor restrictions on locale or type of weapon and where it may be carried.

It's silly to presume that crime can be stopped in the recalcitrant by imposing rules on the law-abiding. To insist that crime in the criminal can be reached by the law that applies only to the law-abiding is a defect in personal integrity because the position comes from reading things through a distorted reality. The insistence on that distorted reality is a danger to the nation.

And it's ignorant to presume that *policy* can take the place of the necessary physical self-defense response resisting of a would-be victim. In legal terms, it fails to stand in the shoes of the victim.

It's just as silly to presume that violence doesn't occur in places where carrying personal weapons is denied the law-abiding, and it's equally stupid to presume that crimes won't occur in schools, churches and other buildings just because the law-abiding are not permitted to carry there. Criminals don't obey the law. Wherever police can be summoned, constituents, too, should be permitted to carry. Opposition to this is just as good – and just as foolish – as saying that they will never need armed police there, ever.

Where many laws recognize self-defense and defense of another by the doctrine of one who stands in the shoes of another, official policy supposedly crafted to protect (such as *gun-free zones*) in fact constitutes an *interference* with self-defense and defense of another by penalties and pre-emptive non-carry laws. It cannot be both ways; law cannot say on the one hand that it is crafted to protect, and recognizes the right to protection in public policy and interest, then on the other hand punish acts of response or even pre-emptively criminalize such foreseeable reasonable response.

Though the law claims to recognize the doctrine of standing in the shoes of another in lip service, it *acts to defy this doctrine* in individual cases (interference) by unreasonable laws such as excessive waiting periods, ammunition restrictions, political discouragement of resolve and resistance, political delays and elitist privilege.

All of these fail to stand in the shoes of the victim.

All of these interfere with the individual's right to self-defense.

States of the Union refusing to follow the model of the right to carry states interfere with their constituents' right to self-defense.

I know that this doctrine applies to individuals who come to the aid of another – to stand in the shoes of another is to defend another person as if you were that person armed – but philosophically and morally, officials speak to self-defense, but interfere with our actions to defend ourselves by refusing to see our realities.

Wherever violent crime occurs or has occurred will not be stopped if the *Citizen's* right to carry is restricted there. Of course not. Only the criminals would be armed, ya dope! Just as the right to carry states' positive records are demonstrable as *constructive*, so the pain and suffering of crime in the gun-free zones is demonstrable as *destructive*.

If officials really believed that the stupid and restraining polices they write, their bodyguards wouldn't be with them half the time when *they* visit churches, schools, and, of course, public buildings.

The superior idea is that a right to carry citizen would be able to stop a criminal act in progress just as *rightfully* and as legally an armed officer would on a school campus, church property or public building. To presume that we would not or should not is to delay intervention, and I'm certain this is the objective in order to retain dependence on officials. Who would *not* want a crime in progress stopped?

Wouldn't it be great if people could carry their personal handgun aboard civil aircraft? Decriminalization of practical armed response *also* means that people who defend themselves with a bat or kitchen knife would also be protected from stupid laws when such responses are necessary.

Let's remember that CCW citizens undergo the application process, and this includes training and background check. Some of us even experience *Hogan's Alley* if we want, and many enthusiasts take more training than required. Many of the weapons training courses available to the Military and to Law Enforcement are available to the private citizen. In fact, it's encouraged. It's also popular. This is not a love of guns as much as it is personal responsibility. You don't have to love driving to be a responsible driver.

Another saying; *violent crime goes down where nobody knows who's armed.* And that should include schools, airlines, you name it, anywhere violent crime is presently committed, anywhere you'd wish to Heaven someone was there.

Nationwide concealed carry. Before it's too late.

The concept of making the predator angrier and thereby more dangerous is taken out of the equation by the facts that, time after time in the right to carry states where the scenario plays out for real, not in theory, situations are pretty much under the control of the homeowner or motorist or other would-be until Law Enforcement arrives. If the perpetrator departs, end of story; CCW (concealed carry weapon) citizens understand the law that they can't just shoot someone fleeing. Mistake or confusion about the facts, such as innocent persons who entered a home because they thought they heard a baby crying, are checked out almost entirely due to the very idea that the matter is under control and facts are then readily available.

Holding an intruder to your home at gunpoint or whatever-point can de-escalate the situation by taking control, and this makes it possible to gets the facts; when the criminal believes he has the upper hand is there an unstable situation, and there is the greater possibility of the homeowner being overcome, injured and perhaps far fewer facts known, now, later or never.

A lot of personal self-defense training emphasizes the 21-foot rule, or the 21-foot gap response. It goes by different names. It's been determined that an aggressor can close the gap between himself and his victim enough to knife you, grapple with you, disarm you, or otherwise injure or kill you *in less than the time it takes you to react* if he's within 21-feet.

If you're holding an aggressor at gunpoint at about 21-feet, you're in control of the situation, as long as he stays there; if he makes an aggressive move and moves within that 21-foot distance, you are about to lose control of the situation, and you have only that distance and time in which to act. Needless to say, if you're holding an intruder at gunpoint within that zone, say at eight or ten feet, you'd better have control of the situation. And, needless to say, *what to do* in a situation like that is part of a good training program.

So, I don't care if he's angry or not; all I need to know is that the homeowner is in control of the situation.

And one other item: there are *already* laws and doctrine in place to sort out who did what to whom, and it's my opinion that many of these could be repealed a bit instead of being expanded against the homeowner who is more likely to have greater assets than most burglars.

For the present, another saying prevails, unhappily: *It's better to be judged by twelve than to be carried by six.* But this saying should be only temporary if we return to the environment of officials taking the side of the homeowner constituent taxpayer against violent crime.

The mistaken, misguided, wrong-headed theory of gun control nuts is that it is better for a woman to be found strangled with her pantyhose than to be alive and well to explain to Police how her attacker got that gunshot wound.

— (Author unknown, but thanked)

We would all benefit from that position.

It's vital to understand, also, that in the concealed carry states, there is more of a philosophy of self-protection throughout than one of so-called Government protection. In many jurisdictions, the idea of Government protection means protecting the Second Amendment, which means, among other things, that what is recognized there is the right to self-defense.

Remember that Law Enforcement is under no mandate to protect you. In these states, the people who want to carry lawfully are of the right heed to obey other laws – they are the law-abiding – including when to draw their weapon, when not to, and so forth.

Naturally, these individuals (myself included) don't have the hot-head mind-set nor do their states have a record of increased outlandish shootings. The idea of responding *in anger,* as the childish liberals and as the majority of Educators put it, isn't as prominent in an act of self-defense as good judgement, training and appropriate lawful and practical response are.

For, insofar as *responding in anger* is concerned, the difference between the philosophies of the right to carry states and the gun-free zone mentality is just another example of how liberals anticipate (project) emotions (i.e. *in anger*) over respecting Liberty, which liberty enables a person to respond in *purpose.* Self-defense enthusiasts aren't thinking of *anger* when we're training on handgun practice, training on understanding the law, appreciating how adrenaline and environment play a role.. It all boils down to developing judgement.

The officials are putting their irrational fears over our safety in spite of our asking, begging and our showing of evidence, not to mention in spite of our rightful authority. This is an important example of how the anxiety-avoidance motivations of ill officials and of ill non-officials profoundly affect the nation.

Remember also, that, though a right to carry individual may be fully prepared to shoot to kill in self-defense, shooting is rare, because the serious-minded drawing down on the aggressor is often sufficient to face them down in time of substantial danger. Many aggressors held at gunpoint are at least smart enough not to enter the 21-foot zone any further and just scamper off, whether they are aware of the zone convention or not. This is a good thing, for many obvious reasons. For readers looking for specific statistics on the question of right to carry shootings versus numbers of licensed-to-carry holders and other questions, please visit *www.studycrime.org* or *www.jpfo.org* on the Internet. A recent article is at *http://www.jpfo.org/commonsense14.htm* as one example of this counterproductive attitude many people can recognize.

Please understand this: no matter where you come down on the issue of self-defense, *the ridiculous laws and rulings, policies and programs against you, the homeowner or motorist, are already in place, painting you as about to respond in anger, presuming that you will act with excessive force.*

So many irrational officials are just sold on this mistaken notion! And their distortions make them so very willing to see *only* that! They love to listen to the so-called experts, but how do they govern properly when they won't listen to the *constituents?*

This kind of intent accusation – assigning an intent where there is none – is horrific, and these are likely to escalate more all the time in the name of so-called social justice, again, proceeding from a distorted read of reality; and since you're nobody special, any act of violence against you could not only hurt you, but place you in a position of further liability even after having done nothing wrong. Lawyers are expensive.

Nationwide concealed carry. Now! Decriminalization of reasonable response. Now.

Washington Potomac Fever

To officials, elected or appointed, in office or on the bench, this brash, gutsy movement is intolerable! It's downright insolent! Where judges and justices say they have their hands tied and refer us to the legislatures, it is a matter of one strain of Potomac Fever referring us to persons of another strain of the same affliction. How do you like that?

This trend of independence, though innocents are not getting hurt in shoot-outs as predicted, is unacceptable. Not only are we having to confiscate less revenue from the taxpayers, we're having fewer bills to sign and less photo opportunities, to boot! It doesn't pay to be a Congressman anymore!

Or does it? Good times in America can be just as rewarding for a Congressperson who isn't so far Left. A physician doesn't have to *create* terminal heart disease to be fulfilled; what he or she sees in a busy practice is more than enough for them and for humanity. A professional enters the profession to help, *not to be needed*. There is a difference in motivation. One is, obviously, to help others; the latter is to help yourself. It's alright to enter any profession to make money, but quite another to feed on need or to loot. This is where the impaired hear a call the constituents aren't sending. Potomac Fever.

We're not to be talked out of our wishes by some official who feels he or she is wiser (Potomac Fever). When officials fall victim to Potomac Fever, they begin to seek more power and prestige, become enormously creative in rhetoric and salesmanship (spiteful, vicious defensive, parsing responses I call malignant issue-spotting as opposed to critical thinking issue-spotting) and become increasingly high-strung and quarrelsome. This is true of both the male and female official. It is true of all parties.

Where it was once an honor to be a Representative, that honor has evaporated for too many officials by dint of scandal, defiant stubbornness, unavailability/absenteeism, and just plain deceit, such as removing archival documents. Where it was once an honor to serve, it has now become opportunity to loot. It's a disgrace.

Potomac Fever puts the patient – excuse me, the official (*Freudian slip!*) – into a frenzy, where he or she believes they are more sophisticated, and certainly not to be argued with, out of touch with reality and furnishing non-sequitur responses in opposition, not because they think we're stupid, but purely because there is no real logical defense anyway of their position and they can't see themselves as we see them; it is an acquired skill, part of an acquired distortion.

Where a sudden largess overcomes the afflicted official, there comes also a sort of constituent credit card chorea, or the writer's cramp kind of inability to relax the hand and elbow to stop spending for special interests; where denial, as a perfectly functioning defense mechanism, won't permit them to recognize within themselves that corruption isn't the fault of constituents and donors, but a character defect of the official in accepting or rejecting monies, as in the matter of restricting *corrupting* donors with campaign finance reform. There's that externalizing, isolating, intellectualization again.

Unlike Judicial Strain / Bureaucratic Strain, Washingtonian Potomac Fever is a disease of prestige and bestowal. They use people, they lie, they have an inflated sense of self, and won't be open to introspection.

It is this complex – this cluster of anxieties and cluster of defense mechanisms – that compels officials irresistibly to interfere, pre-empt and stub out our rights with the unconscious but *complete knowledge* that the national formula, policy, regulation or legislation will never work, not ever, really; the system complex, which, for convenience we can call the disorientation or impairment, makes them believe they are indispensable, and that they are sufficiently important that they must survive at all costs; that they have to fix something that ain't broke. They forget that the clue to this is how they do it behind our backs, or against our wishes when we protest. They say they're in public service, but they run the game their way. The giveaway is that the impaired could never last long with their kind of rhetoric and anti-social behaviors in the kind of world they want.

For them, getting out of the way of Americans is worse than being out of work, it is unbearable; it's to be unnecessary, out of the spotlight, contradicted, unneeded. Maybe even forgotten. This is dreaded by the patient – forgive me, the official – for their *avenue to soothing balm is cut off.* It's not so much that politics is a stage – that's only part of it – it's the change they can effect, destructive, do-it-yerself – do it for themselves – change. That change – that balm – is in *devouring anxiety-producing symbols.*

It's also worth noting that not all Washington officials catch Washington Potomac Fever. Many elected officials from Los Angeles to Washington never catch it. They may know of it, almost certainly, and tolerate it in their peers, or even shrug it off, but they never get it, thankfully.

Unfortunately, most officials do fall victim to one kind of a lesser affliction, and that is that they forget how we have to live with their indolence, and their generally being out of touch with our realities. I'll say it again: though many have written on the subject of Potomac Fever as a popular joke among insiders, it is no joke to us.

The truth is that, with the exception of pure personal introspection, it's not down to them to do anything about it, it's down to *us.* Healthy elected officials can help, sure, but this movement has to come from the People, and they are off the hook only if they will carry out the will of the People. One man or woman in Congress can be poo-poo'd too easily as a Maverick or even as an old timer; they can be too easily ignored as a single voice. The voice of the People says it better.

III. Back To Basics.

Some of the best course corrections have been made simply by going back to basics.

We need a course correction, more precisely a reversal. Remember that things were rational, fairer, safer and generally more sensible before the Left got its hands on things, and began tinkering with its little demons on its shoulder egging it on. Of course, I'm not speaking of any supernatural kind of being speaking in the ear, but of those anxieties within which prompt the reactions that characterize the Left, one's personal demons you might say, the chief danger of the disoriented.

In spite of the clamor about how things were rotten and how a return to basics will bring back, say, Jim Crow, one has to see how things are today (*and* in the distorted minds of the Left) and how we can *pick and choose* what we will toss out and what we will keep, societally.

– Unless they think we're all so stupid as to make it an all or nothing proposition. Of course, that's always a possible explanation for their protest, but they really don't think we're stupid, that is, we the People; they think *they're smarter*, the defense mechanism of *intellectualization*. It appears to be that they believe everybody else is stupid, but the actual dynamic is that the knowledge that people are reasonable makes them anxious (in that they could be defeated), so the mechanism of high ideation does its magic to make them believe we're all stupid, *relatively speaking*. What *we* think of *them* is that they're wrong and disoriented.

The return to basics calls for the return to punishment for crime without the over-analysis of why. *Who cares why criminals commit violent acts?* The idea is to discourage it, not baby it. Liberals claim to care, because it is a tool of obfuscation and delay; translation: meal ticket and contention, contention itself being a perk.

The return to basics calls for the decriminalization of reasonable response, which is presently lawful, but penalized. What a confusing state of affairs. Return to basics calls for de-complicating individual matters that turn the spirit of the law upside down.

*W*ho in their right mind would be against the most direct method of reducing crime? And one of the best ways to do it is to punish criminals, decriminalize resistance to illegitimate violence, and to eliminate the wrong-headed thinking of the confused in society, such as the Robin Hood complex (for lack of a better term) in the liberals. (As you know, Robin Hood took from the rich to give to the poor, but in so doing, he was in fact a robber. No matter how you justify it, it's looting for a payoff to the middleman. As the story at first seems to be compassionate, it misguides and compels people to root for the hood instead of the victim of his robberies. Now that *you're* being robbed, how does it feel?)

Tort litigators love to spot issues on the idea that a criminal can have rights too, usually in accusations of excessive force. But to even contemplate such issues betrays the truth that officials cannot sort things out like they used to. They may argue that society is more complicated today than ever before, but I argue that our society is more obfuscated than before purely by dint of such litigious issue-spotting, and that comes from rotten values. They've disrupted things so they can be summoned to correct them, and charge for it. But the bottom line remains that they say they cannot sort it out. Criminals know this as well as the litigators. It can be sorted out.

Decriminalize moral resistance to violent crime and stop second-guessing and punishing the law-abiding, and see what happens. It's time to stimulate not only the thinking of the would-be criminal, but also his supporters, the politicians, the academics, the reporters and those who drink the Jim Jones Kool-aid.

For those Leftists who don't understand the jab, disciples of the Reverend Jim Jones followed him to the grave in a mass suicide by drinking poisoned grape drink at his instruction. Reportedly a son of a Ku Klux Klansman, Jim Jones forecast an impending third world war, and assembled followers of his self-crafted religion to assemble in Guyana where tubs of grape drink were laced with cyanide and tranquilizers. They knew the drink was poisoned or they didn't know it, but they drank the drink. All died, including young children who were syringe-fed the drink. For liberals, the expression of *drinking the Kool-aid* is to follow something blindly without analysis that a rational, less hysterical person would easily suspect is dangerous. The minions of the Left react emotionally to their marching orders and with a hypnotic-like following, then scream at conservatives without a full comprehension of values; all they know is anger. Hence, the expression of drinking the Kool-aid for those minions who just parrot accusations without a thought as to what they are saying. Or doing.

It's Proven: People Can Be Trusted. The Citizen CPR Model.

Yes, people can be trusted. This is one of the largest differences between conservatives and liberals, the idea that people do best when left alone versus the idea that coercion is needed to bring out the best justice and fairness in people. The fact is that *people* bring out the best in people, and government in this is certainly not needed, and that applies to impaired officials.

Being trustworthy depends largely on the topic, doesn't it? One person who can't be trusted to be at work on time could easily be trusted to pay bills on time. Funny, isn't it? People who may not be trusted with making expensive legal decisions can be trusted with, say, raising children. It depends on our individual priorities in what we see as important to us, a sense of values. Or anxiety-producing symbols or situations.

But, generally, Americans find their way with guidance and invitation a lot better than with coercion. Without coercion, the subject is closed, the public's answer is probably No. Honorable, rational and non-hysterical persons accept this answer. The impaired, hysterical do not take No for an answer and move to coerce their way of thinking from others.

Through coercion, we're not finding our way, but being forced into going someone else's. *Coercion circumvents due process, no matter how it was brought into policy,* because in treating issues as the people do, they have cast their vote. Further information may be allowed, but if the answer is still No, then the answer is No. Think of it as a Vote of a sort.

On the other hand, personal responsibility and the accountability that goes with life choices we make are often thrust upon us, and we adapt. Single men who would never imagine anything but bachelorhood often find themselves becoming loving husbands, doting fathers, growing into the role, and gladly, emphasis on *gladly.*

Suddenly, priorities change. Instead of watching his golf swing, now the father watches his overall health, he gets life insurance, spends time with the kids instead of the links. This is the lesson of the 2004 Presidential election: the Democrats, counting on the youth vote, failed to account for the changing demographics in the intervening last four years; more voters – enough voters – went through a life change that changed their values to take into account the fact that they have now begun to live their lives with and for others. People grew up, and have less need for champions. Adults need fewer champions, and have more need of reliable, trustworthy executives instead. In this, life is good. *Good for whom?* If you're waiting for someone else to make life good for you by removing life's adversities, you may be waiting a long time.

Our job here isn't to prove to *officials* that we can be trusted – our task is to exhibit facts to remind the rest of the constituents that *they the People, their neighbors of shared values,* can be trusted. That the majority of people can be trusted. Barring the criminal and the irresponsible (and the impaired and the hysterical) people can be trusted.

What people will do in a situation and how well they will do it is a tricky thing, but some parameters and performance can be anticipated with very good accuracy. Among these is how some non-medical people will react in a medical emergency if they are willing and if they are trained beforehand; even when they are *not* trained beforehand, as I will explain.

Interested volunteer lay persons, non-medical persons with specific training, are aligned to a single focus or set of technical values with the medical persons of training. Training makes for a most useful homogeneity with everyone on the same page, speaking the same parlance, understanding the same practices and principles and carrying them out with dependable uniformity and convention.

To illustrate this point of personal responsibility of my fellow Americans as it relates us all to one another beyond ourselves, I hold up a national model – in fact, the worldwide model – that clearly exhibits the points of self-restraint, good judgement and character not on the occasion of wedded bliss and family, but in time of medical emergency.

In our own national, dignified example of personal responsibility, I hold up the now well-established *Citizen CPR,* or Cardio-pulmonary-resuscitation *delivered by laymen.*

There is no technical difference between the way CPR is taught to layman and health care providers. How is there a connection between Citizen CPR and the Right To Carry? The answer, my friends, lies in the concept of how it helps individuals and thereby our community and our nation and quality of life, expressed in terms of pain and suffering, personal recovery, legal costs, inundation and choking of the medical and legal system, and recovery of the tax revenues (and the wiser deployment of those saved revenues). Further, the corollary between Citizen CPR and right to carry is in the identity of initial objections from interested parties, which I compare in greater detail below.

As I mentioned at the outset, in my twenties I was one of the early Paramedics trained in Los Angeles. I was wild about EMS and it was very good to me. We wrote history in those days, and we paved the way for training the next generations to work the communities of today. Let me go into great detail now on just how there is an identity of values and objectives, even inquiry, between Citizen CPR and right to carry.

One of the things we did in the seventies was to teach CPR to other healthcare providers. Agencies were always in need of primary instruction and certification as well as re-certification for their personnel every two years. Hospitals required that professionals maintain their CPR Certificates. I was a certified CPR Instructor, as many Paramedics were and even today, I urge people like you to learn CPR and First-aid. Like EMS in general, Citizen CPR shared the mission of reducing morbidity and mortality of acute injury and illness. The enemy was *disability and premature death*, emphasis on *premature*.

CPR was developed at Johns-Hopkins University in 1960. Early on, you see, in the late sixties and middle seventies, EMS was primarily aimed at heart attack patients. EMS systems around the nation in their infancy were hardly even named Emergency Medical Services (EMS) in those days, much less planning curriculum around what we know today. The early Paramedics and Emergency Medical Technicians (EMT's) circa early seventies were trained by physician specialists and specialized Nurses in non-heart emergencies as well as heart emergencies. We were trained in assessing all sorts of medical, surgical and some psychiatric emergencies. We weren't physicians, but officially we were trained to become *an extension of the emergency physician's own senses and skills*. We learned about medical emergency, crime, suicide, trauma, pharmacology, some measure of evidence preservation, multiple casualty management, even baptizing the stillborn of Christian parents, inter-agency collaboration, and today, in the new Millennium (as I am still eligible for re-activation if I choose), Weapons of Mass Destruction and other terrorist attacks, foreign and domestic. EMS has come a long way. EMS faced its own struggle in the early years, *but imagine for a moment if Citizen CPR had never come into existence.*

EMS had its start-up problems in the beginning, but they were overcome thanks to a monumental effort of countless medical and non-medical persons. Scrutiny was absolutely necessary, since Medicine does not admit any process to its methods without proof. This is as it should be, of course. It went well, and I'm recalling the difficulties not in proving the concept, but in getting people onboard to bring it to laymen. The mission of Citizen CPR and professional

EMS is to avert premature death, and like self-defense against violent crime, it applies to everyone in all age groups, in all walks of life, in all circumstances.

Let's Go Technical For A Minute.

In time of heart attack, one out of four patients will die in the first two hours, and they will die of an arrhythmia called *Ventricular Fibrillation*. (American Heart Association CPR Trainer's Manual and elsewhere). In such a case, the heart, being a pump to begin with, simply stops pumping and the heart muscle begins to twitch unproductively instead of pumping as an organized action.

To administer CPR is to manually pump the patient's heart and to breathe *for* them, physically and mechanically effectively, until the EMS arrives to deliver more definitive care. Simple. The patient's cardiac arrest event need not be fatal, then, if someone is there on scene immediately. Without CPR, cardiac arrest is fatal.

Now this is important, because CPR isn't just for heart attacks: it's for *cardiac arrest,* or the heart's stopping, and remember: it's against *premature* death. Cardiac arrest need not be *only* from heart attack. This opens up a whole new realm of discoverable unnecessary losses, doesn't it? Cardiac arrest can result from all sorts of illness and injury. For background, let me name just a few.

Think of the nineteen year-old who takes a lethal electrical shock from his hobby workbench; the epileptic who's had a seizure, and who now has stopped breathing because he or she's come to rest in an unsafe position; the baseball player at bat who takes a fast ball to the chest and suddenly drops into cardiac arrest (such an *external* impact can generate the physiologic equivalent of about 4 Watt-seconds or more of energy *internally* and push the heart into ventricular fibrillation; you might say it's the heart of the precordial thump*)*. There is also the case of overdosage, near drowning, allergic reaction to bee sting or other allergen, choking, burns, falls, emotional shock, traffic accident, complication of pregnancy, including either mother or newborn – the list goes on. Any one of these can lead to cardiac arrest, and in many cases, the death can certainly be *premature.*

In this manner, Citizen CPR has distinguished itself, not only as workable in its lay delivery, but also in its effectiveness. *CPR Saves Lives.* Just who delivers it is of little importance; all that matters is that it be done when needed.

[Author's Note: Defibrillation works best when CPR is administered immediately, and makes the heart receptive to a life-saving countershock. Agencies and communities contemplating portable defibrillation units should explore these for their life-saving potential in connection with CPR training. For further information, www.americanheart.org]

Here's an interesting observation. CPR in time of cardiac arrest is not only life-saving for the individual about to meet a premature death, but prompt intervention can restore the individual to a complete recovery and quality of life under favorable circumstances, such as non-heart disease events. This is an important benefit of embedding trained persons in the community. Not only is the emphasis on preventing *premature death from cardiac arrest,* but also restoring the patient to *quality of life* now more than ever before. This is largely because CPR training involves managing non-breathing encounters, choking encounters, and other cases which, without intervening action, can deteriorate into a full cardio-pulmonic arrest.

Part of disaster recovery is restoration of the tax base on a community scale, including restoring abilities to fulfill contracts, commerce and other business because a local disaster can affect other parts of the country. For those assets of EMS, with delivery on an *individual* level, individual patients, whatever the cost to respond assets may have been or whatever it is today, restoring the tax paying ability of the individual is more than worth the effort and expense of a response of a Squad and Engine Company.

Say, if it costs $500 or more to roll out a Rescue Squad and Engine Company for added manpower as a matter of routine now, the life they save may be restored to pay taxes in excess of tens of thousands of dollars thereafter. Not a bad deal for those who see things in economic terms.

So many instances of cardiac arrest are not related to heart disease *per se*, and can resolve to a complete recovery. Imagine the contribution of handing someone back ten, twenty, or thirty years or more of their life. Imagine the tax revenues they can pay from decades more of earning years. Imagine looking them in the eye to see the twinkle after you delivered a life-saving technique. Imagine looking the whole family in the eye. If you've ever wanted to ask what it's like to save a life, don't forget to ask thousands of *citizens* who have administered CPR before the Paramedics arrived.

Who, then, could ever have opposed it?
And what does the birth and history of Citizen CPR
have to do with Liberty and fighting violent crime in America?

The connection is that a second model exists to demonstrate that individual citizens, not only professionals, are *already* established as responsible in the areas of vital intervention in time of emergency where professionals – the first responders – are not immediately available or otherwise just not able to intervene in time, and that the concept is worth implementing broadly for the national spirit as much as for the cost savings and conservation of assets.

The first model is, of course, the record of the right to carry states of the Union where individual citizens are trained, they are recognized, and they have done well as individuals within the community who, in the criminal emergency counterpart to the medical emergency, are the first line of defense. Mind you, these individuals are not Law Enforcement Reservists nor are they Explorers or in any way connected with Police, but merely individuals who have a civil right which right is recognized and respected by state and local authorities. It is this that the criminal respects in reality much more than a policy subject to unending interpretation.

Law Enforcement in those states doesn't perceive right to carry individuals as a threat, nor as criminals. They perceive criminals as criminals and law-abiding as law-abiding.

And in individual cases, we're not talking about serving up Justice or individuals playing cops, we're talking self-defense. Justice can then come through our due process – Justice can come at all for both victim and aggressor – if the perpetrator is stopped in the act and apprehended and held for Law Enforcement. Then, think of the safer would-be victim; it could have been worse.

Let me say that again: not only can the solution be delivered by Joe and Josephine Taxpayer in their own election to not be a victim, but the societal costs of violent crimes that-would-have-been can be reduced and the savings placed more productively elsewhere. *Isn't that a much more appropriate and more real and reachable social justice?*

Like Citizen CPR – whose success resides in how it helps individuals and thereby our community and our nation, expressed in terms of pain and suffering, legal costs, choking of the medical and legal system and recovery of the tax revenues – so a recapturing of our communities is expressed in conservation on those very same parameters, only more so, because violent crime and the administration of justice take a higher toll on society by billions more than do deaths from cardiac arrest death from non-intervention.

This is because premature death costs virtually nothing to care for thereafter. Yes, there is painful loss, loss of income and protection, loss of a loved one, disruption and recovery; but there are no rehabilitative or convalescing costs for a patient pronounced dead, only burial and losses. But in injury and loss from mayhem and homicide, the administration of justice goes on for the perpetrator and the statistics he creates in his wake in terms of adjusting policing costs, in court costs, incarceration, later recidivism, you get the idea. What is the cost to society in the wake of violent crime when the perpetrator is *not* apprehended, and continues to clone crime after crime? It is no longer a single loss, a multiple of losses.

Let me explain how the status quo presently hurts the nation. Let me explain how we're all in this together, irrespective of where you live. Picture citizens not as cowboys or gunslingers, but as the first line of defense to violent crime for *themselves* to begin with. They are there, on scene. They have resolved for themselves not to become a victim. They are not the aggressors. Each is a human being, valuable as a sovereign, valuable as a taxpayer or parent or child. They are not the takers in our society, they are the givers.

Picture personal right to carry for any age group of adults, then multiply it in any given community. This is not taking the law into your own hands, this is not to circumvent due process – because individuals already have the authority to act in self-defense. Acting in response is to act within due process.

Now see this: affirming right to carry nationwide is the opposite of the broken window theory of urban blight. Right to carry fights crime like beautification fights urban blight. In the broken window theory, the concept is that when you let one broken window remain unrepaired, other destruction grows for lack of opposition. (The broken window is an unchecked, single crime, let's say.) At the heart of the theory is neighborhood or property maintenance (opposition/ resistance) against blight. Keeping walls painted, keeping streets clean and functioning goes a long way in keeping the momentum of beautification and quiet enjoyment. Call it property values, call it attracting business, call it jobs, call it community, call it anything you like, but be certain about one thing: beautification is good for a neighborhood; it requires maintenance, and the neglect of the neighborhood promotes inertia, that unwillingness to move, or, in this case, unwillingness to resist blight. Neglect has its own ballast as it tugs on the life force of a community, it's weight dragged down by sheer gravity. Even when the perpetrator is apprehended immediately, the window must still be repaired, and that's part of the work of it.

This same principle applies to a community in terms of personal security, or even in personal intervention in time of medical emergency, if you will, and this has a direct influence on productivity and spirit of the People. It has a direct influence on certainties and quiet enjoyment. When you're secure, I'm secure, too. We're all more secure. It requires a maintenance, an awakening to understanding the *need* for ongoing maintenance in fighting inertia and ennui, and keeping the momentum of beautification, value and security in preserving the windows as repaired, functioning as they should. Being passive – being indifferent, being impartial – actually contributes weight to the inertia that will eventually bring security to a dead stop.

There will always be someone to drop in, see the unrepaired broken window, then be only too glad to pick up a rock to break the next window. The only real way to stop it is for passers-by to know that they're not in a rotten neighborhood, but a beautiful one, where the beauty itself is a statement that maintenance is important and that that vandalism will be cleaned up *before it has a chance to take hold*. Take that any way you like.

When EMS was developing, Paramedics like myself were tapped on the shoulder to begin a drive for support from the medical community for training non-medical citizens in CPR. Medical professionals were trained in CPR for more than a decade by then, but the drive was for them to get behind the idea of training laymen in CPR now. Though Citizen CPR may be taken for granted today, I'm here to tell you that I was one such person asked to speak to doctors in the private sector to get them behind the concept. In my case, I was supported by the American Heart Association who furnished me and my panel with data, exhibits, props and other details to make the case. I made my presentation in the auditorium of Santa Monica Hospital Medical Center, Santa Monica, California in the middle seventies. Thirty years later, there is a correlation between interrogatory on Citizen CPR then and on the subject of right to carry now.

That same presentation played out at major cities across the nation. I was asked because I was a Chief Paramedic at the time, and I was selected because one statement had to be uttered by a Paramedic, they believed; I concurred; it had to come from me (us). It wasn't stunning especially, and I have no way of knowing just how it all went down elsewhere nationwide, but it did solidify the concept by an interesting field reality to the professional physicians and attorneys attending.

In emergency care, we, as professionals, do the best we can with what we have to work with. This is important for a layperson to understand. Though all professions face this, the consequences are, of course, much more crucial when a life is at stake as opposed to when the situation is a routine non-emergency. We do the best we can with what we have to work with. This means appreciating in colleagues their want for better circumstances we encounter from time to time, an understanding that it happens to all of us, that it is beyond our control, and that there is an acceptance practice-wide that sometimes the situation as it comes to us is hopeless. These are some of the sad realities of all medical professionals and this was the thinking of the era.

In regard to EMS, private doctors and their colleagues know that EMS professionals do their best with what they have to work with, too, and part of this is when EMS is first summoned. It may be too late of a request for aid, it may be a matter of distance, it may be one of many things, but the bottom line is that the medical profession generally accepts that the Paramedics cannot be everywhere at once. This is as true a paradigm for EMS as it is for all professions, naturally. But it is too nebulous. The bottom line for the new talk was that *this wasn't good enough.*

It was a constant endeavor to do better, to learn more, and here was a profound opportunity not to seek out more *science as an area of improvement,* but more spirit and to effect improvement in delivery to the community by community involvement.

What a Paramedic (myself) was summoned to enunciate was the depth of the dilemma in time of emergency and the concept of Citizen CPR as a new tool to remedy the problem identified. What needed to be said in my own words had to come from the field perspective: "Yes, we cannot be everywhere, but the real problem is that no matter how soon you summon us, under even the most ideal circumstances, Advanced Life Support may not be there with *a life-saving response time of under three minutes.*"

That period after which brain death begins (four minutes and later) is the leading edge of what the American Heart Association terms the *resuscitation failure zone.* [See www.americanheart.org on the world wide web and navigate to *Chain Of Survival* and *The Early CPR Link* to learn more. With permission.]

What the Heart Association names today as the *resuscitation failure zone* was in the early years of EMS simply the knowledge that brain death begins in about four minutes. After six minutes or so, likelihood of successful resuscitation and quality of life deteriorate rapidly. Prompt intervention is everything.

This brought the nature of the problem into focus: that the situation of cardiac arrest, by dint of its very nature, indicated that almost no rescue would get there in time when brain death begins within four minutes.

The time it takes to identify the problem, to phone in a request for aid, the availability of the nearest M.I.C.U. (Mobile Intensive Care Unit, the Paramedics) or other aid, to assign the call to the right unit, etc., etc. are all likely to take up most of that four minutes. *And the key is to get there in less than three.* This was why the more precise time quote was most elucidating. They never saw it this way, really. In the world of hospital personnel, CPR-trained persons (e.g. nurses, and all other personnel) were literally only *seconds* away from the patient. This was not the reality of the field, where CPR-trained persons were several *minutes* away. Somehow, that gap had to be reduced to next to nothing, if possible. It was not a medical problem, per se, it was a response / deployment problem.

You see, in time of *most* medical or surgical emergencies, some patients can tolerate the longer wait of minutes due to the nature of the lesser emergency, say, a broken arm where the patient is in the mountains of Los Angeles. But a cardiac arrest patient cannot. Time, the foe of emergency, is not as critical when the patient's heart is beating and circulating blood as it is when the heart has stopped flat and specific, fatal biochemistry goes into action. Emergencies have a habit of deteriorating or they wouldn't be called emergencies, but some emergencies are extreme, deteriorate faster, and already have a horrible head start. In time of cardiac arrest, the running clock is a stopwatch, and seconds are vital. You have three minutes not only to get there, *but to begin treatment.* To a professional Paramedic, that means time to be dispatched, time to drive Code Three to the scene, unload equipment, locate the situs of the call, *then* to see the patient and begin CPR if such is the case.

As one for instance, in the Cardiac Catheterization Laboratory, where radio-opaque contrast media are injected, technicians and surgeons see cardiac arrest all the time as a reaction to introduction of the contrast medium. Naturally, they are on top of it, and the patient resuscitated. CPR works, especially when you're on it in seconds. It ain't no big deal there.

When I enunciated this differentiation in connection with this concept they could all relate to – *the concept of a life-saving field response-time of under three minutes* – I could see the thought reflex in action and I could see the light bulbs coming on throughout the audience. Every professional understands that we do the best we can and that we cannot be everywhere at once; that sometimes we cannot get there in time, and that time was universally, scientifically and conventionally deemed – at that point in time, the seventies – to be a few *minutes or as soon as possible.* It was a matter of more *precise* perspective, to be accurate. All medical professionals, as I said, tend to understand the sorrow of their colleagues who lose patients because of what adverse circumstances they had, or in spite of favorable circumstances they had to work with; *time,* or not enough of it, is one of those. If only one could intervene *sooner.*

This, of course, is the purpose of EMS everywhere: to condense the time frame by creating a Mobile Intensive Care Unit to send *to* the patient, as opposed to the old saw of the grab-and-run getting the patient to the hospital (and, prior to modern EMS, doing little for them en route). Problems are solved with technical wonder all the time, but in the case of the cardiac arrest *in the field,* better treatment was not the answer; it was already excellent; now, *sooner* treatment is the answer. Immediate life-saving intervention is better with trained individuals embedded within any given community – Citizen CPR.

For generations now, family members have been trained in how to inject Morphine and other compounds for an ill spouse at home; family members are trained in how to administer Insulin to their diabetic spouses in time of emergency. Laymen administer Oxygen properly, also a medication, and they administer compounds after being trained by the private doctor. There are more examples of how laymen are trained and trusted to administer care, and this only mentions *medications*. Spouses and others are trained also in maneuvers, assessment and other things to watch for which they can help to mitigate the sudden change in the patient's condition. Such practice – such training, trust, authority, and *reliance* – is commonplace. Interested persons can be trusted with intervention responsibility.

It is vital to understand this: average people are *already* being trusted with vitally important issues. When it comes to self-defense as an emergency of another type, where similarities are extremely close and just as urgent, *trust of the individual* is exquisitely vital to the objective.

Citizen CPR trained persons are trained to discern the emergency from the non-emergency in that they are certainly trained to recognize a pulseless, non-breathing patient, a choking incident, a non-choking incident, other kinds of non-breathing incidents, and some first aid. A good CPR course mentions the history of heart disease, contributing factors and healthy heart advice as part of the program to fight heart disease and stroke. Basic understanding is the gist of a good CPR course.

This temporal component or immediate recognition and rapid reaction time of lay intervention in time of genuine emergency add much to the odds of saving the patient's life, and to the odds of a wonderful recovery and quality of life. This hardly had to be mentioned to the medical professionals in the audience, but what did speak to them was the concept of now delivering help within seconds. They were being asked to get behind the idea of passing this knowledge and technique on in order that the layman may deliver it *without supervision.*

The rest of the presentation fell into place. I had stated the problem. It was now seen in a new light. Now hundreds of EMS Professionals around the country as well as myself had to hear their examination, and it's important to note that modern inquiry on the subject of nationwide right to carry as a loss-prevention tool is most similar to the inquiry of Citizen CPR as a loss-prevention tool.

Interrogatories came from attorneys and private physicians in my audience, and followed a consistent pattern:

1) The training of non-medical professionals – laymen – who may not fully understand the medical concepts and its intricacies, and, further, who lacked the commitment to the long term such a goal would require of them if they were to be a force of passer-by intervention.

2) They'll do more harm than good. Why not let the professionals such as yourself handle it?

3) They'll exceed the scope of their authority and begin practicing Medicine.

4) What mechanism is in place to keep them sharp?

The first issue had the cast of imposing medical professionalism to the volunteer prospects. Namely, that medical persons including firefighters, are career-minded, and the questions was, in part, how one could be trained when they're not likely so career-minded. The answer to that and more components of the issue were actually very simple. These Citizen CPR prospects were volunteers.

Having heard me establish the day-to-day, round-the-clock reality that the M.I.C.U. cannot always arrive with a life-saving response time of under three minutes – *many times we could* – the audience was most receptive to how we answered the rest of the questions when a Rescue was *not* going to arrive inside of three minutes. I answered the first question for them as I just explained in detail above. The value of having a trained volunteer embedded in the community could make all the difference in those vital first few minutes of opportunity. This can overcome the odds that are working against the patient. As to the question of staying power for the trainees, I mentioned that they would enroll as volunteers, and, once trained, would be unlikely to withhold that same volunteer spirit even years later should they encounter a cardiac arrest situation.

The second question was equally important; *They'll do more harm than good. Why not let the professionals handle it?* This is one of the most correlative issues to right to carry weapons.

Let me lay down this preface to the question first: Technically speaking, bad CPR can damage the patient in such a way that it may become a complication of the emergency. That is to say, the patient may recover from the cardiac arrest, but may bleed from a lacerated liver if CPR is done incorrectly. Today, the thinking is different, the medical opinion different.

We understand two ideas in answer to this issue: first, the alternative to no CPR is certain death. When the heart stops, it can be mechanically pumped by CPR, right? But if there is no CPR, the heart remains stopped, there is no pumping action, and the patient expires. There are an extreme few complexes of an arrhythmia that stops the heart and it restarts itself (Stokes-Adams Syndrome, for instance), but this is not knowable at the scene of the emergency, and suspecting it is no reason to withhold CPR to wait and see if the patient recovers spontaneously.

Second, sometimes, when there *is* damage done by the rescuer, lay or professional, and though attributable to the effort itself, it is repairable in most cases, and is infinitely preferable to the alternative of certain death which necessarily follows electing to do nothing. To answer the question of doing more harm than good, any harm the lay rescuer does is certainly preferable to doing nothing. To be conscientious and mindful of such – through realistic practice and testing – is part of primary training.

The second part of the question, the concept of *the Professional,* is broader. Does this mean licensed? Does it mean current? Does it mean full-time? Does it mean active or retired? Does it mean adhering to a code of conduct, to a standard or technology or even to a section of the Welfare and Institutions Code? And, of course, it means nothing if EMS is in any way delayed. Letting the professionals handle it means *to wait – to delay treatment – as if this were preferable to the actual predictable outcome, certain death, because time is the enemy of emergency.* It is identical to doing nothing while life slips away.

Think of this when you think of the model of Citizen CPR and the idea of resistance to violent crime. Remember that to summon help and to wait for it is *to delay intervention, to do nothing on scene while vital time and circumstances destroy.* The emergency – medical or criminal – does not take a time out while you summon aid.

Or, one can do something in the meantime by beginning treatment, the same initial treatment the Rescue will deliver. To intervene without training or to intervene with lapsed certification is the preferred position.

Remember that when care is life-saving, care's response time is *everything*. Letting the professionals handle it may at first seem the wiser thing to do, but choosing the professionals first when CPR trained citizens can be a reality is to compare the incorrect parameters, specifically, *waiting* to do it supposedly *right or better,* compared to beginning it immediately to give the patient the best chances of recovery and better quality of life using the very same techniques as the professional you're summoning. And to reiterate: the emergency, medical or criminal, doesn't take a time out for you to summon aid.

Don't forget that the Citizen delivering CPR is giving the patient circulation and air immediately and keeping the patient alive until the professionals do arrive. Remember, also, that the CPR delivered by a trained citizen is identical to the CPR delivered by a trained medical professional. Remember that CPR delivered even without emergency drugs is better than doing nothing until the Squad arrives. And remember that CPR isn't just for heart disease, but for *any* case of no breathing and no pulse, in any circumstances, any age group.

Let's understand also that someone trained in CPR can become professional-equivalent in their living up to the very same standards as the everyday, full-time licensed medical practitioner who, by the way is in the same classroom to be certified by people like me. The patient assessment is the same; the response protocol is the same; the standard of how to deliver breathing and compressions is the same; you get the idea. Only, it's a lot less to learn since the Citizen isn't going for a paramedic diploma, and just as easy to deliver. It's not brain surgery.

An individual acting in self-defense can also live up to the law in terms of force and purposeful response in time of criminal emergency.

The third question, equally important and reasonable was this: *They'll exceed the scope of their training and begin practicing Medicine.* I noticed this question, because the medical community was just embracing the non-physician medical professional throughout medical practice. They were proving the non-physician professional every single day, from Paramedics to Nurse Practitioners and Physician Assistants. It wasn't at all unrealistic to train a lay person. I answered that it would be hard to imagine just how citizens would exceed the scope of their authority. I took the what-happens-next-thinking through to the logical conclusion. Trainees would be trained in what to do in time of non-breathing, in time of difficulty breathing , and in time of choking and in time of cardiac arrest, and would be pretty much busy until the Squad arrives; you might say they would have their hands full. From then, the patient leaves their care. Simple. What else could they do that would amount to a practice of Medicine? After a few jokes about specific intrusive exams, the crowd agreed. They remembered that medical professionals were at one time non-medical at anything, and what they didn't know, they learned through training. They began to have faith in their lay community. This is the object lesson of Citizen CPR and right to carry.

Finally, one last question: *What mechanism is in place to keep them sharp?* A re-certification schedule of every two years was already imposed, and this answer was satisfactory, but what I gave was this argument: CPR is not a legal concept, but a practical emergency *mechanical* concept, learnable and retainable. Once taught, its delivery is life-saving, and in time of emergency, it's immaterial whether the certification of the lay rescuer is active or inactive. I know that what they were really asking about was deteriorating skills, or just becoming rusty, and, of course, we insist on primary training and on currency of certification as set forth, but let us remember that, speaking practically now, in the new century, even though many, many individuals have permitted their certs to lapse over time, they still were trained at one time, and those persons remain a most useful resource in time of emergency. It's not so much the legality about being currently certified, *it's what they know and remember that saves a life*. Would this expired certification stop a retired physician from delivering CPR on scene? Probably not. Would you want it to?

By the end of the first hour, we had made the case for physician backing of the concept of Citizen CPR. It must have worked around the country; Citizen CPR is a reality today.

Many persons commence CPR without training certification. Their intervention is welcome, helpful and lawful. With such insistence on protocol of licensing, authority and training, how can this be?

It's because *it's important.* It's in the public interest.

Today, more than *20,000,000* Americans are either currently certified or formerly trained in CPR, and others in this total, trained or not, understand its mechanisms and operational objective sufficiently to deliver it *well enough to save a life*. The Heart Association estimates about 8 million persons annually.

This is stunning progress that could develop only when the societal interest theory is grounded on a common, important value system and is given its chance to be proven, and then becomes a proven success. *You might say the selfless opposite of Potomac Fever.* Having the vision and seeing that passerby intervention can save a life, and that it can be successful in defeating *premature* death and restoring the individual to a *productive* life, meant a great deal to communities worldwide, not to mention those individual family members of the loved ones rescued. Saving lives means uplifting spirit. It means increased tax revenues that would have been lost. And it also proved that people willing and who are not excluded can be a critical part of the solution.

How to do this optimally, of course, requires taking training, and I advise learning CPR and First-aid. You may never be thanked by the person you help, you may never meet again, but *they and their loved ones* will know you made all the difference in their world.

Of course, there were no reports of anyone's practicing Medicine without a license or exceeding the scope of their training, for this wasn't about the *practitioner nor the rescuer*, it was about the emergent *patient.*

Today, the motto is, *CPR Saves Lives.* So do armed citizens. And the bottom line is this: *The People have not regretted placing their trust in laymen for such a vital issue.* For decades.

Now let's make the connection between our model of Citizen CPR and the Right To Carry.

In thinking of an identity between response to medical emergency and response to violent crime – is there such a thing as a *violent crime intervention failure zone*?

Yes, there is. Let's identify first a pre-failure zone, that narrow moment of time, that window of opportunity, between the first recognition of an impending violent act and your power to stop it from escalating before it can become a mayhem or a fatality, the actual failure zone being that subsequent time of missed opportunity and its irrevocable consequences of injury or death.

The importance of even recognizing such a concept is in the fact that once that opportunity has passed and the damage begins – and there is a very clear demarcation between life and death – there is a point of no return. That point is the last clear chance where an individual can stop the act before it escalates. And when that opportunity to keep the act from escalating is missed, the results can be unforgiving. Disastrous.

The power to stop this resides almost exclusively with the would-be victim as the first line of defense, and the decisive attitude of refusing to become a victim. The advantage one has over the CPR situation is that where the CPR patient has no choice in a cardiac emergency, resolving not to become a victim of a violent crime is a choice, a civil right. Sometimes, often, that window of opportunity, that pre-failure zone, is all too short, suggesting strongly that the decision must be made beforehand. In preparation and readiness. In resolve. In defeating that PC thinking of non-resistance.

Use of lethal force is permitted in only a limited set of scenarios, so we're not talking about hair-trigger responses to every indignity, but of trained responses from individuals who are entitled to meet dangerous menace with armed resistance. And we are not talking about *designated* persons. The right to carry is a civil right, and shall not be infringed.

Let's restate a few grounds of similarity between the two models and let's take it up a notch.

Having someone in place at the scene of the emergency – volunteers embedded in any given community – who keep the lid on until the Advanced Life Support arrives can be everything, especially in life-threatening medical emergencies. *This medical emergency lay-intervention concept has a direct counterpart in instances of personal resistance to threats of violent crime emergency.*

One difference is that Citizen CPR is a great and workable and proven idea, and the right to carry, also a great and workable and proven idea, *is a Constitutional Right.*

Where CPR saves lives because someone willing is on scene to protect that patient, so an individual can be trained to protect himself or the life of another in time of threat of violence by the right to self-defense, of course, as well as the doctrine of standing in the shoes of the victim and other doctrines.

Especially now, when America is under attack from various corners. As I said before – Nationwide right to carry. Before it's too late.

The immediately corresponding features between the two models are these:

1) *As the First-aid and resuscitation model has an impact on preservation of our tax base and societal loss-prevention and is in accord with public policy, so nationwide right to carry would have an effect on violent crime, would impact our economy for the better and be in accord with public policy.* It is in more than two-thirds the states of the Union. Quality of life is better when criminals don't

know who's armed. Each of these concealed carry individuals is a good will ambassador for the Second Amendment and the entire Constitution.

2) Just as trained laymen weren't ever likely to exceed the scope of their training and practice Medicine, but keep the lid on until the Rescue Squad arrives, so the armed citizen isn't likely to exceed the scope of his or her training and practice Justice, but keep the lid on until Law Enforcement arrives. Newly armed citizens aren't going to practice justice on scene any more than the armed citizens in the right to carry states have over the decades. Self-defense and detaining the aggressor is not taking the law into your own hands, but is permitted by law and it is not circumventing due process; it is not practicing Justice any more than Citizen CPR is to practice Medicine. What reservations some have applies to *criminals they fear and presume that provoking them will somehow worsen the situation*; it does not apply to reasonable, law abiding citizens. The law-abiding are entitled to protect themselves and their families and not to depend on help that would be far too late. See below.

One of the most important ideas is that many, many citizens are already armed, but their hands are increasingly tied it seems from the presently legal protecting themselves in time of violence without unreasonable penalty, both in pre-emptive discouragement and after-incident over-reaction. That is to say, individuals may use lethal force, but the over-scrutiny subjects the defender to great penalties they should never have to go through just because of agendas of impaired officials. I'd be willing to bet, with little fear of contradiction, that, after real thought, and perhaps a little untoward experiences, more people would begin to realize how such penalizing policies affect us all, and therefore, they would never allow them. Pity that it would have to come to that; Some people believe that a conservative is a liberal who's been mugged! Is that trip really necessary? Or can we just as easily learn from tradition and history?

This is where the concept of protecting the rights (so-called, newly discovered rights) of the violent criminal seem to trump those of his victim! This is where government's misguided laws and rulings – so very out of touch with the realities and wishes of the constituents – constitute an interference with its own public policy. In this conflict between individual interest and the misguided desires of officials who insist on over-riding our instructions, the officials have to lose.

Or do I have it wrong?

How would you like to take steps to protect your home against someone who doesn't belong there and you go to jail instead of him or have to mortgage your property to pay legal expenses? Friends, not only are we headed there, we're already here! How would you like a Law Enforcement officer or an officer of the court to make the very same choices you made, but suffer no litigation, castigation or over-examination for their self-defense actions?

Why this elitism? Why this second-guessing? Why the double-standard? I'm not speaking of the indefensible acts of homeowner over-reacting in time of such an encounter, I'm speaking about so-called rights of a burglar in damages of his own doing. Criminals should have no right to claim damages for assumption of risk in criminal acts, hence, I ask for the decriminalization of self-defense responses *except in* excessive over-reaction, *which is rare.* And I ask that officials enjoy no special privilege above what ordinary constituents enjoy.

Let us examine more of the similarities between emergencies of violent crime and the working model of EMS / Citizen CPR in medical emergencies. And please remember one important thing:

the right to defend yourself is becoming increasingly indistinct in certain parts of the country, usually where crime is higher, even though the right to keep and bear arms is a specific Civil Right guaranteed by the Constitution. Self-determination is our right, and actually exercising it without official interference is, too. The concept of taking back our homes and communities, even from our vexing, ill-mannered fellow Americans, begins with these.

First, as you might suspect in the thesis statement, Law Enforcement, like EMS, cannot be everywhere at once, but more to the point, Law Enforcement cannot always be on scene *with the absolutely essential life-saving response time – they may not be there in time at all.* In time of criminal violence, there is our very own *intervention failure zone*, namely those moments when the imminent violence is first recognized (or not recognized at all!) and the window when it can be stopped. When it cannot be stopped, as in the cases of not being able to resist, more specifically, when help cannot arrive in time, violent crime succeeds in committing a mayhem or taking a life.

Of course, response time means nothing without a request for aid. As in making the case for physician backing of Citizen CPR, the concept of clarifying *what is a meaningful response time* is critical, and that, of course, depends on summoning EMS. For EMS, the critical response time *to begin care* is minutes or even seconds, and it's even better if someone is there to administer the same initial life-saving mechanical measures on the spot, the moment they're recognized. Ultimately, the Squad has to arrive *in time*, which is a concept we all understand. *Without a request for aid*, can Law Enforcement arrive in time, *and in time to beat that failure zone?* We're talking about life or death crime violence, quick violence – the kind that doesn't even allow you to even get to a phone.

Second, the very ability to summon aid in time of crime is substantially different from the ability to summon aid in time of medical emergency. Unlike the medical emergency where most people wish to help, the incident of violent crime has the added component of someone present who is most certainly *not* willing to help, but to *stop* you from summoning aid, namely the perpetrator. Police help is only a concept when you cannot even summon them. And what can happen in the meantime from the beginning of the crime and the arrival of assets (assuming you completed a call for aid)? In a medical emergency, you may or may not have friendly assistance at first, but in a violence emergency, you have someone unfriendly working against you, namely the aggressor.

Third, many communities still do not have enhanced 9-1-1 capabilities to immediately display names and originating addresses on-screen in the event of a mute or injured caller. Furthermore, incoming calls are screened and prioritized. How many of us can really calmly and accurately report the incident for the proper prioritization, or even foresee calmly how the threatening situation can then rapidly deteriorate and determine even whether to summon the police before it escalates?

Of course, *cell phones* aren't worth a hoot, unless you program your unit to direct-dial *the* local dispatcher for Fire or Police *where the emergency is* and can utter your location. Furthermore, the crime has to occur within the jurisdiction of the authority you have programmed into your phone for it to work or no soap. It doesn't do a lot of good for you to program your home city's Sheriff office number into your cell phone when your robbery occurs in another city you didn't expect to be robbed in.

Let's take the first point. Law Enforcement, as we know, has no mandate to protect the lives of individuals [See *Dial 911 and Die* by Attorney Richard Stevens, available at www.jpfo.org]. Requests for aid are not without their complications, often waste valuable time in merely placing and completing the call, being prioritized, dispatched and then arrival of officers.

In his book *Dial 911 And Die*, Richard Stevens researches 54 jurisdictions and cites cases where rulings consistently hold against the plaintiff and explain that the police are not liable for their failure to protect individuals.

Here is an excerpt from an interview with attorney author Richard Stevens conducted by author Robert A. Waters for Sierra Times.

RW -- Which cases affected you most (of those you wrote about)?

RS -- Hartzler vs. City of San Jose (California). This one completely shocked me. In law school, we had been learning how manufacturers owe legal duties to buyers of products to be sure the products are safe; how landlords owe legal duties to tenants to protect them from foreseeable criminal attacks; and how homeowners owe legal duties to make sure that visitors don't trip and fall on their property. Then we turned the page and found that governments owe no legal duty to do the one thing that you'd think they are supposed to do: protect citizens from criminal attack.

Another case that really bothered me was the DeShaney Case in Wisconsin. The county welfare authorities placed a young boy with an abusive father who tortured and beat him until he was permanently mentally damaged and had to be institutionalized. There were lots of warning signs and the county case worker saw tons of evidence that the child was being abused, yet the case worker failed to intervene. The Supreme Court ruled that the Constitution does not require states to protect their citizens, such as this young boy. While I have to agree with the court's decision on strict legal grounds in this case, I was horrified by the larger moral issue: why can the government agency charged with protecting children escape legal liability for failing to carry out that duty — when a homeowner can be successfully sued if a would-be burglar trips and falls on the owner's property?In another case, Ford vs. Town of Grafton (Massachusetts), a woman got a restraining order to protect herself from a crazed violent ex-boyfriend. But the police didn't enforce it and the boyfriend attacked her and nearly killed her. This case is particularly appalling because the police actually advised the woman to "get a gun" since they couldn't protect her. The court in that rabidly anti-firearms state later used the "get a gun" warning against her. The court said that the police adequately warned her and therefore had no duty to protect her.

[*Used with permission. The complete interview is available on the world wide web at http://www.sierratimes.com/archive/waters/txt/ edrw101100-t.htm*]

But let's look at something else: what if officers *were* required to protect individuals? Other sources illustrate the history of law enforcement on the subject of personal protection as belonging to the citizen, almost purely because it's just not workable to attempt to protect individuals. And they're right! It just doesn't work! Talk about not being everywhere at once. . .

Exploring the issue, let us make the comparison of the right to carry to the concept of Law Enforcement's efficacy or non-mandate in protecting an individual or intervention in time of violent crime enough to save the citizen. Let's cut our officers a little slack here by re-emphasizing that it would be utterly impractical to expect Law Enforcement to protect individuals or to hold liable Law Enforcement for failure to protect. It just wouldn't work, folks, which not only cuts them slack, but also cements the idea that we will forever be on our own.

Understand, also, that, under the present circumstances, constituents are denied the opportunity to work closely with Law Enforcement in those states which will not recognize right to carry. In these states, such as California, Liberty Enthusiasts are met with suspicion, instead of being appreciated as willing volunteers in support of what officers need, community cooperation. Instead, we are viewed as interfering. Why?

Constituents are perceived as complicating missions, of making police responses more dangerous, and it seems the officers are not able to tell the good guys from the bad guys. But, stay with me on this.

Crime prevention programs that don't work, and all sorts of crime policies and the editorials that encourage them are sapping dollars from our economy. Losses suffered by society are indisputable, painful, increasingly costly and for its emotional toll for some, irrevocable. Losses suffered by society are not essential as a cost of doing business or of living life, and can be stopped. These losses can be stemmed if the right to carry is more properly viewed as a personal safety issue and loss-prevention apparatus that trump the objections of self-interested officials, *irrespective of their predictions and objections.*

If a criminal sues and the court finds against you, then the system is sapping dollars from *you.* You're no longer part of a collective sharing the weight of the hardship. These failed policies take this money out of circulation, in effect, but make for a delightful payday for the officials who administer them. *We're being victimized twice.* We're being victimized *repeatedly, continuously.*

One of the most pernicious and obscene problems with Potomac Fever is that officials view national assets and resources as their own to convert, *our time and energy being one such very common example.* It is vital to understand this mind-set. They think of our time and energy the same way they think of their provided vehicle: it's for their use for the duration. But our time and energy (quiet enjoyment and safety) are not for their use. The impaired official cannot tell the difference between what we as taxpayers furnish them to do their job and what we reserve for ourselves as sovereigns and just why we hire them: quiet enjoyment and safety. They not only fail, they actively rob us of the ability to do what we hired them to ensure.

Officials see our hard work and community wealth (including the concept of our safety) as a resource to tap into by introducing crime policies that will never work, but give the appearance of a full waste basket and working hard so they can administer them and process juicy funds for years and years. We simply have to pick up the tab or else.

The economy, or a good portion of it, can enjoy a much higher prosperity (better ways to spend the same money) if this corner of society were rectified by recognizing the individual's right to carry, and the right of self-protection unfettered by destructive rulings against the victim.

Making The Case For Newlyweds, For Family And For Baby.

In making the comparison of affirming the right to self-defense to the involvement of Law Enforcement, one central two-part inquiry that needs illumination is just what we expect from Law Enforcement in time of request for aid in time of reasonable apprehension of violent crime. That is, presuming that a successful call to the police dispatcher is completed and they send a car, what do we expect from the officers once they're 10-97? Let's revisit those two concepts, *authority* and *force*.

In ejecting an unwanted intruder, a homeowner *already* has all the authority one needs; up against it, a homeowner, or a motorist or passer-by, needs *force*, and sometimes quite a generous helping of it, if he or she is to avoid being a statistic on the police blotter on that watch. I doubt very much if a judge, encountering a burglar in the home, relies entirely on getting to the phone and then waiting for officers. Oh – do they have armed bodyguards? Sorry, it must have slipped my mind.

Digressing momentarily, you may not choose to own a gun, but we do need to repeal laws which punish you *anyway* for defending yourself whether you use a baseball bat, kitchen knife or the nearest thing that's handy. And we need to do something about that presumption that, whatever you do, it will be portraying you as responding *in anger* and presumptively with *excessive force*.

The fact is that the Law Enforcement response time depends on if and when a request for aid is even made and received, whether a unit is available (prioritized and dispatched), and well, the list goes on. So much has to happen just to get the officers on scene and size up the situation, and when they do arrive, they do not even have a mandate to protect you. Mandates they do have involve protecting the public, not individuals, a different legal meaning, preventing crime, detecting crime and so forth, but nowhere is there a mandate to *protect you*. Remember that it is feasible to protect the public, but not feasible to protect an individual. They may certainly have the task of preventing crime, but if they don't protect you in the process, there is no liability to them.

On the subject of violent crime – not traffic accident, flood, barking dogs or a funny smell from the house next door, now – what more do we expect from Law Enforcement when we make an emergency request for aid for a violent crime? How about judgement and experience? How about tactical methods? Let's be clear on this: if they fail to save you, and if you sue them, you probably won't win. [Ibid.] It's important to restate this.

This is the lament of hundreds of women (or more) who trust in restraining orders, the telephone and a clear shot at sprinting to one only to be injured or killed with no legal remedy from the agency she relied on. Thankfully, and properly, more and more women are owning guns and training in how to use them. Thankfully and properly, they are also carrying them.

To reiterate, we cannot be against our police officers, and we must be for them. We need them in the overall administration of justice, but *they* need to support *us* in our being the necessarily unavoidable, undeniable first line of defense in violent crime. They know it; now we need them to actively support it.

They do support us, when responding anonymously as they have responded in this police poll conducted by the National Association of Chiefs Of Police, and published by the American Police Hall Of Fame Newsletter, January, 2005. Of 22,587 respondents, the survey supports the argument that law enforcement is not against private ownership of handguns. It's entirely possible that this includes concealed carry. It also dispels some of the myths of the anti-gun crowd and their go-nowhere policies.

Please look closely at the poll results for FIREARMS, but also take a close look at the section on MEDIA. Don't forget how media omit the other side of the story when it doesn't suit them. They do the same injustice to law enforcement as they do to you and me.

16th Annual National Survey Results of Police Chiefs & Sheriffs

The following survey questions were posed by mail of 22,587 Chiefs of Police and Sheriffs in the United States. It represents a cross section of professional command officers involving every state. The survey was conducted for the 16th consecutive year by the National Association of Chiefs of Police. (321)264-0911. www.aphf.org, policeinfo@aphf.org. Permission to reproduce in whole or part is granted if credit is given to our organization.

		YES	NO
DEATH PENALTY			
1.	Do you believe the death penalty serves as a deterrent to certain types of crimes?	88.5%	
2.	Do you believe that when a law enforcement officer is feloniously killed in the line of duty that the penalty upon conviction should be death?	97.3%	
FIREARMS			
3.	Should any law-abiding citizen be able to purchase a firearm for sport or self-defense?	94%	
4.	Within the past year, has your agency been called upon to arrest anyone who has made a false statement on an application to purchase a firearm?		91.2%
5.	Should anyone (such as a convicted felon) in violation of state or federal firearm possession laws, be prosecuted by the U.S. Attorney and, if convicted, receive a maximum prison term?	87.7%	
6.	Do you believe law-abiding citizens should be limited to the purchase of no more than one firearm per month?		66.4%
7.	Do you maintain that criminals currently are able to obtain basically any type of firearm by illegal means?	96.5%	
8.	Do you agree with H.R. 218 which would enable qualified active and retired law enforcement officers to carry concealed weapons nationally?	93.5%	
9.	Do you believe the application & training process to allow commercial airline pilots to carry firearms in the cockpit is too restrictive and burdensome?		53.6%
10.	Do you agree that a national concealed handgun permit would reduce rates of violent crime as recent studies in some states have already reflected?	65.7%	
MEDIA			
11.	Do you believe the media (TV, radio and print) are fair and impartial in reporting the news?		92.2%
12.	Does your agency have at least one officer assigned to handle media requests?	70.5%	
TERRORISM			
13.	Has the federal government provided or offered your department training to meet the increased threat of terrorism in the wake of the terror attacks of September 11, 2001?	64%	
14.	Has your department participated in any state or local terrorism response simulations?		58%
15.	Would you concur that foreign or domestic terrorist threats or acts will increase in this country in the next year?	88.2%	
TECHNOLOGY/EQUIPMENT			
16.	Do you think anyone convicted of a felony should be required to provide DNA samples to be cataloged in a manner similar to current practices of fingerprinting?	92.4%	
17.	Does encryption technology - the ability to allow electronic messaging to be private and untraceable - hamper law enforcement's investigative efforts?	76.6%	
18.	Does your department require every officer to wear a bullet-resistant jacket while on duty?	60.5%	
19.	Does your department have video equipment in every on-duty patrol vehicle?		63.5%
20.	Does your department issue digital cameras for officers' use?	61.2%	
DRUGS			
21.	Should marijuana be legalized in the United States for those who have a legitimate medical need for the drug?		59.8%
22.	Have you seen an increase in the abuse of OxyContin and other Schedule II Narcotics in your community?	62.6%	
23.	Has the national war on drugs, which has been going on for more than 15 years, been successful in reducing the use of illegal drugs?		82.3%
24.	Do you think the decriminalization of "soft drugs" would allow more resources for violent and property crime management?		68.9%
HOMELAND SECURITY			
25.	Has the current increased threat of terrorist acts and heightened security made it more difficult to obtain new recruits in your department/agency?		93.4%
26.	Have you observed more cooperation between federal and local agencies in the past year?	69.8%	
27.	Is the current "color-coded" terrorist threat level an effective way of informing the public of threats to homeland security?	66.9%	
OTHER			
28.	Does your department have a written and enforced policy against racial profiling?	67.5%	
29.	Does your department currently have at least one active canine unit in force?		67%
30.	If a one-time grant were offered by a non-profit police organization to fund the purchase and initial training of a canine, would your department be able to maintain the ongoing expense in future years?	61.3%	
31.	Do you feel "civilian review boards" are an effective method of handling citizen complaints against law enforcement officers?		76.9%
32.	Does your department provide "sensitivity training" for its officers?	57.8%	

The inference from this poll is important. First, it means that law enforcement does care about constituents. And this clarification is vital.

Am I criticizing law enforcement? In a word, no. I have only this one complaint, and only one: I ask that law enforcement police its own, and no longer tolerate those who bring disgrace to the force. We cannot have high confidence in our cops when they protect their own under positively any circumstances, and sometimes they do; there must be exceptions to that corps spirit when a single officer or cadre of them violates the very mission. This is my only objection.

So much happens in the moments of a crime, even a non-violent one. Burglary may be non-violent, but it is one of the five enumerated felonies for murder for good reason. There are all kinds of burglaries, depending on your state and on the conditions, from daytime to nighttime, from one burglar to a pair or more, each with the potential to escalate. If you wake up and the theft then is committed in your presence, then it's robbery. If he liked your kitchen knife and admiringly holds it, it's armed robbery. If he's with a buddy, it's home invasion. Temptations titillate intruders, and a simple mid-morning or late night breaking and entering can very easily become a rape and worse. The fact is that any one of these, which can range from the pathetic, needy solo intruder to the abusively hostile group, can easily get out of hand. For the intruders, even the most unintentional, opportunistic forays can deteriorate into a rape, mayhem or murder.

But death or severe injury to the homeowner can result during the commission of nearly any small intrusion or on-the-street encounter. Not only is there the reality that a homeowner cannot afford to wait to see what an intruder will do next in escalating the intrusion, but there is also general public confusion about the gravity of such encounters which lead people to take the wait-and-see; there are clues to the idea that laymen have a confusion of what these crimes really are and precisely how they affect the spirit and productivity of our society, hence the you-don't-really-know-what-the-intruder-is-going-to-do   and   you're-not-sure-he's-going-to-hurt-you kind of thinking. For the victims, the experience of these is not at all vague, and are almost forever tormenting. It's time to get people talking. I'd like to see more discussion on the experiences of home invasion targets, rape victims, robbery victims and burglary. We need to hear it from *them*. We need to hear from the field.

Remember that a breaking and entering, for instance, can take a turn for the worse and instantly become a tragedy, and it can be formed in a moment of time, escalating the threat of violence. The very idea of being discovered when one was first planning on being unidentifiable in a quick snatch of some CD's for a little quick cash can change his entire plan from one of getting away to one of no-witnesses. This leaves very little time and opportunity to summon help. This is one of the understated dilemmas that the you-don't-know-the-mind-of-the-intruder thinkers don't get: The worst crimes can start off small and escalate. It can happen very fast inside or outside the home.

The first idea is for an individual to develop an awareness, the experts point out, but it's even more: each individual has to come to understand what can go wrong given a specific environment and opportunity – how it can escalate – in order to smell what is about to happen to them next.

The key is not to prove to others later what you suspect in the mind of the intruder, but to imagine what he can potentially do now and in the next few seconds and prevent it. Think the 21-foot zone.

I also think in terms of a 21-second zone, a period of time in the immediate future. I imagine in mind what someone could potentially do in the next few seconds. I anticipate. It's the same strategy as playing Chess: you think five moves ahead. I try to think 21-seconds ahead, on the road, etc. The professionals call it being alert.

Finally, here is something every person interested in not becoming a victim should know on the subject of what we expect from arriving officers. If you're thinking that your cops are responsible – somehow more responsible than you or your neighbor who might defend themselves – then, do think of this first: don't sell yourself short: persons in Law Enforcement are not *made* responsible at the Academy, applicants are found with the right character *beforehand* in the background check, or they are rejected; their character is not molded by the police academy; they are trained and their judgement heightened, yes, but their *real* qualifications are in the life-long character development to be found in background check or they're dropped early in the selection process.

What it takes to be a good cop was formed long before they chose to become cops, just like *your* character is formed beforehand should *you* want to become a cop. Simply think of what really makes a good cop and how many of these people, perhaps you, live in the community and who simply never wish to apply to the Academy. Good right to carry candidates and other people of good character do not come entirely from the Police Department first, the Police Department comes from the Community first, their very pool of candidates.

For concealed weapons permits, there is not only training as part of the application, but passing a background check.

The Ultimate Homeland Security.

There are authors, commentators, professionals and others who assert that nationwide concealed carry is the ultimate homeland security. They're right, those individuals I read whom I've never met, but would like to meet. I admire their boldness, their clarity and their effort.

They're right because it's not an exaggeration. When we remember that law enforcement cannot be everywhere at once and that police have no mandate to protect individuals, we begin to understand why an individual constituent is the first line of defense against those forces that can rob us of our spirit and net productivity. When we take the position of not becoming a victim, we state that we are the origin of resistance, the first line of defense, and when individuals and institutions strive to *discourage* our resistance, they acknowledge the very same thing, do they not?

When individual constituents do not permit violence to escalate, by meeting menace with force, armed individuals are the least expensive, most efficient, on-scene homeland security.

How this relates to the head of a household is manifold. Families are not only areas of resistance to adversity, both personal and national, but they are made up of productive individuals who should not be injured in any sense of the word, merely because they are human beings. There is actual injury and there is legal injury; actual injury is to be hurt, legal injury is to have your rights compromised or violated, damages to property, etc., all of which can result from an unjust act of violence without police intervention. Americans single or married make up this country, and violent crime is simply not a cost of doing business. It is not some dues we pay to go about our lives.

As I said earlier, providing for family in preserving Liberty for yours and the next generation is another way to say *I love you.* For those newlyweds, new parents and others who plan to protect their family on various aspects, *this is the place to start.*

You don't have to carry a gun, but you might like the option. And one of the first things every constituent should work for is the decriminalization of proper, forceful response. Decriminalization of proper response and nationwide right to carry is the place to start.

Why There Won't Be Vigilanteism and Chaos.

There are tens upon tens of millions of guns out there already. Who is using them properly and who is using them wrongfully, as in the commission of a crime? With about 47,000 persons shot or killed every year compared to the more than two million persons who lawfully use a gun to thwart and discourage a crime, the comparison comes out to be more than 40 to 1. Put another way, it comes out to be about 128 shootings per day on the average, and most of these are suicide, crime-on-crime, and general crime, not law-abiding folks; but just as much on the average, about two million per year divided by 365 days, a gun is lawfully used to thwart a crime about 5,479 times a day.

I not only agree with this affirmation of right to carry, but I want to amplify on it by addressing issues of concern to my fellow Americans. Not only should we be concerned about how officials have fibbed and run interference for decades upon decades and mis-shaped opinion on this issue, but we should look to what would happen if the mistake were to be corrected.

After all, the problem of crime is not with the law-abiding, and it is only the law-abiding who will observe and respect laws, gun laws included. Government officials knows this! There are published reports nearly every day of criminals toting a gun into a posted gun-free zone. [Visit *Operation Self-defense* at *www.keepandbeararms.com* for that repository of under-reported stories.]

The concept of government perceiving *all* constituents as capable of committing crime (lumping the law abiding with the criminal) has not gone unnoticed, it is very insulting, and has been a baffling puzzle for a long time until the very moment you consider the *why:* the truth is that they have their own personal anxieties about you and me, things purely in their own impairment, their own inner experience, and in soothing this anxiety, officials want to control others more than respect our liberties, that all-important balm; they empower themselves with liberties by exemption from the rules we have to live by; they make rulings and regulations we have to live with, which indicates just how out of touch they are with the People and how disrespectful they are, well-meaning or ill-willed.

It is important to remember in assessing policy and in the voting booth that the impaired official sees you and me through their lens of *anxiety-avoidance*, where you and I are symbols of something in need of alteration, repair, and where their perceptions and interpretations put them on such a misinformation input, they cannot resonate with constituents. Right to carry states don't seem to have that problem to the same extent, and there, they enjoy the desired outcome, dire forecasts and predictions never materializing after years and years.

Nationwide Right to Carry is critical to regaining the direction of our nation where more and more individuals will be safer and safer from violent crime, and, thereby taking a great deal of control over the economy out of the hands of the impaired.

As merely one recent example in a long history of concealed carry success, please visit *http://www.dailystar.com/dailystar/dailystar/29510.php* for further details.

For, nothing is more dangerous than a lady with a shotgun. Slide the audible action of a good Mossberg shotgun and the announcement is clear: *"I have a shotgun, probably loaded with one in the throat right now, and it could go off!"* I could say that I'll call the cops, but the perp might be gone before I could finish the sentence. If not, then he takes his chances the gun is loaded. This kind of scenario is replicated hundreds of thousands of times a year, most of which is tragically and incompetently unreported by the media. I'll say it again: For a compendium of reports not generally appearing in the mainstream Press, please visit *www.keepandbeararms.com* Home Page and navigate through it to locate the topic of Operation Self-defense.

Now picture this: when individual constituents are more deeply concerned – let's say involved – with their personal safety and they act responsibly because in their core values they are more concerned about that issue when they elect not to be a victim, these people tend to remain focused, irrespective of which weapon they choose, and not deteriorate into an abyss of power over others or of aggression, another conclusion drawn from the experience of the concealed carry states.

It may be a baseball bat by the door; it may be a shocking device by the bed. For me and for millions nationwide, it's just a tool. The Second Amendment isn't about hunting – it's always been about defending the nation, and today, we're defending it on our shores like never before. We're battling violent crime as a path to recapturing our homes and communities, and that's a lot more useful and important than shooting for shooting's sake or hunting.

The issue is not the choice of weapon, friends, the issue *is our governance and the determination not to be a victim.* The concept then takes a sensible position on the list of priorities, and people tend to take it seriously in those states. *This is why CCW gun-owners around the nation are a safe bet for community and personal custody of personal safety: they value Liberty more, and the status of the right to carry is only a measurement of official respect for the constituent.*

Many owners who buy also often take additional courses from experts and see their ownership more as a statement about Liberty and taking more responsible action by learning more about their safety than something about shooting or hunting. Classes involve personal safety and the law, among other things, in and outside the home.

And for those making the case against guns as inherently dangerous, remember that guns don't go off by themselves. Any good training class mentions the how-to's of gun safety, including education for those who don't intend to own and proper safety education for children.

For adults, training includes familiarity with the firearm, its mechanical operation, what it can do and how it is to be handled. Rule number one is that all guns are to be treated as loaded. Some owners simply shorthand it to *'all guns are loaded.'* The next inviolable rules include never aiming the muzzle of the gun at anything you don't intend to destroy, and that means that you don't draw until you intend to shoot. Even when you do draw, the best safety is the hi-technology straight finger over the trigger guard; never put your finger on the trigger until you intend to shoot. It's put in clear terms and discussed in detail by Instructors. They're taught, and they're observed in practice before certification. Students are *told*. Students are told that alcohol and guns don't mix; we're told on the record what happens if... and we're taught case studies. We're taught by experts, including Military and Law Enforcement persons.

Gun safety isn't accomplished by trying to get guns off the street, a *futile* endeavor; gun safety is accomplished by getting education into the minds of owners, a *proven* formula. Gun control isn't making it hard for honest people to obtain self-defense tools; gun control is safe handling of the gun in both attitude and training.

With this consistency in mind, most individuals are not on the offensive, but the defensive, and they would not behaviorally fall into a category of likely suspects for vigilanteism, nor of paranoia or over-reaction. There's no evidence that they have. Without going into an essay of legal theory, let me simply point to the reality of the Right To Carry States with yet another recent example at the time of publishing, namely to visit *http://legallyarmed.com/decade.htm* for further details.

In reading any story's comments about crime going down or not going down, please let me emphasize that for crime to *be one way or the other*, the aggression not only has to be completed as a successful act and then reported as such, but data needs to be assembled. Thus, saying that there is no evidence that crime is down would be a true statement, *for now*. The jury's still out until more analysis is completed, *but the raw data is in.* I'm interested in how many crimes are *stopped* by right to carry, but then we have the data on that already: the right to carry states.

The Average Reasonable Person doctrine still permeates our society and our law *(I hope!)* and presumes that persons are reasonable until proven otherwise. This endures *because* most people *stay* reasonable. And that means that *enough* people stay reasonable. The impaired never seem to want to give people that kind of credit.

The bottom line is that *we're either going to fight Crime, Terror and Terrorism as a unit, or we're going to be elitist and ambiguous and not be able to fight at all.* This is not a diversity issue subject to the forces of Political Correctness – this is a *unity issue*, subject to the needs of individual and societal survival. It is not the People who are confused and mistaken, it is officials who balk at their instructions. And where the People are respected, as they are in the right to carry states, you can expect to see many such stories if you know where to look outside the mainstream media.

Let The Heavens Fall.

Medicine observes that some illnesses cannot be cured, but they can be treated. Crime, a plague on society, won't be cured entirely, but it can be suppressed. The goal of *really* reducing crime is resisted by nearly every impaired official from City Council to Congress and in nearly all of the larger cities, though of some exception in the right to carry states. Each pays lip service to crime, crime prevention, justice, you name it, but they continue to make policy that completely boomerangs, and which they insist on keeping in place; all that's needed is more time, more money and more patience. More prestige is more like it. Or wrong-headedness, or malice.

In the treatment of violent crime, the right to carry can have a direct impact on reducing severity and frequency substantially and realistically within a very short time, I would guess about a year when we would begin to see positive results. I'm speaking of encounters that could escalate, but don't because the victim is armed; this kind of encounter hardly ever gets reported *(publicly, anyway) entirely because* it didn't escalate. You don't have to be familiar with the inner workings of the average police station or newsroom to know why you should be ready to defend yourself in your personal sovereignty, and to see that if everyone defended himself, completion of violent crimes would diminish, and with it, the nature and degree of the violence and victim injury. Hence the bold forecast.

And another thing would happen: people would begin to discern once again the difference between illegitimate violence and legitimate force. This is a moral, societal outcome I predict. This would mean, of course, that the idea that violence is bad would be exposed to all for the lie that it is.

In summary, we don't especially need more *authority* to protect ourselves at the moment of threat. We don't need to hear official or editorial board explanations on why it wouldn't work: officials need to hear *our instructions* that this is what we want, and that we expect it without argument, or we will be convinced that Government is out of control, and that, truly, their resistance to this indicates that they have something in mind for us that explains this decades long, unreasonable ideation in officials. The long history of stifling right to carry has to have something in mind as much as right to carry has something in mind, namely Liberty and restoration of the nation.

Instructing officials to carry out what we want, not what they think, is to summon them to their duty, and is part of the environment that has to change in order to defeat liberalism's true anger – to take that axe they grind out of their hand.

If you are interested in changing America back to the safer, more courteous, good taste nation you would like it to be, if you understand that a family is a pocket of resistance to life's adversities, and if you would like to help shape that, then please consider the following involvements.

Speaking to officials is Step One. Instructing them on one simple position: that reclaiming our national direction now is imperative and that stemming violent crime is the beginning of recovering wasted revenues toward that. We insist. The Nationwide Right To Carry is essential to personal self-defense as the most sensible, economical and direct method of beginning this endeavor. Resistance, with lawful, lethal force if necessary, is the first line of defense in stopping violent crime where Law Enforcement simply cannot.

Specific House Resolutions are on the record as we speak, and need to be passed. Among these are nationwide right to carry, such as HR 47, the "Citizens' Self-Defense Act" and others, involving the recognition or reciprocity of various states in honoring the concealed carry permits of others states so that a licensed individual may legally carry his or her weapon anywhere in the country. www. CCRKBA. COM reports this excerpt about progress of House Resolution 47:

> Rep. Roscoe Bartlett (R-MD) has introduced a bill protecting the right of law-abiding Americans to use guns in self-defense.

> HR 47, the "Citizens' Self-Defense Act", would specifically protect the right of law-abiding citizens to use handguns, rifles and shotguns in defending themselves, their families or their homes. It would also allow people whose self-defense rights have been violated by any government entity to bring legal action in federal court.

Remember the news stories over the last couple of years, about husbands, wives, fathers and mothers who were arrested after shooting home-invaders, because the "homeowner" possessed a firearm for protecting their family? This bill could put an end to that kind of nonsense.

(Source: Citizens Committee for the Right To Keep And Bear Arms, www.ccrkba.com. Used with permission.)

Talk about sensible legislation, it's about time.

President Bush has already signed a similar resolution into law to become Public Law authorizing former police officers nationwide right to carry. This was The Law Enforcement Officers Safety Act of 2003, which in 2004 became Public Law 108-277. This is important, since these individuals are no longer police officers, but *private citizens* now. In essence, President Bush didn't sign a bill to put more officers on the street – he signed a bill that put more *armed private citizens* on the street. In this same spirit, constituents have the right to such immediate self-defense, too.

These resolutions should be passed without further delay.

It's important to understand that more than two-thirds the states of the Union respect the individual's right to carry – they acknowledge and respect the Second Amendment to the Constitution of the United States of America – and that in those remaining states where it is needed most, it is frustrated the most. Contact your Representative and urge nationwide right to carry now for all qualified adults as the indicator – as the confirmation – of the health of all our other liberties.

Some people say *talking to people* is another step, but I modify it to *getting people talking*. Raising the issue and permitting people to explore it all is a great start. Getting people talking – comparing notes – empowers us all, and permits all sides to be heard. If people wish to defend themselves without having to justify it repeatedly to the District Attorney or a civil lawsuit or to face off the castigation of others, then this is the will of the People. How many other rights of the Bill of Rights do you have to *show cause* to exercise?

If they wish to be sued for defending themselves or to be cooperative victims and hoping the alligator eats them last, that too, could be the result of the will of the People. Which do you think we want? The point is that officials should not have initiative which trumps the desires of the people they serve because they-say-so. And if officials cannot survive without societal problems, either taking advantage of them or even creating them, then let the heavens fall in correcting it. Remember that the children who run the education institutions don't really want parents to compare notes. Getting together – getting people talking – is to get constituents to compare notes, and will help us to work it through.

Step Three is to be alert to signature gathering venues. If new laws are proposed at any time throughout the year to further curtail your Second Amendment right, *it is your right to self-protection and way of life which are necessarily being curtailed.* Officials cannot resist the temptation to convert your safety to their marketable prestige (looting), specifically, to market your safety as an issue, then administer programs which really do nothing for you, but serve to perpetuate the problem, and give the appearance of doing something, just to keep the need for the official alive. If you see signature gatherers in favor of self-protection as the first line of defense in recovering our national direction, specifically concealed carry, or if you see signature gatherers collecting signatures for repealing no-fault divorce or anything else we can use, then please sign. And urge others to sign.

Next, Register to Vote! Many Americans do a lot of talking about the weather, but do nothing about it. Here's your chance to change the climate for the better. **Register to vote.** It will put you on the mailing list for information you can use and permit you to sign petitions you want to see come into law. Step four is to get out the Vote, then get out and Vote.

And for those who don't like being on lists, understand that we're all *already* on a list. Whether you dislike lists or whether you're just discouraged – don't fall for the atomic stink bomb of discouragement – it's time to balance that by being on some good lists where you want to be counted and heard. Register to vote, get out the Vote, and then you, yourself, get out and vote!

*F*ive, remember how infuriated you can be at the time officials insultingly won't carry out your wishes. In the case of the Los Angeles County Board Of Supervisors who refused to resist the ACLU's demands to remove the cross from the County Seal, many constituents stated publicly at the microphone that they would remember the Supervisors come election time. Things have a way of losing steam, and the Left counts on this enormously, so that when it's time to vote, constituents will not want to appear to be petty, one-issue voters and can become forgetful and forgiving in the polling booth. Item Six is to *keep an election diary.* Keep a *journal* of official misfeasances to remind you when you go into the polling booth of just how they defied your wishes, lost their hearing and talked down to you, and how they governed against the wishes of the People. Keep this book handy and make entries on the last few pages of this book to use as your Election Diary for just that purpose.

*S*ix, *reform the State Department.* Individuals in the Foreign Service are far too generous with our rights, far too loose with our liberties and far too far away to even care anymore. Careers in the Foreign Service changes Americans, it seems, to make friends with persons we should be firm with; we should be heard more there, and with less listening to them. Our rights and liberties, including our right to self-defense, is being counterproposed with nearly every meeting.

Where some Liberty enthusiasts are concerned about state and federal laws here at home – and we should be, of course – we're ignoring international law and how it can take away our right to self-defense as a matter of coming more into accord with the beliefs of other nations. The Oval Office by law has little influence over affairs of the State Department. Key to maintaining our interests at home by making them less subject to the wills of Foreign Service appointees, and thereby the influence of foreign interests, the State Department is in need of reform and fast. Getting involved here is a long-term but vital mission for the continued sovereignty of both individual *and* nation. The approval and appointment of Dr. Condoleezza Rice to Secretary of State is a move in the right direction.

Seven, strengthen watchdog laws such as the WPA, the Whistleblower Protection Act. Many of these laws have teeth in them, but as watchdog legislation, they could also have bite and more heart. Too many details in a watchdog law such as WPA are toothless, and must be reinforced. These are laws which protect individuals from retaliation in reporting abuses, lingering and loitering and general indolence in government's obligation to protect the nation, as one for instance. Internal punishments remain legal and permitted under such language, and make the law almost nothing in terms of improvement. Whenever opportunities present themselves, take the time and energy to do what you can to improve these; the Whistleblowers have the guts, now they need *our help* in the protection they need against retaliation. Wouldn't it be great to have Whistleblowers in the Media?

Step eight is to respect our Troops. The Left's statement that they support the troops is one of the best examples of political lip service today. Lip service is the act of speaking to a subject, but knowing (consciously or unconsciously) that you'll never really fulfill it. It is a self-deception.

Supporting our troops doesn't mean to say it, but to do it. It means that we respect our Military by welcoming individuals and thanking individuals we see in the Mall, on the street, anywhere we meet them. There is a convention we honor that goes like this: when we thank the soldier or sailor at home, we reach the soldier or sailor in the field. When you thank one, you thank them all. For their present service, or their past service, Step Eight is to respect them all.

*A*nd finally, *meet the hate where you see it.* Recognize that anti-safety rhetoric is hate and contempt for the law-abiding, that's you *and that means your household.* And recognize that hatred for you is because you are a symbol to them of something long ago that really has nothing to do with you; that's unjust, and so is their political position.

Meeting the hate means correcting erroneous information crafted to mislead when you know otherwise, either from the due diligence of your own research (and your own critical thinking) or from personal experience. Whoever hears the hate is getting only one side of the story and isn't hearing yours. Things will continue to get worse if the undecided hear only the Hate side – that's how things got this far! – and make no mistake: tying your hands so you can't fight back and discouraging you from fighting back is to have nothing but hate for you by presenting you to the predators. When their hate and disinformation spread into our Liberties, we need to engage them.

And when you meet the hate with philosophical truths and facts, don't forget to mention how many incidents are under-reported. Though there may be 128 shootings per day nationwide, there are an under-reported 5,479 thwartings per day by the lawful and proper use of a gun. Keep it simple.

If someone says that carrying concealed weapons for personal protection will promote chaos and vigilanteism, tell them that we'll cross that bridge if and when we get to it, and don't forget to add, by the way, that in the right to carry states, it hasn't happened in proven decades.

If the Left says that we should let the Police handle it, or that it's all *just your opinion,* remind them that Law Enforcement has no mandate to protect individuals, nor can they always arrive in time (presuming they have a completed request for aid and are available). Remind them that good character, the very kind they turn to policemen for, is developed in the individuals long before even putting in an interest card, and that such character is discovered in background check or the officer candidate is rejected as unfit or undesirable.

The real idea is that you never know who may be hearing your truths for the very first time.

Irrespective of what statistics show for reduced murder and other violent crime, there will still be painful losses in communities. Though the odds of a cow being struck by lightning while under a tree at midnight may be a .0001%.. for the cow that gets struck, the loss is 100%. Crime hurts in ways statistics can never show. It is not a number, it is a cost to an individual and all the lives he or she touches, and thereby the community in ways the figure cannot ever compare. Weakening an individual this way – by making them a victim of violent crime by tying their hands – takes its toll on his or her spirit and productivity, and thereby is an immeasurable loss to the community, one of those body blows that keep tearing down our nation. Yes, violent crime may be viewed as a disease, but this doesn't mean that we don't stop it with the method we have in hand.

Summary.

Looking at the ideas of liberal policy-making and progressive rulings as having a cost tries to appeal (and sometimes succeeds in appealing) to the public's sense of bargain and investment. This is the incorrect parameter to use to measure our Liberties, this sense of *exchange.* The fact is that we have gotten *nothing* in return for our sacrifices, and, of course, we cannot return the item or get out of the deal. We have cooperated, and we regret it. We have given them way, way too much time, not for policy to work, but way too much time for the angry to finally come around.

The *real* measurer of our liberties is in how responsive our government is to our wishes, irrespective of what they believe or say. Governance is that measure; responsiveness, cooperation, reaction time, cheerfulness and consistency, all work to indicate how officials serve us, and not the other way around. Right to carry is a graduation on that scale of cooperation and respecting the will of the People, and it presently indicates far too low a performance; it also exhibits a betraying area of emphasis and focus for those loathing us.

This is the solution. The real measure of our liberties is in our governance. For, even though we may never cure a very stubborn Potomac Fever and violent crime everywhere, it can be treated and overcome by identifying the angry. Courageous persons triumph over their demons all the time. We simply contact officials in adequate numbers and make it easy for them to comply. Or we unseat them.

The 2004 election started that mechanism.

And what of 2008? Will Hillary Clinton run for President? She'll face much of the same forces the two Johns faced in 2004, namely a more values-oriented constituency than expected (denial or other misread) and a shifting demographic where constituents, as I've said, now begin to live their lives for others and begin to make decisions based on those values for the sake of their families. Not *jobs*, but values.

On liberal anger, let me say a few parting words: in my assessment of angry people – people so wrapped up in their own anxiety that they make soothing that anxiety part of every personal and political choice – it's important for any reader to understand further that America has tolerated liberalism's anger for a very long time. Older liberalism was a values-based morality belief system, and there was a time when it was welcome anywhere in the world, as it should have been. It was not an angry system then, and as the nation improved on so many fronts in such a relatively short time, there was really never any political reason for anger over the decades. Perhaps political *frustration*, yes, but this is not even close to personal, inner experience, long standing anger that has nothing to do with the nation and which drives people to erase our own history and to justify habitual prevarication along the way.

When the angry seized the Democrat Party, when individual, personal, inner experience anger laid a hand on America, liberalism was hijacked by persons with that very axe to grind. Those persons are today, not surprisingly, the products of three generations or so of broken homes by now, of graft and corruption next, temptation and self-indulgence, anger, and revenge – members who are not of the same beliefs of Democrats of generations past. They are no longer the conscience of the People, they are the Angst of the People. This distinction is important, because the complaint to today's unhappy and angry I say to their face. And not to be insulting, but to be clear. This is why it is we distrust you.

Today's liberal is a child, stuck in time because they elect to dwell on anxieties people can get past. As I've said, the respect Americans have for one another derives from the truth that if one can do it, another can do it, too, and that Liberty is the ultimate respect of an individual who wishes to do anything. This ability to work through the anger, to mend, and yes, to *heal it,* is a personal decision, and it would mend the country. We've been trying to say this kindly and politely for a very long time. That time is over.

Perhaps later will the modern chip-on-the-shoulder liberals realize that we have been doing our best to spare their feelings and to point the way as gently as we can. And, most of all, to give them *time.*

A very kindly America has known all along, and deep down inside, that liberals are children who hurt, people stuck in time, traveling in circles emotionally, and that many of these can make their way into areas of influence, with tons of money, many connections and an insular lifestyle for guaranteed safety of never shutting that intellectualizing super-computer off.

Now, the adults will have to take over. Liberal guilt and hurt cannot be allowed to hurt us anymore.

There *is* Justice if the People will become more involved in their *governance*. Law enforcement officers sympathetic to our plight continually point out how they can react only to the law, and that it's up to us to change the law. They're right. A single California Recall has proven not only that it can be done, but done easily. The message would then be most clear worldwide: the one-two punch the impaired really fear most is *due process* (the dignity that we will do it by the law and nothing else will do) and *follow-through*, the certainty that we are an irresistible force to be reckoned with.

In baseball terms, constituent involvement would mean *we swing for the fence*. If you like sixties television, *you pitch one for the angels*. And if you understand launching carrier-based fightercraft, you *turn the ship into the wind*.

We will *always* be under attack, from without and from within.

Defeating the Beast first is imperative. Nationwide concealed carry is necessary to defeating violent crime everywhere, including schools, churches, civil aircraft, anywhere police can be summoned but where only constituents are, individuals who resolve not to be a victim, individuals who are in fact the first line of defense. The rest, then, would take care of itself or be otherwise simpler to defeat and discourage; the criminal among us and our ill-mannered fellows supporting them would then be much more cooperative – not out of admiration for us, certainly – but from the absolute knowledge that we are much more likely now to complete every single mission we undertake.

Epilogue

This Is Huge.

In December of 2004, the U.S. Department of Justice released a 93-page report completed August 24th, 2004 detailing exhaustive research studying the history of legislation and court cases in an examination of the original meaning of the Second Amendment, specifically on the issue of whether that amendment provides a *collective right* or an *individual right*.

As part of the debate against guns, the gun control movement had argued in its parsing that they acknowledge the Bill Of Rights, but that the Second Amendment was merely a collective right, and that individuals did not have the right to own guns. This of course, by extension, constituted a substantial interference with a person's ability to protect himself. The significance would have meant confiscation of personal weapons. Liberty enthusiasts, plagued by answering issue after issue on what rights we all have are now able to celebrate the fact that our beliefs have not been anti-social as claimed by the gun control movement, but in fact affirmed by the

Department of Justice's Office Of Legal Counsel and it is the gun control crowd now outed as anti-social.

This affirmation is huge.

First, the gun control crowd has not played by the rules; not only has gun control proven to be an abject failure wherever it is tried, but jurisdictions are rethinking their gun-ban policies for the safety of their constituents. The District of Columbia and the United Kingdom for the present. Throughout the debate, the gun control movement has misinterpreted rules and spirit of people, and in that debate they have stalled and interfered with a single, specific civil right.

Second, and this should be first, perhaps, the Liberty enthusiasts have observed only the law and due process to win this affirmation. This is an example of how not only due process must be observed, but why follow-through is so very important.

The importance is what Liberty enthusiasts have sought for generations, not to oppose Law Enforcement, but for Law Enforcement to work with constituents in a synergy of personal protection of the individual as a sovereign.

In excerpting a December 17th, 2004 report,

"This report confirms what the gun rights community has known to be true for many years," said Second Amendment Foundation founder Alan M. Gottlieb. "The right to keep and bear arms is a right to be enjoyed and exercised by every citizen. Henceforth, all Americans will know that the claim by anti-gunners that the Amendment only protects some mythical right of the states to form militias and the National Guard units is an outright fraud."

"For too long," stated Joe Waldron, Executive Director, Citizens Committee For The Right To Keep And Bear Arms [CCKRBA], "enemies of individual liberty have lied to the American public. They've tried to convince us that we have no right of self-defense, no right to own firearms as personal property, and no right to have the means to resist tyranny, which is what the Founding Fathers specifically had in mind when they wrote the Second Amendment. There is nothing in the Amendment about 'sporting purposes,' duck hunting or target shooting, and the anti-gunners know it. Now all Americans know it, too.

"There should be no doubt," Gottlieb concluded, "that those who have campaigned for restrictive gun laws or outright gun bans have been working to rob Americans of a constitutional right, a civil right. The time has come for America to re-examine every restrictive federal and state firearms statute, every local ordinance and every regulation, and start erasing those that were written solely to infringe on the rights of individual, law-abiding citizens to peaceably own firearms of their choice, without ever again having to explain why."

[used with permission]

But the battle is far from won. It is only the hopeful, encouraging, optimistic beginning of reversing all the ill-manners, bad taste in art, education-indoctrination and immature anxieties that plague us.

It is to help us to take on the Beast first.

Through due process and follow-through.

As Americans, we do not need to show cause to enjoy our civil rights. And, as Americans – and because America is not a place but an idea – that battle we fight will never end.

References / Recommended Reading

Jane Fonda – [See Jane Fonda's interview with Oprah Winfrey available at www.jane-fonda.net and elsewhere.] Visit specifically Part I and Part II at:

http://www.jane-fonda.net/Feature_2003/Feature_Pages/L_dec_b_oprahinterview.htm

http://www.jane-fonda.net/Feature_2003/Feature_Pages/L_dec_c_oprahinterview_pt2.htm

Injustice Collectors, a name coined by Anna Freud in her book, *The Ego And The Mechanisms Of Defense. Injustice collector* is a common, somewhat derogatory but accurate term in psychology (if not erased for political correctness) for persons who not only perceive injustice after injustice somewhat selectively in others, but who describe being wounded by everyday, otherwise harmless experiences.

More Guns, Less Crime. Understanding Crime And Gun Control Laws by John Lott, Jr. (Highly, highly recommended for facts and figures you may be looking for.)

Visit the FBI at www.fbi.gov and navigate through the Uniform Crime Report there.

Visit www.Keepandbeararms.com on the world wide web. Look for *Operation Self-defense.*

Visit www.studycrime.org on the world wide web.

Visit www.Pinkpistols.org on the world wide web.

Visit http://www.nraila.org/Issues/FactSheets/Read.aspx?ID=18

On the 21-foot rule, Visit http://www.theppsc.org/Staff/Tueller/Dennis.htm

Visit http://www.firearmsandliberty.com To read *Police have no mandate to protect individuals*, visit also http://www.firearmsandliberty.com/kasler-protection.html

Visit www.jfpo.org on the world wide web.

Dial 911 and Die- The Shocking Truth About The Police Protection Myth, by Attorney Richard Stevens, available at www.jpfo.org.

Divorce Won't Help, by Edmund Bergler, M.D., Harper & Brothers.

A Boy Named Sue, recorded by J.R. Cash on 2/24/69, written by Shel Silverstein.

Visit www.americanheart.org and visit their Early CPR page at http://www.americanheart.org/presenter.jhtml?identifier=3012022

Learn CPR and FIRST-AID.
The life you save may never thank you – you may never meet again – but you and they will know you did your very best.

Visit the American Heart Association near you for further information.

To view the entire report of the Department Of Justice's Office of Legal Counsel, visit:
      http://www.usdoj.gov/olc/secondamendment2.htm

For any broken links, please contact the author at John@nationwideconcealedcarry.com

Election Diary Page

Use this form as your journal of official misfeasances
and issues to remind you when you vote in the very next election.

Official	The Issue	The Outcome Before Election

The merit of our Constitution is not that it promotes democracy, but checks it.

—Horatio Seymour

The NRA has a point about the inadvisability of simply taking guns away from the populace. If that were possible, it would not disarm that small percentage of the population willing to break the law.... Punishing people who obey the law is backward thinking.

— Hugh Downs, Veteran ABC newsman.

It is not the function of our government to keep the citizen from falling into error; it is the function of the citizen to keep the government from falling into error.

— Justice Robert H. Jackson

He may be President of the United States, but he still takes my socks.

— Joe Kennedy speaking of his son, John F. Kennedy.

www.ingramcontent.com/pod-product-compliance
Lightning Source LLC
Chambersburg PA
CBHW030259290526
45785CB00001B/150